SEPARATING THE MEN FROM THE BOYS

◆　◆　◆

SEPARATING THE MEN FROM THE BOYS
The First Half-Century of the Carolina League

Jim L. Sumner

JOHN F. BLAIR, PUBLISHER
Winston-Salem, North Carolina

Design by Debra Long Hampton
Printed and Bound by Maple-Vail

The paper in this book meets
the guidelines for permanence
and durability of the Committee
on Production Guidelines for
Book Longevity of the Council
on Library Resources.

Library of Congress Cataloging-
in-Publication Data

Sumner, James, 1950–
Separating the men from the boys:
the first half-century of the Carolina League /
Jim L. Sumner.
p.   cm.
Includes bibliographical references and index.
ISBN 0-89587-112-2   (alk. paper)
1. Carolina League (Baseball league)—
History.   I.   Title.
GV875.C37S86   1994
796.357'64'09756—dc20   94–5564

To Ann, Lauren, and Mark

Contents

◆ ◆ ◆

PREFACE

♦ ♦ ♦

The year 1994 marks the 50th season of the Carolina League. Anniversaries such as this are always a good time to sit back, take stock, and see where you've come from and where you're going. When Carolina League president John Hopkins contacted me several years ago for ideas to commemorate this anniversary, it seemed logical to think about a league history. The league's ancestors, such as the Piedmont League, the Bi-State League, the Virginia League, and the North Carolina League, date back to the early years of the twentieth century. Minor league baseball has been a significant part of the sports scene in North Carolina and Virginia for quite a while. At the present time, the Carolina League is one of many leagues undergoing a resurgence of popularity equal to that of the pre-television era. Yet relatively little has been written on the subject. It is my hope that this book will help fill that gap.

Minor league baseball has traditionally served two purposes.

The vast majority of major league players polish their skills in the minors. The

Carolina League has an enviable record in this regard. The relationship between the major leagues and the minor leagues in developing players has evolved over the years, and not always in ways beneficial to the minors.

But minor league ball has always been more than just a way to train major leaguers. Before television and major league expansion, most baseball fans outside the urban Northeast and Midwest received their greatest exposure to professional ball in the minors. Neither North Carolina nor Virginia has ever had a major league team; leagues like the Carolina League have been as good as it gets. The Carolina League has entertained fans with top-quality baseball, fevered pennant races, and exuberant personalities since the closing days of World War II. This is also part of the Carolina League story.

A note about statistics. Baseball is our most heavily quantified sport. I've included as many statistics as was possible without interrupting the narrative, in large part because this information is not otherwise available under one cover. In order to simplify this information, I have used a standard shorthand. A mention of a position player followed by (.300, 17, 71) stands for a .300 batting average, 17 home runs, and 71 runs batted in. Statistics for other offensive categories, such as doubles, runs scored, and stolen bases, are specifically identified. Likewise, mention of a pitcher followed by (13–8, 2.71) is shorthand for 13 wins, eight losses, and a 2.71 earned-run average. Other statistics, such as saves and strikeouts, are specifically identified.

ACKNOWLEDGMENTS

◆ ◆ ◆

This book could not have been written without the assistance of Carolina League president John Hopkins and *Baseball America* owner (and former Durham Bulls owner) Miles Wolff. Both offered their files, their time, their expertise, and their encouragement. I also wish to thank other present and past league and team officials, particularly Jim Mills, Bill Jessup, Calvin Falwell, Rob Dlugozima, Al Mangum, Kevin Heilbroner, North Johnson, John Rocco, and Dave Shonk. I also want to thank Jack Horner, Tony Riggsbee, Steve Massengill, Brad Sullivan of the Society for American Baseball Research, archivists and librarians too numerous to name, and the late Willie Duke for their contributions. Most of all, I want to thank my wife, Ann, for putting up with endless Carolina League folders, phone calls, and research trips.

SEPARATING THE MEN FROM THE BOYS

♦ ♦ ♦

Raleigh Capitals, 1913   N.C. Division of Archives and History

INTRODUCTION

♦ ♦ ♦

It's easy to take minor league baseball lightly. After all, how important can something be if the word *minor* is a prominent part of its name? Alternative names such as "Bush League" and "The Sticks" don't inspire much confidence, either.

Yet minor league baseball has made profound contributions to the evolution of the national pastime. The most obvious is the development of talent. Virtually every major league player of consequence has apprenticed in the minors, honing skills later demonstrated in the big time.

The minors have also been more prone toward innovations than have the majors. Ladies' Day, night baseball, and the post–World War II racial reintegration of professional baseball all took place first in the minors.

There's also geography to consider. Until the 1950s, major league baseball was confined to the heavily urbanized areas of the Northeast and the Midwest, leaving minor league ball as the highest level of baseball in the rest of the country. Despite the undeniable attractions of the distant major leagues, the minor leagues have been able to develop their own stars, their own fans, and their own rivalries.

This has certainly been the case in North Carolina. A 1952 publication by the governing body of the minor leagues asserted that "people in North Carolina place professional baseball next only to home, church and school." Over 70 North Carolina cities have hosted a minor league team at one time or another, a total surpassed only by Texas.

The Carolina League was founded in 1944 as a predominantly North Carolina circuit. The league flourished during the brief postwar minor league renaissance and survived the subsequent collapse that saw two-thirds of the minor leagues disappear nationwide during the 1950s. The league's center of gravity gradually moved north into Virginia, with the circuit eventually expanding north of the Mason-Dixon line. In the 1980s, the Carolina League helped spearhead a minor league revival that continues to this day. Throughout its existence, the Carolina League has maintained a reputation for high-quality baseball and knowledge-able, enthusiastic fans.

At first glance, 1944 seems a peculiar time to start a professional baseball league. World War II still raged in Europe and the Pacific. Professional baseball occupied a curious position during the war. Shortly after the Japanese attack on Pearl Harbor, President Franklin Delano Roosevelt gave the game a green light to continue play. In his opinion, professional baseball was an important morale booster for troops abroad and workers at home.

Yet if the game was special during the war years, its players weren't. Professional players were given no special exemption from the military draft. As a result, most either were drafted or volunteered for service. Further complicating matters were travel restrictions. Gasoline and tires were rationed, and military travel took rail priorities. Both teams and fans had a difficult time traveling to games. The major leagues survived the war, but only with a noticeably inferior product, using graybeards, 4-Fs, teenagers, and players who managed to slip between the cracks one way or another. The situation was even more precarious in the minors, which lost several thousand players to military service. Most minor leagues simply shut down for the duration, including such area leagues as the Bi-State League, the Coastal Plain League, and the North Carolina State League. The Piedmont League, the upper South's most prominent circuit, continued play only by reducing its membership. Asheville, Greensboro, and Winston-Salem dropped out of that circuit after the 1942 season, followed the next season by Durham. North Carolina was without a single minor league baseball team in any league during the 1944 campaign.

Why, then, would anyone contemplate starting a league under such bleak circumstances? One reason was the encouraging progress of the war in Europe. The successful Allied invasion at Normandy in June of 1944 promised an early end to the war against Hitler—at least to optimists. Although the war against

Babe Ruth in North Carolina

1914 Baltimore Orioles with Babe Ruth in center   Maryland Historical Society

Babe Ruth is probably the best-known athlete in American history. Although the Bambino never played an official game in North Carolina, the state did play an important role in his career. In February and March of 1914, the young Ruth and his Baltimore Orioles, then a minor league team, took spring training in Fayetteville. Ruth had signed his first professional contract only months earlier. In his autobiography, Ruth related that he spent his first day in Fayetteville riding the hotel elevator up and down, over and over again. After all, it was the first time he had ever been away from Baltimore.

It was in Fayetteville that George Herman Ruth acquired his enduring nickname. The story goes that Ruth attached himself to Baltimore owner and manager Jack Dunn. Early in spring training, one exasperated Orioles veteran saw him tagging along with the owner-manager and remarked, "There goes Dunn and his new babe." Thus, America's most famous sports moniker was born.

Ruth hit and pitched well enough that spring to draw newspaper attention back in Baltimore and leave a lasting impression on the locals. For years afterward, Fayetteville baseball fans amused themselves comparing the youthful exploits of Jim Thorpe, who had played minor league ball in that city in 1910, and Babe Ruth, a combination few cities of its size could match.

Japan seemed certain to continue for some time, it appeared likely that large numbers of discharged ballplayers would be ready to resume play by the spring of 1945.

The major leagues offered encouragement of a different kind. The shortage of minor leagues during the war was delaying the development of young talent, and the majors desperately wanted to reverse the trend. There were no Class C minor leagues in operation during the 1944 season. Any minor league that dared to operate in 1945 was certain to receive major league support.

The Bi-State League therefore decided to resume play in 1945. Having made one bold move, the league elected to make another. The temporary absence of North Carolina cities in the Piedmont League presented an opportunity not likely to be duplicated soon, since it was probable that the league would move back into the Tar Heel State after the war's conclusion. The Bi-State League could beat its rival to the punch, grab the larger cities in North Carolina, and step up in class. That is precisely what happened.

Who were the Piedmont League and the Bi-State League? The answer goes all the way back to the baseball played in North Carolina and Virginia from the time of the Civil War.

Amateur baseball exploded across the United States after the Civil War. Teams sprang up in cities throughout the South, including virtually every city in North Carolina and Virginia. By the late 1880s, many colleges fielded intercollegiate baseball teams. Baseball rivaled football in campus popularity well into the 20th century.

Meanwhile, professional baseball was establishing an organizational structure. Several leagues during this period declared themselves "major leagues," including the National League, founded in 1876 and still in operation today. The major leagues were concentrated in the urban Northeast and Midwest, leaving the South wide open for the minors.

Relatively few minor leagues operated in the South until the 20th century, although Richmond and Roanoke were members of the Atlantic League in the late 1890s. The first direct progenitors of the Carolina League were a group of early-20th-century leagues which were more adept at starting seasons than completing them. Among the first of these was the Virginia League, which operated ineffectively and at irregular intervals in the 1890s, disbanded, and reappeared in 1906. This circuit had teams in the larger Virginia cities, including Richmond, Norfolk, Petersburg, Lynchburg, and Danville.

Although the Virginia League eventually included a handful of North Carolina cities, including Wilson, Rocky Mount, Edenton, and Elizabeth City, the first attempt to combine minor league teams from Virginia and North Carolina was the 1901 Virginia–North Carolina League. This league failed to complete its season, as did the 1902 North Carolina State League and the 1905 Virginia–North Carolina League.

Despite this litany of failure, minor league magnates in the two states learned valuable lessons in building financial reserves, controlling rowdy play and gambling, and developing a fan base. Leagues began to complete seasons and achieve continuity. The Virginia League returned in 1906, this time prepared to stick around. It was joined two years later by two leagues located to the south. The Carolina Association was a six-team league which consisted of teams from the North Carolina cities of Charlotte, Greensboro, and Winston-Salem and the South Carolina cities of Greenville, Spartanburg, and Anderson. This league lasted from 1908 to 1912. For its time, it was a remarkably stable group—five seasons without a single franchise failure or transfer. Farther east, the Eastern Carolina Association operated the same years in such cities as Raleigh, Wilmington, Kinston, Fayetteville, Rocky Mount, Goldsboro, and Wilson.

In 1913, Tar Heel organizers put together another North Carolina State League, with teams in Asheville, Charlotte, Durham, Greensboro, Raleigh, and Winston-Salem. By this point, the Virginia League had expanded into North Carolina; Rocky Mount won the 1915 title, the first North Carolina–based team to win that league's pennant.

Most of the minor league players of this era are long forgotten. The North Carolina and Virginia leagues were close to the bottom of the organized-baseball totem pole and were located far from the media centers of the North. Yet a few players made their mark on baseball history. Jack Chesbro pitched for Roanoke's Virginia League entry in 1896 and for Richmond in the 1897, 1898, and 1899 Atlantic League campaigns. Chesbro posted what is still a major league record 41 wins for the 1904 New York Highlanders (now Yankees) and gained election to the Hall of Fame. Only one year removed from Bucknell, pitcher Christy Mathewson, whose sterling career with the New York Giants also led to his induction into the Hall of Fame, went 20–2 in an abbreviated season for Norfolk in 1900; he ended the season with the Giants. Burleigh Grimes won 23 games for Richmond in 1914, while Sam Rice batted over .300 for Petersburg in 1914 and 1915. Rice began pro ball as a pitcher for Petersburg but starred in the majors as an outfielder. Grimes and Rice are both in the Hall of Fame.

Durham Bulls, 1913

American involvement in World War I shut down minor league baseball in 1917 and 1918. With players facing a work-or-fight order, the pool of available professional-caliber talent dried up almost completely. The major leagues were forced to cut the 1918 season short, and most minor leagues disbanded for the duration. The North Carolina State League threw in the towel early in the 1917 campaign and did not even bother to attempt a 1918 season. The Virginia League began play in both 1917 and 1918 but shut down both seasons after a few weeks.

The Virginia League resumed play in 1919, with teams in Richmond, Petersburg, Newport News, Norfolk, Portsmouth, and Suffolk. Two more future Hall of Famers passed through the league. Pie Traynor made his professional debut for Portsmouth in 1920, while Lewis "Hack" Wilson hit a league-leading .388 for Portsmouth in 1923.

The Virginia League had a new challenger, however. The North Carolina State

Jim Thorpe Comes South

During the early years of the century, it was common for top-notch college baseball players to earn a few extra dollars by playing minor league baseball during the summer. Most played under an assumed name, but the best-known player to officially grace the local minor league fields neglected that precaution, an oversight for which he paid a terrible price.

In the summer of 1909, Carlisle (Pa.) Indian School football star Jim Thorpe came south with several teammates to play for the Rocky Mount Railroaders of the Eastern Carolina Association. Although Thorpe possessed enough baseball ability to eventually reach the major leagues, he was only an average player for the Railroaders, batting .253 while winning nine of 19 decisions as a pitcher. The

local newspapers knew who Thorpe was and made numerous references to his college football exploits and his Indian heritage. Thorpe came back the following summer, playing first for Rocky Mount and later for Fayetteville.

Baseball and football were not Thorpe's only sports, of course. In 1912, he won Olympic gold medals in the decathlon and the pentathlon, becoming in the process the acknowledged greatest athlete in the world. When news of his summers as a professional baseball player became public, Thorpe was stripped of his Olympic medals. Despite a widespread and persistent public outcry, they were not returned until well after his death in 1953.

League did not resume play in 1919 but emerged in 1920 as the Piedmont League, one of the most successful minor leagues of the period. This ambitious circuit was founded by Durham's William G. Bramham, an attorney, political figure, and minor league administrator. Bramham led the Piedmont League throughout the 1920s and at one time late in the decade was president of four minor leagues simultaneously. The Piedmont League was predominantly a North

Carolina circuit during its early years. Its inaugural membership consisted of High Point, Winston-Salem, Greensboro, Raleigh, Durham, and Danville—all cities that would later be represented in the Carolina League.

The Piedmont League won the battle for baseball fans in North Carolina and Virginia during the 1920s. Part of the credit goes to Bramham, whose forceful leadership kept club owners and players in line and gave the young league surprising stability. Yet Bramham became president of the Virginia League in the middle 1920s and was unable to arrest its decline. The older organization suffered from population imbalances between its largest and smallest cities. Throughout the 1920s, the populous cities of Richmond and Norfolk sought affiliation with a higher league, while smaller cities such as Tarboro, North Carolina, and Suffolk, Virginia, suffered poor attendance. The Virginia League declined throughout the decade and ceased operation following the 1928 season.

While the Virginia League was struggling, the Piedmont League was producing a number of crowd-pleasing sluggers. Two of the best had names that were especially evocative in the Tar Heel State. Durham Bulls outfielder Tom Wolfe batted .351 in 1930 while leading the league with 39 home runs and 154 runs batted in. However, these impressive marks pale beside those compiled by Dan Boone, the Piedmont League's most accomplished slugger. Boone, a High Point outfielder, had successive batting averages of .399, .342, .419, .372, and .385 from 1926 to 1930. He drove in over 100 runs in four of those seasons and hit 46 home runs in 1929. Boone was preceded as a Piedmont League .400 hitter by Greensboro's Lloyd Smith, who hit .404 in 1921, and Raleigh's Carr Smith, who batted .418 in 1923.

With the failure of the Virginia League and the Eastern Carolina League, the Piedmont League had the local professional scene to itself entering the 1930s, a decade that saw more dramatic transformations in minor league baseball. Many of these were a direct result of the economic cataclysm that began with the collapse of the stock market in the autumn of 1929. Not surprisingly, the Great Depression devastated the minor leagues. Thirty-one minor leagues started the 1928 season; less than half were still in operation five years later.

In the fall of 1932, the National Association of Professional Baseball Leagues, the governing body of minor league baseball, elected Bramham president and gave him broad powers. Bramham moved the organization's headquarters to Durham, tightened up on fly-by-night operators, came down hard on fighting, rowdy play, and gambling, and promoted minor league ball fervently. By 1940, some 44 minor leagues were in operation.

Not all changes came from the commissioner's office. In order for minor league teams to survive the Depression, it was necessary to attract as many fans as possible. Teams in the area expanded their fan base in two important ways. Night baseball was introduced to the minor leagues in the spring of 1930 and was an immediate success. Within a few years, virtually every minor league ballpark in the country had lights. More controversial was Sunday baseball. At the beginning of the 1930s, professional Sunday baseball was against the law in North Carolina and Virginia, as was Sunday operation of such attractions as moving pictures, swimming pools, and amusement parks. As social mores changed, the minor leagues overcame opposition to Sunday ball in most communities by the end of the decade.

What were perhaps the most far-reaching changes in minor league ball, however, had nothing to do with the Great Depression.

The majors had always needed the minors to develop talent, while the minors had always needed the money generated by selling player contracts to the majors. There was an inherent conflict here—the majors wanted to pay as little as they could for player contracts, while the minors wanted to receive as much as possible. The relationship between the two being what it was, the various National Agreements between the majors and minors generally gave the major leagues the right to draft a limited number of players for a set price. The majors occasionally "loaned" young players in need of seasoning to minor league teams with the understanding that they would be returned when needed. After 1921, this became more formalized, as a provision was introduced whereby a major league team could use a limited number of "options," sending a player to the minors with the option of bringing him back later.

In 1918, Branch Rickey became president of the St. Louis Cardinals, a perennial National League doormat. In an attempt to make the Cardinals competitive, Rickey redefined the relationship between the major leagues and the minor leagues. Since the major league draft only covered a limited number of players, many minor leaguers continued to be sold to the highest major league bidder. The financially strapped Cardinals were chronically unable to compete for this talent. The innovative Rickey came up with an alternative, the so-called farm system, in which a major league team either owned minor league teams or created working agreements with existing teams which gave them contractual control of players. Eventually, the Cardinals controlled hundreds of players and had teams at every minor league level. In their peak year of 1937, the St. Louis farm system consisted of 33 teams. It produced enough stars of the caliber of Dizzy Dean, Enos Slaughter, and Stan Musial to enable the Redbirds to become one of the dominant teams of the pre–World War II period. The Cardinals also managed to unload surplus players for a tidy profit. Although the farm-system concept was opposed vehemently by baseball's commissioner, Judge Kenesaw Mountain Landis, it proved so successful that other teams adopted it in short order.

Most Piedmont League teams became part of a major league farm system during the 1930s. The Cardinals were affiliated with Greensboro and later with Asheville. The deep pockets of the New York Yankees turned Norfolk into a league powerhouse. Rocky Mount became a Boston Red Sox farm team; Charlotte became affiliated with the Washington Senators; the Detroit Tigers and Winston-Salem hooked up; and Portsmouth became a Chicago Cubs farm team.

Piedmont League membership continued to shift during the 1930s. Greensboro, Durham, Winston-Salem, and Charlotte all dropped out of the league in the 1930s and later rejoined. Raleigh and High Point dropped out for good following the 1932 season. Wilmington was a league member from 1932 through 1935. With the North Carolina teams in a state of flux, the league expanded its Virginia representation. Richmond joined the league in 1933, Norfolk in 1934, and Portsmouth in 1935.

Bolstered by its major league affiliations, the league gained a national reputation. A number of future major league stars passed through the Piedmont League on their way to the majors. One of the most notable was slugging first baseman Hank Greenberg, baseball's first Jewish superstar, who played for Raleigh in 1930. Johnny Mize batted .337 for Greensboro in 1931 and .360 with 22 home runs in 1933. Early Wynn pitched for Charlotte in 1938, 1939, and 1940, winning a total of 34 games; Wynn did much better in the big leagues, winning 300 games in a career that lasted until 1963. Yogi Berra batted a mere .253 for Norfolk in 1943, his first year in professional baseball, before going into the military. Berra made the big leagues late in the 1946 season and remained there until the mid-1960s. Also getting in a season in the Piedmont League before joining the military was Duke Snider, who played for Newport News in 1944. Greenberg, Mize, Wynn, Berra, and Snider are all members of the Hall of Fame.

Just below that lofty standard were a number of other players who graduated from the Piedmont League to major league stardom. For example, the 1936 Durham Bulls were led by two of the best-known players of the era. First baseman Frank McCormick, who batted .381 with 138 runs batted in for the Bulls, later captured the National League's Most Valuable Player award in leading the Cincinnati Reds to the 1940 pennant. Pitcher Johnny Vander Meer won 19 games and recorded 295 strikeouts for Durham in 1936. Vander Meer is best remembered for pitching consecutive no-hitters for the Reds in 1938. In addition to Berra, Norfolk sent shortstop Phil Rizzuto and second baseman Gerry Priddy to the Yankees. The 1937 Portsmouth team featured first baseman Bill Nicholson, second baseman Eddie Stanky, and pitcher Harry Breechen, all National League standouts during the 1940s. Tommy Holmes (Norfolk, 1937), Johnny Pesky (Rocky Mount, 1940), and George Stirnweiss (Norfolk, 1940) all batted over .300 in the Piedmont League before going on to solid big league careers.

Not all Piedmont League stars went on the majors, however. Frank Packard (Charlotte, 1931), Jim Bryan (Norfolk, 1934), Bobby Estalella (Charlotte, 1938), and Luis Olmo (Richmond, 1942) all won the Piedmont League triple crown, leading the league in batting average, home runs, and runs batted in. Of the quartet, only Estalella, a diminutive Cuban-born outfielder, ever played in even a single contest in the major leagues; he played in 680 games for three American League teams.

As the minor league situation stabilized in the mid-1930s, several smaller leagues were established in Piedmont League territory. After a hiatus of more than a decade, a reformed Virginia League resumed play in 1939, with teams in Lynchburg, Salem-Roanoke, Staunton, and Harrisonburg. It expanded to the east in 1941 with the addition of Petersburg and Newport News. The Bi-State League was established in 1934, with teams in the Virginia towns of Danville, Martinsville, and Fieldale and the North Carolina communities of Leaksville-Spray-Draper, Mayodan, and Mount Airy. Bassett, Virginia, and Reidsville, North Carolina, joined the league in 1935, while South Boston replaced Fieldale in 1937. Several new leagues operated exclusively in North Carolina, including the North Carolina State League, the Tar Heel League, and the Coastal Plain League. None of these circuits challenged the Piedmont League in popularity or quality of play, although they all had their loyal fans.

Baseball was at the apex of its popularity during the first half of the 20th century. No other sport challenged its stature as the national pastime. Fans could follow the game in person, in their daily newspaper, and, beginning in the 1920s, on the radio. Professional baseball was atop a hierarchy that included college, high-school, business, church, and sandlot nines. Most baseball fans knew the game not just as spectators but also as participants. Newsman Charles Kuralt, who grew up in several North Carolina towns before World War II, remembered, "Wherever you lived, no matter what school you went to or what you did for a living, there was a baseball team playing nearby. The smell of a catcher's mitt was universal, as were the crack of a good hit, the smell of a hot dog, the dust on your britches." Writer Paxton Davis, who grew up in Winston-Salem about the same time, confirmed baseball's primacy: "Baseball lay so deep within us we played it reflexively, with none of the thought or planning we gave football; it was as natural as breathing, and as easy."

Many games were characterized by the kind of hoopla and passionate fan intensity more often associated with college basketball and football later in the century. In 1941, Raleigh newspaper editor Jonathan Daniels used baseball as a point of comparison in describing North Carolina's wild tobacco markets: "It is a competition for the tobacco between the towns which exceeds even the wildest moments in the Coastal Plain Baseball League."

Daniels's offhand observation is clear evidence of the passion of minor league baseball. When the Bi-State League transformed itself into the Carolina League in the autumn of 1944, it was counting on this passion, along with four decades of minor league experience in North Carolina and Virginia—decades in which minor league ball had become an integral part of the fabric of everyday life.

◆ ◆ ◆

Devereaux Meadow, Raleigh, September 1947   N.C. Division of Archives and History

CHAPTER ONE
1944 — 50

♦ ♦ ♦

The Carolina League came together at a series of meetings in the autumn of 1944 involving business leaders, local baseball men, and minor league officials. Dr. Thomas Wilson, a dentist from Draper, North Carolina, and former head of the Bi-State League, was elected president. By the time the dust settled, the North Carolina cities of Raleigh, Durham, Winston-Salem, Greensboro, Burlington, and Leaksville and the Virginia cities of Danville and Martinsville had signed on, confident that the war was winding down.

This confidence was misplaced. The war in Europe dragged on well into the spring of 1945, and the expected influx of demobilized ballplayers did not materialize. With an estimated 4,000 minor leaguers still in the military, only a dozen minor leagues answered the call in the spring of 1945. The Carolina League was the only Class C minor league in a system that included AA (the highest level),

A, B, C, and D. National Association official Leroy Addington admitted that the minors were running with "the aid of considerable green and inexperienced talent, large numbers of teen-age youngsters being employed in the lower classifications."

The Carolina League's best-known figures were its managers. Former Washington Senators outfielder Heinie Manush, who would be elected to the Hall of Fame in 1964, managed Martinsville and played in a handful of contests. Longtime minor league star and Greensboro native George Ferrell was player-manager for Winston-Salem during the second half of the season. In a pro career that started in 1926, Ferrell had played mostly in the South, especially for Memphis and Richmond, but had batted .330 for Winston-Salem's 1930 Piedmont League team. He ended his professional career in 1945 with almost 3,000 hits but without ever playing in the big leagues. The 41-year-old Ferrell batted .289 as a player-manager for Winston-Salem's inaugural Carolina League team. He was the brother of Hall of Famer Rick Ferrell and former big-league pitching standout Wes Ferrell. The latter started the season as the Greensboro manager but was forced to quit early in the campaign when the draft board advised him that his deferment as a full-time farmer was in jeopardy. Fans also recognized 38-year-old Cliff Bolton, a native of High Point and a former major leaguer, who played 41 games for Martinsville and batted .371.

Most of the rest of the players were less distinguished. Many didn't even shave. Durham's Tom Poholsky was a teenager. He later recalled his first trip to Durham this way: "I was just fifteen years old . . . so for me to go to Durham was incredible. I could have been going to Singapore or Paris and it would have seemed just as strange and new." At the other end of the spectrum was 34-year-old Ossie Buckner, who was advertised as baseball's oldest rookie. Buckner started the season with Greensboro but finished with Raleigh.

Herb Brett managed to corral most of the good players for his Danville Leafs. They won their first two contests over the Raleigh Caps and never looked back. In fact, they won their first 10 games and held first place all season, although Leaksville did tie them for one day early in the campaign. On May 12, the Leafs scored 17 runs in one inning against the Caps. By the beginning of July, they were 44–19 and led second-place Raleigh by 7. At the end of the month, they were 68–28 and led by 10½. Only Raleigh was even remotely competitive. For much of the season, the other six teams had losing records.

Despite Danville's dominance, the Leafs were forced to win the championship in a four-team playoff. The Leafs were matched against the third-place Martinsville Athletics in a best-of-seven first-round matchup. The Athletics won two of the first three contests before losing the last three games and the series. Danville ace Art Fowler was the key performer. The right-handed pitcher struck out 14 in a game-one victory and won the crucial fourth game 4–0 with a three-hitter.

In the other playoff series, Raleigh fell behind Burlington two games to none

The Father of the Carolina League

The appellation "Father of the Carolina League" invariably followed the name of Herb Brett during the 1940s and 1950s. No one was more responsible for the establishment of the league than the Virginia native.

Herb Brett was born in Lawrenceville in 1900 but was raised in Portsmouth. He started his long baseball career as a pitcher. Brett had cups of coffee in the big leagues with the Cubs in 1924 and 1925, winning one game and losing one. He became a manager in 1934 after a sore arm ended his playing career. He guided Boston's Danville farm team to the Bi-State League championship in 1934 and 1935. Brett stayed at Danville until 1938, when Boston moved him up the ladder to the Piedmont League and Rocky Mount. He managed at Little Rock in the Southern Association in 1940 and served as a Red Sox scout in 1941. He got back in uniform in 1942 and managed in the minors through the 1944 season.

After finishing the 1944 season managing Hagerstown, Brett decided to come back home to Virginia. His years in the Bi-State and Piedmont leagues had given him an intimate knowledge of the area and a wealth of contacts. Brett purchased the inactive Danville team and worked tirelessly as an owner-manager to build up his team and convince seven other franchises to join him in establishing a new league despite the uncertainties of war.

Brett was the prime mover behind the October 15, 1944, meeting held in Burlington, in which the Danville, Leaksville, and Burlington franchises of the inactive Bi-State League voted to reopen for the 1945 season, move to a higher classification, change the name of the league, and accept five new members. Raleigh, Rocky Mount, and Greensboro were granted membership at the first meeting, while a decision was deferred on the final two teams. Rocky Mount had been a member of Bi-State League, while Raleigh and Greensboro had been members of the Piedmont League.

Herb Brett
Greensboro
News & Record

Brett had help, of course. Among those attending this meeting was National Association publicity director Leroy Addington, who assured all concerned that the minors' governing body approved the proceedings. Although National Association president William G. Bramham did not attend, there seems little doubt that he favored the idea. Also attending were representatives of the Chicago Cubs and the Philadelphia Phillies. An optimistic statement was released maintaining that "all those present at the meeting agreed that the fans are ready for the return of baseball and expressed their belief that enough players would be available and that transportation could be arranged."

A follow-up meeting was held two weeks later in Durham. The league's membership was completed when Winston-Salem and Durham were voted in, to the disappointment of representatives from Wilson and Martinsville. The circuit was named the Carolina League, and Dr. Thomas Wilson, a Draper, North Carolina, dentist, was elected president; Wilson had been president of the Bi-State League. Brett could have had the job for the asking, but he preferred to stay in uniform.

Herb Brett continued in the Carolina League as a manager or general manager well into the 1960s in Danville, Reidsville, Raleigh, and Winston-Salem. He was instrumental in moving the Carolina League from Class C to Class B and was a prime mover in establishing the league All-Star Game. Throughout his tenure, he impressed observers with his astute baseball knowledge, his dedication to the game, and his amiable disposition.

before coming back to win in seven. The comeback was keyed by staff ace Roy Pinyoun, who won games three and six.

Danville handled Raleigh easily in the championship series. Fowler threw another three-hitter in the opener, winning 7–1. After Pinyoun won game two for the Caps, Danville won the next three games and the championship. Fowler closed out the series with a 3–2, 11-inning five-hitter. Altogether, he was the winning pitcher in four of Danville's eight playoff victories.

Fowler's postseason excellence was simply a carry-over from the regular season, when he won 23 decisions against six losses, compiled an earned-run average of 2.56, and struck out 177 batters. Fowler later pitched in the major leagues for nine seasons. He was supported by outfielders John Carenbauer (.320, 121 RBIs) and Glenn Brundis (.366, 132 runs) and shortstop Jaime Almendro (.350). Other Danville standouts were outfielder Daniel Siracusa (.302), second baseman Lewis King (league-leading 65 stolen bases), and pitcher Nicholas Andromidas (16–4, 2.81). The formidable Danville sluggers scored 998 runs and compiled a team batting average of .286.

The Caps were led by two outstanding pitchers who would become league mainstays in years to come. Pinyoun finished 21–10, joining Fowler as the league's only 20-game winners. Charlie Timm was 17–10 with a league-leading earned-run average of 2.36. On August 30, Timm beat Martinsville 7–3 and struck out 20 batters, establishing a league record which has been equaled but never surpassed.

Seventeen-year-old Winston-Salem pitcher Johnny Klippstein only won eight games in 1945 but went on to tally 101 victories in the majors.

The league featured lots of high batting averages in 1945. Seventeen men with more than 100 at-bats hit over .300. However, few of these hits left the ballpark. Burlington led the league with a modest 71 homers. Greensboro hit only 24 home runs, Raleigh 25. Four players collected 12 home runs, easily the lowest total to ever lead the league.

The atrocious fielding statistics demonstrate clearly the subpar quality of ball played that season. Last-place Greensboro committed a staggering 479 errors, a dubious Carolina League record that with any luck will never be challenged. Greensboro third baseman Leo Northrup committed 64 errors and fielded .828. Raleigh shortstop Eddie Jackson made 71 errors. His teammate, second baseman Owen Friend, committed five errors in a single July game against Danville. Martinsville committed 14 errors on May 14 in a 26–10 loss to Greensboro and a dozen on May 1 against Durham.

Not all performances were so dismal. Greensboro's Roy Williamson scored six runs on May 14 in the same game in which Martinsville made 14 errors. Winston-Salem's Louis Sander had seven hits, all singles, in a July 11 game, a 19–6 rout of Burlington. Both marks are still league records. Durham and Martinsville played the league's endurance contest. On July 17, they battled to an 18-inning 1–1 tie in a game called at midnight because of a Durham curfew. Bulls hurler Wallace Mitchell lasted all 18 innings.

Considering problems with travel, preoccupation with the end of the war, and the mediocre quality of ball, league attendance was probably about as good as could be expected. Regular-season crowds averaged just under 1,000 per game.

1945 Final Standings

* Danville	94–44	playoff winner
Raleigh	78–60	
Martinsville	69–67	
Burlington	67–70	
Leaksville	66–70	
Winston-Salem	61–76	
Durham	59–77	
Greensboro	53–83	

—◆—

Nineteen forty-five was a dress rehearsal for a much different 1946 season. The half-decade following World War II was a golden age for minor league baseball. For the first time in nearly two decades, there was no Depression or war to cast a shadow on the baseball world. Although challenged increasingly by football and other sports, baseball was still the undisputed national sport. Fans were starved after years of makeshift wartime ball and flocked to the ballparks in record numbers.

Players were almost as numerous as fans. The war years had delayed the careers of thousands of ballplayers and created a logjam at the major league level. In effect, an entire generation of professional ballplayers lost its chance to enter the major leagues at an appropriate stage of development. Many 23-year-old al-most-ready-for-the-majors prospects from 1941 had become 28-year-old former prospects by 1946. Faced with an abundance of choices, big-league clubs invari-ably chose the current crop of young prospects over the older former prospects, dooming some major league–quality players to a lifetime in the minors.

As unfortunate as this was for the players, it was a boon for leagues like the Carolina League, which fielded a blend of grizzled pros and hot prospects. So enthusiastic were minor league fans that they were able to support 42 leagues in 1946. By 1950, this number increased to 59 minor leagues and over 400 teams. Unable to fully stock this many teams, the big leagues gave the minors more autonomy in signing players than would be the case in a few years. Carolina League teams, even those affiliated with major league clubs, could sign a fair number of local players. This created a strong bond between team and community. Players and fans interacted with each other in a much stronger way than in later years, when increasing big-league control began to funnel a new group of outsiders into the community every year. Communities and fans had a strong emotional investment in the fortunes of the local team. Occasionally, this investment overflowed its appropriate channels; league fans attacked umpires and opposing players more than a few times during this period.

This community involvement can be seen in attendance figures, which reached levels in the 1940s that the Carolina League wouldn't approach for almost a half-century. It was also reflected in newspaper attention. High-circulation dailies like the Raleigh *News and Observer* and the *Greensboro Daily News* routinely sent reporters to cover the road games of the local teams, gave box scores of every league game, and devoted more column inches to Carolina League ball than at any time in history. Hot pennant races even generated front-page features.

The 1946 Carolina League returned with the same eight clubs as the previous season. Martinsville continued to be owned by the Athletics, while Winston-Salem was a farm team of the St. Louis Cardinals. Raleigh had a handful of players on option from the Boston Braves. Although there were some holdovers from 1945, such as Roy Pinyoun and John Carenbauer, the majority of players were new to the league, and the quality of ball improved significantly.

League president Wilson set the tone early in the season when he cautioned players, umpires, and managers against slow games, especially the habit of throwing the ball around the infield after every out: "This monkey business certainly slows up a game and the fans are strong for a short, snappy, and fast game." The complaint seems quaint from a 1990s perspective. Games in the 1940s rarely took much more than two hours, and 90-minute games were not unheard of. Still, this shows the league's early concern with keeping its fans happy.

The Greensboro Patriots and the preseason-favorite Raleigh Capitals jumped off to a lead in the early part of the season. On May 1, Greensboro mauled Danville 22–5 even though it only garnered 12 hits; four Danville pitchers walked 25 Patriot batters. The following day, the Patriots found out how the other half lives when Raleigh beat them 21–1. The powerful Caps were led by pitchers Al Henencheck, Roy Pinyoun (19–12), and Charlie Timm (16–10), outfielder Jim Mills (.318), second baseman Glenn Lockamy (.320), catcher Harry Sullivan (.303), first baseman Dave Baxter (110 RBIs), outfielder Emile Showfety (a former Elon College star and Greensboro native who batted .343), and former Danville player John Carenbauer (106 RBIs).

At the end of May, Raleigh was 1½ games ahead of Greensboro. On June 2, the Caps won a dramatic game over Winston-Salem when Dave Baxter hit a three-run inside-the-park homer with two outs in the bottom of the ninth for an

8–7 victory. Yet Greensboro continued to hang tough. Not even a 10-game Raleigh winning streak in mid-June opened significant ground for the Caps. At the end of the month, Raleigh led Greensboro by only a game.

Greensboro took over first place on July 1 by scoring two runs in the bottom of the 13th inning to beat Leaksville 8–7. The Caps fell farther behind when they lost two games to archrival Durham on July 3 and two more during a big Fourth of July double-header. Raleigh lost its sixth straight in bizarre fashion to Leaksville on July 5. A rain shower led to a 45-minute delay. Leaksville officials burned gasoline on the field in an unsuccessful attempt to dry it. When the game resumed, the disgruntled Mills and Lockamy took their shoes off and played barefoot.

Greensboro threatened to break the race open in July. The Pats had a solid club, led by veteran shortstop Matt Topkins (.314), outfielders Tig Harris (.307, 124 RBIs), Bob Falk (.355), and Don Butzer (.305), and pitchers Bill Plummer (17–5) and Bernie Keating (18–7). By July 20, Greensboro had a record of 58–30 and a 6½-game lead over Raleigh.

Greensboro's margin over Raleigh continued to range from three to six games as the race entered its stretch run. The Durham Bulls then went on a hitting spree to make it a three-team race. The Bulls ran their record from 50–45 on July 27 to 70–52 on August 21. The Bulls featured a fearsome lineup of hitters. Veteran outfielder Woody Fair hit .344. His outfield running mate, future major leaguer Tom Wright, led the league with a .380 average and drove in 116 runs.

1946 Durham Bulls

Courtesy of Miles Wolff

Woody Fair

Woody Fair
Courtesy of
Miles Wolff

Players, fans, and media people who remember the early years of the Carolina League agree that the league's best player was slugging outfielder Woody Fair. Yet because of the intrusion of World War II, Fair never played a single game in the big leagues.

Woodrow Clark Fair was born in 1914 in Turner, Washington. He made his professional debut in 1934 in the Arkansas State League. Despite compiling solid batting statistics year after year, Fair had a hard time breaking out of the lower minor leagues of the Deep South. He spent five years in Louisiana's Evangeline League. A modest five-foot-ten and 165 pounds, Fair simply didn't look like a big-league hitter and was an ordinary fielder. Good statistics notwithstanding, there were lots of Woody Fairs in the crowded minor leagues of the late 1930s.

Still, Fair persevered. He finished the 1943 season with Toronto of the International League, only one small step from the major leagues. Of course, there was a war going on, and Fair could hardly escape its impact. He spent 1944 and 1945 putting together B-29 bombers in Wichita, Kansas, and playing a little semipro ball. By the time Fair got back into gear after the war, the major leagues and high minors were flooded with returning war veterans with big-league credentials who were looking to make up for lost time. Major league teams had little use for 32-year-old might-have-beens.

Fair settled down in the Carolina League, where he was the league's dominant force in its first half-decade. He gained a reputation as the kind of clutch hitter no pitcher wanted to face with the game on the line. His best year undoubtedly was 1946, when he hit .348, collected a still-standing league-record 51 doubles, and hit 24 home runs for Durham. Most extraordinarily, he scored 161 runs and drove in 161 that year. Fair batted .324 in 601 Carolina League games, with 123 home runs and 559 runs batted in. For his 17-year minor league career, he batted .306, hit 275 home runs, and stole 263 bases.

Second baseman Lee Mohr (.327) and first baseman John Streza (.299, 116 RBIs) supported Fair and Wright. On August 21, Durham defeated Leaksville 22–13, as Wright drove in seven runs and Fair went five for five, with a home run, three doubles, a single, and four runs batted in. The Bulls ended the season with still-standing league records for batting average (.305), hits (1,573), and runs (1,050).

Yet the key to the Durham surge was pitcher Hal "Skinny" Brown, ironically a native of Greensboro and a former Greensboro High School star. The 21-year-old right-hander lost his first four decisions before winning 15 straight. He ended the season with a 15–5 record and a 2.42 earned-run average. Brown won one big game after another as the Bulls closed in on Greensboro. On August 22, he defeated Raleigh and former big leaguer Max Butcher in front of a home crowd of 5,100.

When Durham beat Raleigh again the following day, the two were tied for second, four games behind Greensboro. Durham and Raleigh continued to close in on Greensboro as the season neared its conclusion. On August 26, Brown won his 13th straight, a 23–3 victory over the collapsing Pats, who committed five errors and walked 10 batters. Two days later, Raleigh scored nine runs in the last two innings to beat Greensboro. When Greensboro lost to Danville on August 31, it dropped into a tie for first with Durham, with Raleigh only two games back.

Having dissipated a substantial lead, it would have been only natural for Greensboro to continue its collapse the last week of the season. So, of course, the Pats righted themselves and regained first place. They were aided immeasurably by Raleigh's 15–3 thrashing of Durham on September 1 and a Caps double-header sweep of the Bulls the following day, Labor Day. Raleigh then lost a backbreaker on September 3 when Danville scored eight runs in the top of the ninth for an 11–9 win. The next night, Raleigh turned the tables, overcoming a 10-run deficit to beat Danville 14–13 in 12 innings. It was too little, too late, however, as the rejuvenated Patriots held off Raleigh and Durham by five games.

There was also a close race for fourth place and the final playoff spot. Winston-Salem won 14 of its last 17 to make a late run but fell just short. The final spot went to a Burlington team that featured league home-run leader Gus Zernial (.336, 41, 111). The muscular Zernial went on to hit 237 home runs in the major leagues.

The tight race for fourth place was enlivened by what has become known as the "Lights Out" game. In Burlington on August 27, Winston-Salem held an 8–1 lead in the third inning when the lights went out. By all accounts, the home team didn't try very hard to get them fixed, and the game was called within 15 minutes.

Winston-Salem made a futile protest to Dr. Wilson. The league directors met on the season's last day and voted to overrule their president; Wilson subsequently quit, but the directors refused to accept his resignation. The directors wanted the two teams to replay the game from the beginning, not from the point where it was interrupted. A Winston-Salem victory would result in a tie and force a game for the final playoff spot. Before the contest could be played, however, National Association president Bramham expressed his "opinion" that the league directors could not overrule the president on this issue. The game was never played, and Burlington held onto the last playoff spot.

Since the rather illogical playoff format called for the regular-season champion to play the third-place team and the second-place team to play the fourth-place club, it was necessary for Raleigh and Durham to break their second-place tie in a single postseason game. Raleigh edged Durham 8–7 in 11 innings, meaning first-place Greensboro was forced to play the dangerous Bulls in the opening round, while second-place Raleigh got a relative breather against Burlington.

The Caps lost the first two games to Burlington but came back to win the next four.

In the other playoff, the Bulls upset Greensboro. Patriot nemesis Skinny Brown won the opener, and Ed Robertson lengthened the Bulls' lead with a shutout in game two. Staring elimination in the face, the regular-season champs rallied with three unearned runs in the top of the ninth for an 8–6 win in game three. Brown beat Greensboro again, however, and Durham finished off Greensboro four games to two.

In the championship series, Raleigh overcame the Bulls in six games. The Caps scored 23 runs in winning the first two games with ease. The Bulls came back with victories in the third and fourth games; Raleigh aided its rival considerably in game four by committing five errors, which led to eight unearned runs. The Bulls reciprocated with five errors in a 9–4 loss in game five. Raleigh then won game six 3–2 to take the title. Roy Pinyoun threw a five-hitter, while Glenn Lockamy singled in the winning run in the eighth inning. According to Raleigh players, the Caps' impressive total of 51 runs in six games was at least partially the result of stealing signs from Durham's catchers.

The final statistics for 1946 demonstrate how dominant the hitters were in the Carolina League. Twenty-five batters with more than 100 at-bats hit over .300, while 11 men drove in more than 100 runs. The Durham Bulls set batting records that have never been equaled in league play. Their star, Woody Fair, scored 161 runs and hit 51 doubles, both still league records, and his 161 runs batted in has been surpassed only once. Other batting stars included Martinsville shortstop Willard Nance (.321, league-leading 61 stolen bases), Martinsville outfielder Joe Socey (.375, 115 RBIs), Martinsville third baseman Bill Hockenbury (.327), Leaksville outfielder W. L. Hobson (.350, 126 RBIs), and Burlington first baseman Jim Blair (.331).

One pitcher who endured this onslaught was Leaksville's Frank Paulin (19–18), who pitched 31 complete games and 303 innings, both still league records.

Clearly, the fans loved all this offense. The league claimed an impressive attendance of 930,000, led by Greensboro with 171,000. The Bulls drew 6,237 on September 2 for a crucial late-season matchup with Raleigh. This game attained a measure of fame in the 1980s, when tradition-minded Bulls owner Miles Wolff intentionally underreported several larger crowds in order to let the old mark stand as a stadium and franchise record.

1946 Final Standings

Greensboro	85–57	
*Raleigh	80–62	playoff winner
Durham	80–62	
Burlington	69–71	
Winston-Salem	68–72	
Martinsville	67–75	
Danville	60–82	
Leaksville	57–85	

—◆—

The Carolina League began its third season with its lineup intact. Winston-Salem was still owned by the St. Louis Cardinals, Martinsville by the Philadelphia Athletics. Burlington had a working agreement with the minor league Atlanta Crackers, while the Bulls had a working agreement with the Detroit Tigers. The other four teams were independent.

Raleigh, Durham, and Winston-Salem were the early league-leaders in 1947. Raleigh fell off the pace after some crucial personnel losses. Veteran Roy Pinyoun suffered a sore arm, Charlie Timm left the team, and outfielder Jim Mills suffered a broken nose and cheekbone when he was hit by a pitch from Leaksville's Tal Abernathy on June 1.

The Bulls again featured a potent lineup, led by outfielder-manager Willie Duke (.385, 13, 117), first baseman Cecil "Turkey" Tyson (.349, 105 RBIs), and Fred Pacitto (.368, 112 RBIs). The ace of the pitching staff was Claude Weaver (18–8, 3.93), a Bulls mainstay from their Piedmont League days. Weaver had his ashes scattered over Durham Athletic Park after his death in 1967.

On May 20, the Bulls leveled Leaksville 35–8, keyed by a 17-run seventh inning. Tyson, normally a tough out, made the first two outs in the inning and came to bat a third time with a chance to achieve baseball immortality by making all three outs in an inning. He walked, however.

Despite a formidable array of slugging talent, the Bulls were unable to pull away from Winston-Salem. The Cards featured the league's two best young prospects, pitcher Harvey Haddix and crowd-pleasing 18-year-old first baseman Steve Bilko. Haddix won the league's Rookie of the Year award with a 19–5 record, a league-leading 1.90 earned-run average, and a no-hitter. He went on to win 136 games in a 14-year major league career. In 1959, he became the principal figure in one of baseball's most famous games when he pitched 12 perfect innings against the Milwaukee Braves, only to lose his perfect game, his no-hitter, and eventually the game in the 13th inning. Bilko (.338, 29, 120) was a burly power hitter who became a minor league legend. In 1956 and 1957, he hit 55 and 56 homers for the Los Angeles Angels of the Pacific Coast League. Bilko ended his pro career in 1963 with 313 minor league homers and 76 major league homers.

The 1947 Cards also had 24-year-old outfielder Frank Gravino (.310), who would end his minor league career with 271 home runs, including back-to-back totals of 52 and 56 for Fargo-Moorhead in 1953 and 1954. Unlike Bilko, Gravino never made the majors.

The free-swinging Cards were mastered once, however. On June 30, Danville's Thurman Lowe struck out 19 in a 2–0 win over Winston-Salem.

At the end of May, Durham led second-place Winston-Salem by 1½ games

Mr. Baseball

Willie Duke   N.C. Division of Archives and History

One of the most storied names in the history of North Carolina minor league baseball is that of "Wee" Willie Duke. Duke graduated from North Carolina State College in 1933 and began playing minor league baseball the following year in Nashville. He advanced as high as Minneapolis, where he briefly batted cleanup behind a young slugger named Ted Williams. Duke delighted in telling the story of a game against Milwaukee when Whitlow Wyatt struck out Williams four times but allowed a double, triple, and home run to Duke.

Willie Duke served in the military from 1943 to 1945. Like so many other once-promising talents, he was too old to be considered a major league prospect by the time the war ended. He spent the remaining years of his career playing and occasionally managing in the Carolina League and the Tobacco State League. After batting .393 in 1946 for Clinton in the To-

bacco State League, Duke hit .385 for Durham in 1947. Incredibly, this mark, the second-highest single-season batting average in Carolina League history, did not lead the league; Raleigh's Harry Sullivan batted .391.

The extroverted Duke was a crowd-pleasing favorite. A talkative sort, he made friends throughout the league. He played through the 1950 season, retiring with a lifetime .331 minor league batting average.

Duke stayed active after his playing career. He was a moving force behind youth baseball in the Raleigh area, particularly American Legion ball, and founded the Raleigh Hot Stove League. In 1970, he was awarded the *Sport* Magazine Service Award "for outstanding contributions to the advancement of the community sports programs and activities." At his death in 1993, he was eulogized as North Carolina's "Mr. Baseball."

and Greensboro by two. As the season progressed, Raleigh and Burlington climbed into the race and Greensboro dropped out. Raleigh's surge was sparked by the return of Mills in early July and the efforts of pitcher Red Benton, a former University of North Carolina football and baseball star, who started the season 6–5 but finished 16–10.

The most dramatic turnaround was in Burlington. The Bees started the season slowly and were in last place on May 15 with a record of 8–14. However, pitcher Lamar Chambers got hot, winning 16 consecutive games, a league record equaled but never surpassed. Chambers finished the season with a 21–6 record. He was ably supported by manager–center fielder Buddy Bates (.361), Charles Woodail (.323, 12, 118), and pitchers Pete Bryant (22–12) and Ken Deal (23–7, 275 strikeouts). Chambers, Bryant, and Deal made the 1947 Burlington Bees the only team in Carolina League history to have three 20-game winners in a single season.

On July 22, Burlington blasted slumping Greensboro 20–1. The same day, Winston-Salem broke a nine-game Raleigh winning streak, as Haddix outdueled Benton 3–1. At that point, the Bees led Winston-Salem by 1½ games and the Caps by five.

The pitching-shy Bulls were dropping out of contention. They also had some defensive problems. Shortstop Frank Sturm committed an appalling 85 errors, a record that still stands. However, the Bulls did have one memorable day in the regular season. On August 30, they stole a still-standing league-record 12 bases against Martinsville.

Burlington, Winston-Salem, and Raleigh continued to stay close through August. Raleigh bolstered its chances when it purchased slugging third baseman Bill Nagel (.290, 30, 128) from the cash-poor Leaksville Triplets. Nagel had played for several major league teams in the late 1930s and the 1940s. The Caps got two exceptional pitching performances in mid-August. On August 18, former North Carolina State star Ray Hardee pulled an iron-man performance by pitching all 14 innings of an 8–0, 7–1 doubleheader sweep of Greensboro. (Most minor league doubleheader games are seven innings.) Three days later, Al Henencheck no-hit the Pats 13–0. Unfortunately for Raleigh, Hardee's feat took something out of him. On August 29, he was hit hard in a crucial 10–1 loss to Haddix and Winston-Salem.

Despite the heroics of Hardee and Henencheck, Raleigh was unable to catch Burlington and Winston-Salem, who traded first place throughout the final month. The two were tied following the games of September 2, after which the Cards went into an untimely slump, losing their last four contests and handing Burlington the regular-season title.

The playoffs had the same format as the previous two seasons. The Bees jumped to a 2–0 lead over Raleigh, as Deal won the opener and Chambers won game two. Raleigh came back to send the series to a decisive seventh game, and then upset the regular-season champs by pounding Deal 11–6.

In the other playoff series, Durham reversed its second-half slump and stunned Winston-Salem four games to two. The Bulls' big bats exploded against the Cards for nine runs in game two, 13 in game four, and 16 in the final contest.

The championship matched the two rivals of the previous year. Although no one knew it at the time, Raleigh and Durham would never again meet in a Carolina League championship series. The rivalry this year was enlivened by bad blood, which had existed between the two clubs since a May 27 fight between Hardee and Tyson. Jim Mills went five for six with four runs batted in as Raleigh won the opener 14–4. After that, the pitching for both teams became surprisingly effective. Durham won games two and three and Raleigh game four by identical 2–1 scores. Ray Hardee won game five for the Caps, who then took the title in game six by a 1–0 score. Al Henencheck won the final game, with late-season acquisition Nagel driving in the game's only run in the sixth inning.

Raleigh's championship team had many heroes. Catcher Harry Sullivan led the league in hitting with a .391 average and drove in 109 runs. Not only is Sullivan's batting average still a league record, but Willie Duke's runner-up mark of .385 remains the second-best single-season average in league history, despite not even winning a title. Sullivan was supported by first baseman Dave Baxter (.308, 20, 117) and second baseman Glenn Lockamy (.302), while Henencheck, Hardee, and Benton combined for 49 victories.

Other top players included Greensboro outfielder Emile Showfety (.328, 26, 121), Greensboro shortstop Matt Topkins (.305), Leaksville shortstop Walter "Teapot" Frye (.308), Danville's Gene Petty (.314, 31, 107), Martinsville outfielder Pat Cooper (.376, 23, 108), and Martinsville's Art Wellman (.368).

Carolina League attendance continued to increase. In 1947, the league became the first Class C league ever to exceed a million in attendance, led by Winston-Salem's 223,000. The league would not go over the million mark again until 1989, while no Carolina League team would surpass the Winston-Salem mark until 1988.

There was one dark cloud on the horizon, however. The Leaksville franchise folded at the end of the season. None of Leaksville's three Carolina League teams had been very good, and the small community, which merged with nearby Draper and Spray in 1967 to form Eden, was unable to compete financially with the larger cities in the league. In early July, club president J. M. Norman announced that the team was $8,600 in debt and could not continue. Only league intervention allowed Leaksville to complete the season. Raleigh *Times* columnist Neale Patrick observed that it does not take "a cagy business man to witness the fact that the organization of some of the leagues which pits some of the smaller towns against baseball-crazy cities isn't quite cricket for the gate receipts of the little fellow." He predicted that Martinsville would be next.

Among the possibilities mentioned for replacing Leaksville was Charlotte, then a member of the Tri-State League. North Carolina's largest city would continue to be mentioned as a possibility for the Carolina League for years to come, but the move never happened, largely because of the city's relative distance. High Point and Sanford were also mentioned. The final result was considerably more mundane than Charlotte. The Leaksville franchise moved only a few miles down the road to the equally small tobacco town of Reidsville. The team was named the Luckies in honor of Lucky Strike cigarettes, one of the town's leading products. In a league whose other nicknames over the years have included the Bulls (from Bull Durham chewing tobacco), the Leafs, and the Tobacconists, the Luckies were right at home. Nonetheless, it's hard not to think that the Carolina League missed a great chance to move into a bigger neighborhood.

1947 Final Standings

Burlington	87–55	
Winston-Salem	85–57	
* Raleigh	81–60	playoff winner
Durham	70–71	
Greensboro	65–75	
Danville	65–77	
Leaksville	59–82	
Martinsville	53–88	

———♦———

Minor league baseball continued its postwar expansion in 1948, with an unprecedented 58 leagues in the National Association. In addition to a new franchise, the Carolina League had a new president. Dr. Wilson resigned because of ill health and an inability to devote enough time to the league. He was replaced by Carroll Brown of Martinsville, the former business manager of that town's team.

Brown presided over one of the league's closest pennant races, with only 6½ games separating the top five teams at season's end. Winston-Salem drew first blood in the race, winning 10 of its first 12 games, 15 of its first 20. The Cards were led by first baseman Harvey Zernia, catcher Ed Lippeatt, and pitcher Jack Frisinger.

Eventually, Danville and Raleigh closed the gap on Winston-Salem. On May 1, Woody Fair, now playing for Danville, hit a pair of homers, one a grand slam, and drove in seven runs in an 18–5 thrashing of Raleigh. By the middle of June, the hot-hitting veteran had propelled the Leafs into first place. On July 3, he took over as player-manager. With a solid supporting cast which included league Rookie of the Year Russell Sullivan (.335, 35, 129), outfielder

Gene Petty, and pitchers Melvin Adams (18–11) and Pete Angell (14–9), Danville had the look of a winner by midseason.

The most effective managerial change took place in Raleigh. The Caps slumped in June and dropped nine games behind Winston-Salem. On June 26, player-manager Bill Nagel, a solid hitter but novice manager, was replaced as manager by second baseman Glenn Lockamy. The change energized Raleigh. Lockamy, who batted .328, skippered a team which included outfielder Charlie Fitzgerald (.362), shortstop Jimmy Edwards (.304), pitcher Al Henencheck (22–9, 2.24), and former Leaksville pitcher Frank Paulin (17–8).

The pennant race continued to take unpredictable turns. On July 8, Fair injured his leg. Only five days after becoming player-manager, the Danville star was reduced to being just a manager. He missed much of the rest of the season, and, predictably, the Leafs struggled in his absence. He finished the season with a .336 average, 29 homers, and 110 runs batted in.

Late in July, the Burlington Bees won 13 straight to climb into the race. In early August, Martinsville got hot and made it a five-team race. Martinsville took over first place on August 12, at which point fifth-place Burlington trailed by only three games.

The tension of the tight race took its toll on players, fans, and umpires. The

The Un-Luckies Scandal

Most baseball fans are familiar with the so-called Black Sox scandal of 1919, in which eight members of the Chicago White Sox accepted money from gamblers to throw the World Series, and the recent controversy surrounding Pete Rose's gambling activities. Baseball gambling crises have not been restricted to the major leagues, of course. The Carolina League faced one tawdry such episode in 1948.

The principal figure was Reidsville Luckies manager-pitcher Barney DeForge. On May 10, DeForge met at a Reidsville hotel with W. C. McWaters, a Greensboro man, and Ed Weingarten, an official with the nearby Leaksville team of the Blue Ridge League. The three discussed the possibility of gambling and the money that could be made from that activity. Four days later, McWaters offered DeForge $300 to make sure that his team lost that night's game against Winston-Salem by at least

three runs. DeForge accepted.

DeForge placed himself on the mound in the eighth inning of that contest with his club trailing 2–0. He then proceeded to give up three more runs on four walks and a wild pitch, ensuring a 5–0 loss.

That night, an unidentified fan went to the office of *Winston-Salem Journal* sports editor Frank Spencer and told him that he had overheard talk in the stands that the game was fixed. Winston-Salem officials began investigating, and within days, DeForge confessed.

The reaction of National Association president George Trautman was quick and decisive. Only three years earlier, his predecessor, William G. Bramham, had issued a lifetime ban against a dozen men for throwing games in the Evangeline League. Trautman's response was identical. DeForge and Weingarten were banned from baseball for life.

1948 season may have been the roughest in league history. Ejections were common, fights frequent. On June 18, several hundred fans at Raleigh's Devereaux Meadow repeatedly threw seat cushions on the field to protest the umpiring of Bull Davis. When some of the fans switched to pop bottles, Davis called the game, which Raleigh was losing 7–0 to Martinsville, and declared a forfeit for the visitors. A police escort was necessary for Davis and the other umpire to safely escape the field.

As ugly as this incident was, things got worse as the pennant race entered its stretch run. On August 12 in Greensboro, Raleigh manager Lockamy was ejected for arguing and required a police escort to leave the playing field. Ten days later, a near-riot occurred at Winston-Salem. With Greensboro ahead 1–0 and Winston-Salem at bat in the bottom of the ninth, baserunner Ed Lippeatt became caught in a rundown between third and home. When he threw up his hands to deflect the ball, he was called out. The game ended 1–0, whereupon several hundred disgruntled fans chased the umpires into their dressing room. A dozen Winston-Salem policemen were needed to escort the arbiters away from the ballpark. During the fray, umpire Bull Davis was punched by a fan, as was a Greensboro player.

On September 1, Martinsville manager Edwin Morgan almost came to blows with the umpiring crew following a close play at the plate in a crucial 2–1 loss to Durham.

Martinsville and Raleigh traded first place throughout the middle of August, while Burlington, Danville, and Winston-Salem stayed close. On August 21, only 2½ games separated the top five teams. Winston-Salem faded from contention in the season's last weeks and ended up in fifth place, out of the playoffs. Raleigh, Martinsville, and Burlington were all tied for first as late as August 27. The Caps pulled away down the stretch, winning nine of their final 12 games, while Martinsville edged Burlington for second place.

Raleigh had won the postseason championship in 1946 and 1947 despite not winning the regular season. In 1948, the tables were turned, as third-place Burlington upset the Caps four games to two in the first round of the playoffs. The key for Burlington was pitcher Maxie Wilson, who started the season in the Coastal Plain League as the manager of the Wilson team. When he was fired by Wilson, he signed as a pitcher with Burlington and keyed its stretch run with a 13–3 record and two wins over Raleigh in the playoffs. The Bees also featured outfielder Dick Woodard (.336), outfielder-manager Buddy Bates (.332), catcher Norm Wilson (.311, 102 RBIs), and pitchers Larry Hartley (11–5) and Tal Abernathy.

In the other half of the playoffs, Martinsville handled Danville easily, losing only once in five games.

The Athletics followed this up with a hard-fought victory in the title series.

Burlington won the first two games, but Martinsville took the last four and the title. Led by Bill LaFrance (.327, 29, 94) and George Wright (.307), the hard-hitting A's scored 33 runs in their four victories. The surprising championship came amidst widespread rumors that Philadelphia was anxious to get out of the small Virginia town. In addition to LaFrance and Wright, Martinsville's surge to the title was led by first baseman Eddie Morgan (.373, 30, 116) and outfielder Pat Cooper, who had a league-record 31-game hitting streak and finished the season with a .330 average, 20 home runs, and 123 runs batted in. Several players have challenged Cooper's record in the years since, but no one has equaled it.

The three noncontenders all had some outstanding performers.

Despite the heroics of Sullivan, Cooper, Morgan, and others, the league's Player of the Year was Reidsville southpaw Lewis Hester, who won 25 games against 13 losses. Hester set a league record for wins in a single season, a spectacular accomplishment for a team that won only 57 games. What little offense Reidsville produced was supplied by Dick Sipek (.318), Bob Downing (.304), and Bill Nagel (.313, 28, 120), who finished the season with Reidsville after being fired as the Raleigh manager. The hearing-impaired Sipek had played in the major leagues in 1945.

Durham player-manager Willie Duke batted .355, veteran second baseman Lawrence "Crash" Davis hit .317 and led the league with 50 doubles, and outfielder Malcolm Stevens batted .317.

Greensboro's miserable season was enlivened only by outfielder Emile Showfety (.337, 19, 105), who had a 27-game hitting streak, and first baseman Bob Falk (.308).

League attendance in 1948 declined precipitously from the dizzying heights of the previous season. The league total was 777,000, led by Winston-Salem with 141,000. Champion Martinsville brought up the rear in attendance with less than 60,000.

1948 Final Standings

Raleigh	84–58	
*Martinsville	81–61	playoff winner
Burlington	80–62	
Danville	77–64	
Winston-Salem	76–65	
Durham	63–79	
Reidsville	57–85	
Greensboro	49–93	

The Carolina League decided to make a dramatic change for 1949. In August, the league voted to jump from Class C to Class B, a change that raised the salary limit $100 per month (to $4,000 per month), increased the maximum number of veterans (defined as anyone with three or more years of pro experience) from seven to 13, and created the possibility of better baseball. In Herb Brett's words, "If we could have more veterans, we would be able to give the public better baseball, and that's what the fans want."

Not everyone agreed. Durham, Martinsville, Burlington, and Reidsville all voted against the move. President Carroll Brown broke the four-four tie in favor of Class B. The larger cities hoped to use the change to lure Charlotte into the league but were again unsuccessful.

Brown's tie-breaking vote was one of his last acts as league president. He resigned and was replaced temporarily by Herb Brett. On February 20, the league named Glenn E. "Ted" Mann as its third full-time president. Mann was the sports information director at Duke University. He took over the league in a year when minor league baseball reached its peak, at least in terms of the number of leagues; 59 leagues were members of the National Association that year.

The Carolina League returned with the same eight teams as the previous season. The Danville Leafs dominated most of the 1949 regular season. Unlike the previous year, player-manager Woody Fair was healthy the entire season. He finished with a .325 batting average, 38 home runs, and 117 runs batted in. Outfielder William Brown (.361, 18, 99, 199 hits), catcher Hugh Taylor (.313), and third baseman Bill Nagel augmented the attack. A first-rate pitching staff included Adam Twarkins (22–9, 2.07), Pete Angell (20–9), and Fred Guiliani (16–6). The Leafs won 15 of their first 21 games and took over first place for good by mid-May. The surge was sparked by Brown's 23-game hitting streak, which was broken by Reidsville on May 21.

The rest of the league responded by firing managers. Reidsville dismissed Johnny George on May 2. Around the same time, it signed a working agreement with the lowly St. Louis Browns, which didn't do it much good. The other teams followed suit in firing skippers. Before the season ended, every team except Danville, Durham, and last-place Martinsville changed managers. One of these moves helped the Leafs. On June 12, Winston-Salem fired player-manager Willie Duke. Danville picked up "Wee Willie," who ended the season with a .349 average, 22 homers, and 106 RBIs.

Danville led second-place Greensboro by 1½ games at the end of May. The Patriots faded in June and dropped out of the race for good. Danville went 20–11 that month, opening up an 8½-game lead. The Winston-Salem Cards, in sixth place at the end of May with a 17–22 record, got hot in early July and moved into second place. Winston-Salem featured one of the league's outstanding young prospects, 21-year-old outfielder Eldon "Rip" Repulski (.300,

20, 88), who went on to hit 106 home runs in the major leagues. Lee Peterson (19–10, 2.22) and Hisel Patrick (10–1, 2.71) anchored the Winston-Salem pitching staff. Despite the improved play in the Twin City, Danville still appeared to have the race in hand. On August 10, it was nine games ahead of second-place Winston-Salem.

Even with an apparent runaway, fans had plenty to get excited about in the exploits of 32-year-old Reidsville first baseman Leo "Muscle" Shoals, one of the most exciting players in Carolina League history. A powerfully built left-handed first baseman, Shoals was definitely a major league–caliber hitter. Unfortunately, an affection for parties and a propensity for getting into trouble kept him in the minors permanently.

Shoals hit 14 home runs in his first 40 games and never let up. On June 12, he slugged three home runs, a double, and a single against Greensboro, amassing a league-record 15 total bases. Shoals hit three home runs and a single on August 25 in a 20–8 win over Burlington. He scored six runs and drove in six in that game, in which Reidsville scored 10 runs in the sixth inning to overcome an 8–4 deficit. Shoals finished the season with a .359 batting average, 55 home runs, 131 runs batted in, and 365 total bases. He received his share of $100 handshakes from Reidsville supporters. Late in the season, the team gave him a "Muscle Shoals Night," during which he received, in his own words, "a truck load of gifts." He had a chance to finish the season with the St. Louis Browns as a pinch hitter but turned it down because his wife was expecting a child in October.

Late in the season, Danville succumbed to a bad case of overconfidence. A cocky Fair declared that the Carolina League consisted of Danville and seven second-division clubs. Not surprisingly, this didn't go over too well with the rest of the league. When the streaking Cards made a late run, it appeared that Fair might have to eat his words. On September 2, Winston-Salem took a doubleheader from Martinsville, while Danville lost to Reidsville ace Mike Forline. This reduced Danville's once-imposing lead to four games.

It remained at four on September 5, when Danville journeyed to Winston-Salem for a crucial three-game series at Southside Park. The September 5 twin bill was one of the league's most memorable nights.

An overflow crowd of 8,147 jammed the ballpark. So large was the throng that it spilled onto the edge of the playing field. Before the game, the umpires ruled that any fly ball hit into the crowd would be a ground-rule double, whether it was caught or not. In the sixth inning, with a runner on first base and Danville ahead 1–0 behind Angell, Winston-Salem's Al Neil hit a fly ball that was caught in the crowd by right fielder Al Clark. The umpires called Neil out, leading to a major rhubarb. They refused to change the call, and Angell ended up with a one-hit, 2–0 win.

Muscle Shoals

If Hollywood ever makes a movie about a true minor league legend, it could do worse than select Leo "Muscle" Shoals, a larger-than-life figure if ever the Carolina League had one.

Muscle Shoals was born in West Virginia in 1916. He made his professional debut in 1937 in the Pennsylvania State League for the St. Louis Cardinals organization. A muscular 220-pounder, Shoals quickly established himself as a formidable slugger. In 1939, playing for Johnson City in the Appalachian State League, he hit .365, with 16 home runs. Two years later, he hit 26 home runs in the Cotton States League.

Muscle Shoals

Greensboro News & Record

The gregarious Shoals also gained a reputation for being difficult to manage. He had run-ins with managers, and sometimes with the law as well. He told one newspaper reporter, "I did Hell around, there was no question about it. Any advice I'd give a ballplayer today would be lay off them bars at night." In 1939, Shoals was shot and seriously wounded in a dispute with a bartender.

By World War II, Shoals had been blacklisted by the Cardinals and was playing for independent teams. He served in the Pacific during the war and saw combat on several desolate islands.

In 1946 and 1947, Shoals played for Kingsport of the Appalachian League, where he batted .333 and .387. His only full year in the Carolina League was in 1949, and it was the best year of his career. The enormously popular Shoals pounded out 55 home runs for the Reidsville Luckies, a league record never equaled and not seriously challenged since Tolia "Tony" Solaita's 49 homers in 1968. Shoals also led the league in runs batted in and missed the batting title by only two percentage points. The highlight of his season was a three-home-run, 15-total-base game against Greensboro on June 12. In his last at-bat, Shoals lined a single off the wall, only inches from his fourth homer. No Carolina League player has ever hit four home runs in a game.

Late in the season, the hapless St. Louis Browns offered to bring Shoals up to the majors. He declined for several reasons, including his wife's pregnancy. He also would have taken a pay cut. Shoals was the beneficiary of so many passed hats, $20 handshakes, and merchant discounts that he couldn't afford to leave.

The Cincinnati Reds, a much more prestigious major league organization than the perennially inept Browns, drafted Shoals and signed him to a minor league contract in 1950; he was sent to Columbia, South Carolina, of the South Atlantic League. Shoals subsequently disappeared for several games on a road trip to Jacksonville, Florida. When he finally showed up, he was released. Reidsville signed him for the remainder of the season, but the magic was gone. He batted only .224 in 116 at-bats.

Shoals finished his career back in Kingsport. When he retired after the 1955 season, his career minor league stats included a .337 batting average, 362 home runs, and 1,529 runs batted in. As of this writing, he ranks 10th on the all-time minor league home-run list.

A common assessment of Shoals was offered several years ago by another noteworthy minor leaguer, Lawrence "Crash" Davis: "He was compassionate. You would think a big guy like that might be mean. But he'd give you the shirt off his back."

In the nightcap, Danville rode the momentum of its controversial first-game win to an 8–3 lead in the bottom of the ninth, when, incredibly, Winston-Salem rallied for six runs and a 9–8 win. The winning run scored when Red Long stole home.

Despite the gutty comeback in the second game, Winston-Salem still trailed by four games with only six to play. When Danville won the third game in the series, the pennant race was over.

By that time, Raleigh had settled securely into third place, but the race for fourth and the final playoff spot was contested to the very end by Burlington and Greensboro. Going into the season's last day, Burlington led by 1½ games, with both teams facing scheduled doubleheaders. When Burlington lost twice to Winston-Salem, the door was open for Greensboro. The Patriots beat Danville in their first game, but with a playoff spot on the line, they lost the nightcap 10–3.

The Carolina League made a slight modification in its playoff format for 1949. Now, the first round more reasonably matched the regular-season champion against the fourth-place team, while the second- and third-place teams squared off.

Danville and Winston-Salem entered the postseason as clear favorites. The Leafs had led virtually the entire season, while the Cards had made a late run for first. Yet the Cards had their share of distractions. Ted Mann denied their appeal over the controversial Danville game. He also suspended manager Roland LeBlanc for the first two games of the playoffs for bumping umpire Lou Bello in a late-season argument. The Cards were without star first baseman Andy Philip, who had left the club in August to prepare for his professional basketball season with the NBA's Chicago Stags. Finally, the Cards were involved in a messy dispute with former manager Willie Duke, who had not been paid all the money owed him at the time of his termination; Duke eventually collected.

Given these problems, it is probably not surprising that Winston-Salem was swept by Raleigh. The key player was Salisbury, North Carolina, native and former major league pitcher Wes Livengood, who won game one 6–2 with a two-hitter and game four 4–1. The versatile Livengood broke a 1–1 tie with a three-run homer in game four.

If Raleigh's win over Winston-Salem made sense, what happened in the other first-round series was completely inexplicable. The Bees jumped to an early lead over Danville with a 5–4 win in game one and a 4–1 win in game two. The Leafs fell apart in the second game, committing six errors. They rallied to an 11–1 win in game three, as Fair drove in four runs. The teams split the next two games before Burlington closed out the regular-season champs 6–5 in game six.

Even with their upset victory over Danville, the Bees still entered the finals as underdogs. Raleigh featured third baseman Don Siegert (102 RBIs), well-traveled second baseman Crash Davis (.296), and pitchers Charles Miller (18–11) and Eugene Kelly (16–11). Burlington countered with four .300 hitters—former Martinsville star Pat Cooper (110 RBIs), outfielder Billy Evans, outfielder Don MacLean, and second baseman Mike Hafenecker—along with hurler Larry Hartley (13–6).

The two teams turned out to be evenly matched. Raleigh won the first two games before Burlington took the next three. A crucial throwing error by the usually reliable Crash Davis in the ninth inning of game five gave Burlington the winning run in a 3–2 thriller. Livengood evened the series at three games apiece with a 4–0 five-hitter in a 10-inning sixth game; Burlington's Lou Bush retired the first 20 batters in that contest but tired in the 10th. Burlington broke open the decisive seventh game with six runs in the eighth to win 9–3. Raleigh committed five errors.

Greensboro and Durham missed the playoffs by a narrow margin. Both boasted some fine individual performances.

Greensboro featured outfielder Emile Showfety (.347, 35, 120), first baseman James Halkard (.313, 21, 96), and second baseman Fred Vaughan (85 RBIs). Left-handed pitcher Luis Arroyo pitched a no-hitter and won 21 games against 10 losses. Arroyo later achieved a brief measure of fame as a relief pitcher for the New York Yankees in the early 1960s, after a long career in the minors.

The Bulls were sparked by diminutive southpaw Eddie Neville, who went 25–10 with eight shutouts and a 2.59 earned-run average. Neville matched the league-record 25 games won the previous season by Lewis Hester. Like Hester, Neville accomplished this for a losing team. Much of his team's offense was provided by outfielders Carl Linhardt (.311, 23, 114, 108 runs scored) and league stolen-base leader Pat Hagerty. The best-known Bull, however, was player-manager Clarence "Ace" Parker, who batted .299 in limited action. Parker, a former Duke All-America football standout, played in the major leagues in the 1930s but was better known for a football career that included the 1940 NFL Most Valuable Player award.

Reidsville and Martinsville demonstrated the adage that pitching is three-fourths of baseball. Both featured formidable batting attacks, but poor pitching doomed them to miserable seasons.

Led by Shoals, Reidsville batted .278 with 132 home runs. Outfielder Dick Sipek batted .321, outfielder Jim Miller hit .319, and third baseman George Souter hit 25 homers and collected 99 RBIs. Reidsville's only solid pitcher was "Magic" Mike Forline (19–9, 2.33, 5 shutouts).

Martinsville's last-place team hit 139 home runs, 27 of them by first baseman Joe Mangini.

1949 Final Standings

Danville	86–57	
Winston-Salem	84–61	
Raleigh	76–68	
*Burlington	72–72	playoff winner
Greensboro	72–73	
Durham	70–72	
Reidsville	63–80	
Martinsville	52–92	

—◆—

Martinsville's cellar finish in 1949 marked its swan song in the Carolina League. Fayetteville, Martinsville's replacement, became a farm team of the Philadelphia Athletics. Unfortunately for Fayetteville baseball, the Athletics in the 1950s were one of baseball's worst franchises and were chronically unable to supply their farm teams with competitive players. Martinsville's departure left Danville as the only Virginia city in the eight-team league.

The Winston-Salem Cards dominated the 1950 Carolina League season. Early in the campaign, their manager, George Kissell, boasted that his club would be "the hustlingest and runningest ball club" in the league. He did not exaggerate. The Cards ran constantly. They stole four bases in their opener against Fayetteville and 16 in their first 10 games, eight of which were victories. Twice in the opening weeks, Winston-Salem baserunners scored from second base on infield outs. On May 4, the Cards bolstered their slugging attack when they purchased veteran minor league outfielder J. C. Dunn from Omaha of the Western League.

The aggressive Cards broke the race open early, winning 19 of their first 23 games. At the end of May, they were 30–11 and led second-place Danville by six games. On June 14, a crowd of nearly 5,000 jammed Southside Park to see Winston-Salem pitching ace Wilmer "Vinegar Bend" Mizell win a pregame cowmilking contest involving players and managers from Raleigh and the home team. Mizell then took a 5–0 lead into the eighth inning before tiring—presumably from the exertion of milking cows—and giving up six runs. Jim Neufeldt then hit a two-run homer in the bottom of the ninth for a 7–6 win. The victory was Winston-Salem's 13th straight, equaling the league record set in 1948 by Burlington. The streak reached 16 before being stopped on June 16 by Durham. It remains the longest winning streak in Carolina League history.

By that time, Winston-Salem was 46–12, 11½ games ahead of Danville. The Cards then put together a 12-game winning streak in mid-July. At the end of that month, they had a superlative won-lost record of 78–27 and a 16½-game lead.

Fayetteville was Winston-Salem's polar opposite. In fact, the A's were a first-class disaster. The newest member of the league gained an unenviable spot in the record books by losing its league-record 14th straight on May 10. The streak reached 19 before ending May 19, surprisingly with a 3–2 win over the power-house Cards; that victory was sparked by newly acquired six-foot-seven pitcher Long John Davis. Later in the season, Fayetteville had a 13-game losing streak. The A's followed a time-honored tradition by dismissing their manager, former big-league standout Mule Haas, in mid-May, but replacement Tom Oliver had no more success than his predecessor.

With a one-sided pennant race, league fans turned their attention to other attractions. One was the return to Reidsville of Muscle Shoals. After his spec-tacular 1949 season, Shoals was signed by the Cincinnati Reds organization and assigned to Columbia of the South Atlantic League. He disappeared for several days on a road trip to Jacksonville and was released. Reidsville quickly signed him, but Shoals was unable to duplicate the magic of 1949. He split time at first base with Bill Nagel and batted only .224, with five homers and 16 RBIs.

Another attraction was the deteriorating relationship between Winston-Salem and the rest of the league, the sort of thing that sometimes accompanies a run-away pennant race. One particularly ugly incident took place on June 12 in Burlington, when a pitch thrown by Al Cleary broke J. C. Dunn's arm. Burlington fans pelted Dunn with debris as he left the field. Home-team officials reportedly refused to provide a car or call a taxi for the injured player, forcing the Cards to transport Dunn to the nearest hospital in the team bus.

One Winston-Salem player who was more popular than Dunn was 19-year-old Vinegar Bend Mizell, whose easygoing country ways endeared him to fans across the league. After being named the most popular Cardinal late in the sea-son, Mizell serenaded the home fans with an impromptu rendition of "Country Boy." He went on to win 90 games in the major leagues before becoming a United States congressman from North Carolina. At a time when Carolina League teams routinely scheduled pregame square dances, milking contests, beauty pag-eants, and stunts with mules in an attempt to attract rural fans, Mizell was right at home.

Despite Winston-Salem's dominance, everyone knew that no regular-season champion had captured the playoffs since Danville in 1945. Thus, the real drama involved the other teams jockeying for a chance to knock off the Cards in a short series. Danville held second place most of the season; Burlington nipped Reidsville for third; and Greensboro and Durham came up short in the fight for fourth place.

The Winston-Salem Cards were so talented that they were able to overcome the postseason jinx, although not without a struggle. Third baseman–manager Kissell aided his cause by batting .312. His potent lineup included outfielder

Russ Rac (92 RBIs), outfielder Bill LaFrance, first baseman Neil Hertwick (94 RBIs), outfielder Jim Neufeldt (42 stolen bases), and shortstop John Huesman (league-leading 43 stolen bases). J. C. Dunn batted .307. An excellent pitching staff included Lee Peterson (21–10), Mizell (17–7, 2.48, 227 strikeouts), George Condrick (15–6), and relief ace Bob Tiefenauer (66 games, 16–8, 2.51). Tiefenauer eventually pitched in 849 minor league games and 179 major league games in a pro career that lasted until 1969.

In the first round of the playoffs, Winston-Salem squared off against fourth-place Reidsville, managed by the always-mobile Herb Brett. Unaffiliated with any big-league team, the Luckies had a number of Carolina League veterans, including Shoals, third baseman George Souter (.291), first baseman Bill Nagel (.290, 19, 85), and pitchers Joe Micich (18–8) and Mike Forline. Mizell and Tiefenauer staked Winston-Salem to a 2–0 lead over the Triplets, but Reidsville won the next two games to even the best-of-five series. The suddenly pressed Cards won the fifth game easily, however, by an 11–2 score, with Mizell getting the victory.

The other first-round series matched second-place Danville and third-place Burlington. The Leafs, managed by fiery former major league outfielder Ben Chapman, were led by the always-dangerous Woody Fair (.300, 23, 103), out-fielder John Rothenhauler (.297, 17, 92), and pitcher Pete Angell (21–10). Burlington's best player was speedy center fielder Bill Evans (.338, 111 runs, 207 hits), who set a still-standing league record of 466 put-outs on the way to a league Player of the Year award. Fellow outfielders Don McLean and Jim Maynard batted .328 and .310, respectively, while veteran Pat Cooper hit .302. Mike Kash and Tony Polink each won 15 games to pace the pitching staff. Led by Evans, Burlington pulled off a 3–1 upset win over Danville in the first round.

Burlington was no match for Winston-Salem in the finals, however, winning only once in five games. The best game of the series was the opener, in which Neil Hertwick's 13th-inning home run gave the Cards a 1–0 victory. Burlington won the next game but Winston-Salem took the final three contests, the league title, and acclamation as the best Carolina League team of the period.

Fifth-place Greensboro ended the season with a winning record and just missed the playoffs. Second baseman Fred Vaughan (.320, 27, 75) and pitcher Woody Rich (16–9, 2.41) had stellar seasons for the Patriots.

The same can be said for Durham pitchers Bob Cruze (11–8, 2.31) and Lacy James (16–9).

Little positive can be said about the hapless Raleigh Caps, who were kept out of the cellar only by the unprecedented ineptness of Fayetteville. Raleigh pitcher Charles Miller went 14–21 despite a decent earned-run average of 3.18, becoming in the process the only 20-game loser in Carolina League history.

Fayetteville ended the season with a .228 team batting average and a .307 winning percentage, the worst in league history until 1974. Fayetteville finished 59 games out of first place.

League attendance dropped slightly to 738,000. Attendance in Raleigh was especially poor at 52,000, a sign of bad things to come for the Capital City.

1950 Final Standings

* Winston-Salem	106–47	playoff winner
Danville	87–66	
Burlington	83–70	
Reidsville	82–72	
Greensboro	78–74	
Durham	73–79	
Raleigh	55–97	
Fayetteville	47–106	

♦   ♦   ♦

1952 Carolina League Beauty Contestants

N.C. Division of Archives and History

CHAPTER TWO
1951 — 56

♦ ♦ ♦

The postwar minor league boom went bust in the early 1950s. The minor leagues began a slide that lasted for almost three decades. The numbers tell the story. Fifty-eight minor leagues were in the National Association in 1950. The following year, there were 50. By 1954, there were only 36.

There were a number of reasons for this decline. Certainly, minor league baseball was overextended in the late 1940s, and a winnowing-out process was neither unexpected nor undesirable. There simply were not enough professional-caliber baseball players, umpires, coaches, and front-office personnel to staff over 400 professional teams. It is also doubtful if there were enough fans to support this many teams indefinitely.

There were other factors, however. The culprit cited most often in the decline of minor league ball was the development of television. For the first time, minor league baseball fans in the Carolina League area could see such major league stars as Mickey Mantle, Willie Mays, Stan Musial, Ted Williams, and Warren Spahn without having to make a long trip to a big-league city. The local minor league stars began to look a little less stellar. The minor leagues fought major league broadcasts—even going so far as to look to Congress for legislative relief—but to no avail. Big-league games weren't the only competition on television. When shows like "I Love Lucy" and "You Bet Your Life" became popular, they drew their audiences in part from people who otherwise would have gone to a professional baseball game.

The fevered postwar construction of highways added another recreational option. The easier it became to go to the beach, or to the mountains, or to visit grandmother's, the easier it became to forget about the local baseball team.

Baseball, both major league and minor league, also suffered from the rising popularity of other sports. The postwar development of professional stock-car racing created a serious summertime rival for recreational dollars in North Carolina and Virginia. The constant images of President Dwight Eisenhower playing golf helped expand that sport's popularity beyond the country clubs. Football and basketball enjoyed new heights of popularity. Although these sports had little seasonal overlap with professional baseball, they increasingly attracted the kinds of superior athletes that had theretofore automatically played baseball. The most serious rival was the National Football League, which exploded in popularity in the middle and late 1950s. By the end of the decade, many pundits were arguing that the fast-paced, violent sport of pro football more accurately mirrored the realities of mid-twentieth-century America than the prosaic sport of baseball. It was widely argued that pro football was the new national pastime.

The attrition of the minor leagues was evident in North Carolina and Virginia. The venerable Piedmont League went under after the 1955 season. The Virginia League folded following the 1951 campaign. The Tri-State League, the North Carolina State League, the Tar Heel League, and the Tobacco State League all disappeared in the 1950s.

It's not clear why the Carolina League survived when so many other leagues didn't. Many knowledgeable observers believe a critical factor was the compactness of the league, which kept travel expenses at a minimum. Furthermore, the league had gained a reputation for solid baseball by the early 1950s. Most of the league's cities were traditionally good minor league cities with large-enough populations to support the professional game.

As the number of minor leagues dwindled, the quality of ball improved in those leagues that survived. Major league teams had fewer places to develop their prospects. More Carolina League teams signed working agreements with major league teams, and more future major leaguers passed through the league on the way up. Of course, this also reduced the number of veterans in the league.

The over-30 Carolina League player became an endangered species by the end of the 1950s.

Despite the improved caliber of ball and the disappearance of rival leagues, Carolina League attendance continued to fall during this period, graphic evidence of the expanded recreational opportunities in North Carolina and Virginia. In 1952, five years after the league broke the million mark in attendance, it barely surpassed a half-million.

The league began play in 1951 with no franchise changes from the previous year. Five of the eight teams now had working agreements with major league teams. The Durham Bulls began a profitable relationship with the Detroit Tigers that would last into the 1960s. Greensboro became a farm team of the Chicago Cubs, while Burlington became affiliated with the Pittsburgh Pirates. Winston-Salem and Fayetteville retained their agreements with St. Louis and the Philadelphia Athletics, respectively.

Yet the independent Reidsville Luckies drew first blood, winning 13 of their first 18 games and leading most of the first half of the campaign. The fast start was keyed by pitcher Mike Forline (21–8, 2.83) and outfielder Carl Miller (.311, 28, 114). On May 24, Forline threw a one-hit shutout against Durham. The following day, Miller began a memorable streak when he got a hit in his last two at-bats against the Bulls. He then went six for six on May 26 against Winston-Salem, with two home runs, two doubles, and seven runs batted in. When he singled in his first at-bat the following day, Miller had hit safely in nine consecu-

Mike Forline   Greensboro News & Record

tive trips to the plate. Forline and Miller were supported by outfielder Dick Sipek (.322) and third baseman George Souter (.283, 15, 74).

Things weren't going as well in Fayetteville. The faltering Philadelphia Athletics again failed to stock a competitive team, and the Fayetteville fans were not pleased. The *Fayetteville Observer* blasted the parent organization: "The Fayetteville baseball fans . . . are fed up with the worthless promises of the Philadelphia Athletics front office. . . . In the future any utterance coming out of Philadelphia of player strength here to the local A's will be taken for what it's worth—almost valueless." Philadelphia delivered enough new talent to Fayetteville to enable the A's to climb out of the cellar into seventh place, but the relationship remained strained.

This was not the only strained relationship. On June 2, Danville shortstop Mike Romello slugged umpire Emil Davidzuk after being called out for leaving third base too soon on a sacrifice fly. A judge in the stands in Durham arrested Romello. Several days later, Romello pleaded guilty to assault and was fined $25 and costs. League president Ted Mann suspended him for the remainder of the season.

Fireworks also erupted frequently when the Raleigh Capitals played. Their new manager was Joe "Ducky" Medwick, a former major leaguer whose considerable batting skills eventually led to his election to the Hall of Fame. Medwick also was hot-tempered and verbally abusive. He won few friends around the league, particularly among the umpiring crews.

Reidsville's lead over second-place Raleigh reached four games on June 10. Durham and Winston-Salem were also close. The Bulls made a run for first place in early July, which caused some interesting complications. At that point, the league All-Star Game matched the first-place team against a team representing the rest of the league. The team in first place after the games of July 4 was designated to host the game on July 15. On July 4, however, Durham and Reidsville were tied for first at 43–32. The league directors voted to move the All-Star Game back a week and scheduled a bizarre game between Durham and Reidsville on July 15 to settle the question; this game was not to be part of the regular season. Reidsville won 3–1. Ironically, the slumping Luckies had by that time dropped 4½ games behind the Bulls.

That still didn't settle the All-Star Game. Although Sunday ball had been common in North Carolina since the 1930s, Reidsville still had a local ordinance prohibiting games on the Sabbath. Reidsville general manager–manager Herb Brett assured the league that the ordinance would be waived. When the Reidsville City Council declined to follow Brett's recommendation, the game was hastily moved to Greensboro. *Greensboro Daily News* sportswriter Smith Barrier accused Brett of misleading the league, and the two feuded the remainder of the season.

Reidsville faded in late July despite the best efforts of ace pitcher Forline. On July 30, he ran his record to 17–5 with a win over Durham. He beat the Bulls again the next day in relief. Nonetheless, Durham began August with a one-game lead over Raleigh. Durham and Raleigh traded the top spot throughout August, while Winston-Salem stayed close. The Bulls were managed again by the legendary Ace Parker, who batted .269 in limited action. His top players included outfielder Gordon Bragg (.346), shortstop Henry Navarro (.306), and pitchers John McPadden (20–10, 2.93) and J. C. Martin (14–6). The veteran Raleigh team was led by third baseman Joe Tedesco (.299, 15, 115), outfielder Ted Browning, Crash Davis, and pitchers Jim Benes (10–5, 2.80) and Claude

"Dizzy" Voiselle (14–4, 2.87). Manager Medwick batted .285 in limited action, while Woody Fair spent most of the season in the Florida International League. He wrapped up his five-year Carolina League career with 123 home runs and 559 RBIs, records not likely to be challenged.

In the midst of this close race, also-ran Danville made league history. On August 10, the Virginia team introduced the league's first black player, outfielder Percy Miller, Jr., a 20-year-old local product. Miller got a two-run single in his first game, a 5–4 win over Durham. The league's newspapers reported this matter-of-factly, while fans appeared to take a wait-and-see approach. Miller was no great player, batting .184 in his only Carolina League season. Yet he helped transform the Carolina League. That same month, Granite Falls of the Western Carolina League became the first minor league team in North Carolina to racially integrate.

Raleigh faded from contention in late August, but Winston-Salem mounted a late challenge to Durham. The Cards won 10 of 12 to pull within three games of the Bulls before journeying to Durham for a crucial four-game series. Winston-Salem won the first three games to move into a tie for first on August 30. With 13 wins in 15 starts, Winston-Salem was poised to move into first on the last day of August. The Bulls prevailed 4–3, however, on a bases-loaded single by Ralph Caldwell in the 10th. The Bulls closed out the season with two wins over Fayetteville and a pair over Raleigh to finish 2½ games ahead of Winston-Salem.

League fans had become accustomed to upsets in the playoffs. They would not be surprised in 1951. The regular-season-champion Bulls took their five-game winning streak into a first-round ambush by Reidsville. Although the Bulls won the second game by a 22–3 margin, Reidsville captured the other four contests behind Forline, George Souter, and Sipek.

In the other first-round series, Winston-Salem swept Raleigh.

Winston-Salem continued its hot run in the finals. The first game may have clinched the title. Reidsville took a 5–1 lead into the bottom of the ninth, only to lose 6–5. Star first baseman Joe Cunningham (.311, 11, 72) won the game with a two-run, two-out triple. Winston-Salem captured game two and Reidsville game three. A three-run homer by Cunningham keyed a 9–6 Winston-Salem win in the fourth game. The Cardinals clinched the title with a 2–0 win in game five, with relief pitcher Steve Grozdecki striking out Reidsville's Souter with two outs and the bases loaded in the bottom of the ninth.

The champion Cardinals produced three first-rate future major leaguers, the best showing to that date by a Carolina League team, and evidence of the increased importance of young prospects in the league. The 20-year-old Cunningham went on to bat .291 in a 12-year major league career. Stu Miller (13–10, 2.88) became one of baseball's best relievers, pitching in 704 big-league games. Both had better major league careers than 1951 Carolina League Player

The Carolina League Integrates

Any baseball fan knows that Jackie Robinson was the first black player in organized baseball during the 20th century. His Carolina League counterpart is not so well known. Percy Miller, Jr., was a native of Danville, Virginia, where he starred in baseball, football, and basketball at all-black John Langston High School. He graduated from that school in June 1950.

During his high-school years, Miller played baseball during the summers for the Jacksonville (Fla.) All Stars. The summer following his graduation, he was playing for a local black team, the Danville All Stars, when Danville Leafs officials decided to add him to their club. Miller's signing came after a concerted effort by the local black community.

League president Ted Mann gave cautious approval: "There's nothing in the league constitution to prevent any club from using a colored player and as far as I'm concerned it's perfectly legal." Ace Parker, the manager of Miller's first opponent, the Durham Bulls, was more upbeat: "I think it is all right to play Negroes. I played with them in professional football and once the game is underway you don't realize that you have them on your team." The Danville players were more circumspect, many giving no comment to press queries concerning Miller.

There were apparently no instances of overt hostility toward Miller. Danville fans gave him a courteous reception, and team officials noted with pleasure that black fans were turning out to see him. One stockholder noted that "it was one of the biggest thrills of my life—that roar of applause they gave him when he came out on the field." A Winston-Salem newspaper optimistically predicted that Miller "may have pointed the way toward a new chapter in Southern race relations."

As it turned out, the 20-year-old outfielder was overmatched against Carolina League competition. He batted only .184 in the few weeks left in the 1951 campaign and did not return in 1952. Yet Miller opened a door that more talented black players crashed through. Bill White, Leon Wagner, Willie McCovey, and Jose Pagan played for Danville prior to the dissolution of that franchise following the 1958 season, and inroads were made in other league towns as well.

Racial integration was not without problems. The black players, many from the North, moved into a segregated society where even so simple a task as eating a meal on the road with teammates became a nightmare. Some players looked the other way at racial harassment, while others lashed back. One of the latter was Bill White, an outstanding 19-year-old first baseman for Danville in 1953. In the early 1980s, White told sportswriter Frank Dolson of a time in Burlington when he made an obscene gesture to taunting fans: "I had to put up with the crap from the fans, which had never happened to me before. I was called names I had never heard. I just got tired of it." The Danville team had to run a gauntlet of angry fans just to escape.

This sort of thing continued into the 1960s. When Cleon Jones joined the Raleigh Caps in 1963, he was dismayed to find out that the stands at Devereaux Meadow were segregated and that his wife could not sit with the other players' wives. The policy was changed quickly. White, Jones, Rod Carew, George Scott, Curt Flood, and Dock Ellis are some of the black players who have complained in print of racially hostile fans during their Carolina League days.

In fairness, it should be pointed out that the Carolina League had racially integrated teams well over a decade before college teams in North Carolina and Virginia, and almost two decades before most Southern public schools had more than token integration. It should also be noted that, unlike other Southern minor leagues, no club in the Carolina League ever refused to play against black players.

of the Year Ray Jablonski, Winston-Salem's standout third baseman. Jablonski led the league with a .363 batting average, 28 home runs (equaling Carl Miller's total), and 127 RBIs. To date, Jablonski, who batted .268 in eight major league seasons, remains the only triple-crown winner in Carolina League history. Outfielder Delton Childs (.315) and pitchers Jim Lewey (19–7, 2.647) and George Condrick (18–9, 2.651) also had fine seasons. Lewey edged Condrick for the league's lowest earned-run average by .004.

Greensboro and Danville were respectable also-rans. The fifth-place Patriots were led by outfielder Malcolm McKeithan (.325), while sixth-place Danville featured outfielder Joe Socey (.322, 20, 73).

Seventh-place Fayetteville and cellar-dwelling Burlington were not competitive, despite their major league affiliations.

1951 Final Standings

Durham	84-56	
* Winston-Salem	81-58	playoff winner
Raleigh	78-62	
Reidsville	76-64	
Greensboro	67-73	
Danville	66-73	
Fayetteville	59-79	
Burlington	47-93	

—◆—

Winston-Salem began the 1952 season in search of a third consecutive title. That year, the league's list of independent clubs diminished by one, with Danville becoming a farm team of the Washington Senators. Only Raleigh and Reidsville remained unaffiliated. Both featured a healthy number of minor league veterans, and both were competitive.

Danville, Greensboro, and the two independent clubs took turns in first place until early June. Raleigh took over first place for good on June 2 with a 27–17 record. The independent Caps were managed by Herb Brett, who used his keen knowledge of the minor leagues to make several key in-season moves that solidified his team's hold on the top spot.

In late May, the Caps purchased the contract of Norman Small from Hickory in the Western Carolina League. The 38-year-old minor league veteran was in the latter stages of a career that carried him to a dozen different cities, from Waterloo, Iowa, to Mooresville, North Carolina. When he finished the 1953 season at Mooresville in the Tar Heel League, Small retired with a .320 minor league batting average and 2,073 hits. He never played a game in the majors.

On June 10, the Caps purchased hard-hitting Canadian-born outfielder Don MacLean from the financially strapped Burlington team. MacLean went on to bat .312, while Small hit .270. At the end of June, Raleigh acquired another old reliable, pitcher Al Henencheck, from Wilson in the Coastal Plain League. Small, MacLean, and Henencheck joined a team that included veteran second baseman Crash Davis. Raleigh's best performers were pitchers Ben Rossman (18–10) and Al Cleary. Rossman threw three consecutive shutouts in June before giving up a run in a 7–1 win over Danville on June 26. The run ended his consecutive-scoreless-inning streak at 38⅓.

Raleigh's high-water mark came in the first game of a doubleheader against Fayetteville on July 27. Cleary not only beat the A's by a 15–1 score but also hit three home runs, a double, and a single, with six runs batted in. The pitcher's 15 total bases equaled the mark set by slugging star Muscle Shoals. The win gave Raleigh a 66–36 record and a nine-game lead over Durham. The Caps lost the second game of the doubleheader to begin a five-game losing streak. They stabilized briefly behind Rossman and Cleary. Cleary beat Reidsville with a one-hitter on August 10 to push the lead to 10. The Caps then slumped again, losing more than they won in the season's final month.

None of their rivals could put a sustained run together, however. No one got closer than four games before the Caps clinched first place on August 28. They then lost their last five games, ending the season 2½ games ahead of Durham. Winston-Salem edged Reidsville for third place, while early leaders Greensboro and Raleigh finished out of the playoffs.

The regular-season champions started the playoffs in bad shape, having lost 19 of their final 32 games. Making matters worse, they were minus the heart of their infield. Light-hitting but strong-fielding shortstop Bob Richardson broke his hand on August 7 and missed the remainder of the season, including the playoffs. Crash Davis left the team in late August to resume a teaching position in Gastonia. The wounded Caps opened with Reidsville, the league's other independent. The Luckies were managed by outfielder Ralph Hodgin, who had played for several major league clubs. Hodgin skippered a team which included outfielder Joe Pancoe (.304, 19, 85), slick-fielding shortstop Walter "Teapot" Frye, George Souter, and pitching standout Mike Forline (18–11).

Walter "Teapot" Frye
Greensboro News & Record

Grateful Raleigh fans presented manager Brett with a new Studebaker as the Caps

Ray Jablonski and the Carolina League Triple Crown

One of the most difficult individual challenges in baseball is winning the triple crown—that is, leading a league in batting average, home runs, and runs batted in. In the Carolina League's first half-century, several players have come close to this goal, but only one has succeeded.

Ray Jablonski was a highly regarded 24-year-old when he began the 1951 season in Winston-Salem. Winston-Salem was in the sixth year of a working agreement with the St. Louis Cardinals, and Jablonski was one of its top prospects. In 1950, he had batted .289 for St. Louis's Lynchburg club in the Piedmont League, with 17 home runs and 83 runs batted in. In a preseason assessment of Winston-Salem's prospects, St. Louis minor league director Walter Shannon predicted that Jablonski would hit a lot of home runs and "will do the job" in left field. Shannon's prediction was incorrect in one respect. Manager Harold Olt moved Jablonski to third base early in the season and left him there.

Jablonski went two for four on opening day and continued to hit for a high average. By midseason, he was hitting .376 and had left his competition far behind. He was never challenged for the batting title, ending the season with a .363 mark; runner-up Gordon Bragg was 17 percentage points behind.

Winning the home-run and RBI titles were more difficult for Jablonski. For much of the season, he trailed Reidsville's Carl Miller in both categories and Fayetteville's Hector Lara in home runs. Jablonski passed Miller in RBIs in late July and maintained that lead through the end of the season. At the end of July, Jablonski had 19 home runs and 95 runs batted in, while Miller had 23 homers and 92 runs batted in; Lara had 20 homers.

Of course, Jablonski's efforts took place in the context of a closely contested pennant race which saw Winston-Salem chasing Durham and Reidsville much of the season. Winston-Salem started August in third place, 1½ games behind the league-

Ray Jablonski   Greensboro News & Record

leading Bulls. Jablonski closed the home-run gap on Miller at the same time Winston-Salem tried to close its gap with Durham. Jablonski hit his 20th home run on August 2 in a 6–4 win over Danville. The following night, he hit a pair of two-run homers and two singles as Winston-Salem pounded Durham 11–2. Jablonski shared the headlines with Cardinals pitcher Dennis Reeder, who ran his scoreless-inning streak to a league-record 34²/₃ before giving up two late runs. Both shared the fans' attention with the eight beauty contestants—one for each league club—hoping to be named Miss Carolina League.

Jablonski had another two-homer game on August 6 in an 8–6 win over Fayetteville; he also singled twice and drove in five runs. His rival Lara also hit two homers. That effort gave Jablonski 24 home runs, only one behind Miller. But the Reidsville outfielder hit his 28th home run on August 19 in his club's 121st game, an 8–7 loss to Winston-Salem. At that point, Jablonski and Lara had 26. Miller did not hit another home run the remainder of the season, a drought of 19 games. Lara likewise went homerless down the stretch.

Jablonski hit his 27th on August 29, a dramatic two-run blast in the bottom of the ninth that tied Winston-Salem with Durham 4–4. The Cardinals went on to win 5–4 in 13 innings, cutting Durham's lead to a single game. The next night, Winston-Salem beat Durham again to tie for the lead. Winston-Salem could not maintain its late run, however. The following night, the Bulls won the final game of the pivotal series in 10 innings to regain the lead for good.

Jablonski hit his 28th home run, tying him with Miller, on September 2 in a 7–3 win over Raleigh. The next day, the Cards closed out their regular season with a scheduled doubleheader against Fayetteville. Jablonski went hitless in two at-bats in the opener and lost a chance to improve his stats when the second game was rained out. Meanwhile, Miller also came up empty on the last day. The two men ended the season tied with 28 home runs.

Jablonski drove in 127 runs, 13 more than runner-up Miller. He also led the league with 200 hits, 45 doubles, and 335 total bases and was an easy choice for league Player of the Year.

Two years later, Jablonski was in the majors, playing third base for St. Louis. His rookie year was his best, as he posted career highs of 21 home runs and 112 runs batted in. Jablonski went on to play eight years in the majors, batting .268, with 83 home runs and 438 RBIs. It was a solid career, although not quite as productive as those of his Winston-Salem teammates Joe Cunningham and Stu Miller.

In the more than four decades since Jablonski left the Carolina League, a number of outstanding prospects have taken aim at the triple crown, only to come up short.

Greensboro catcher Guy Morton led the league in 1954 with a .348 average and 120 RBIs. However, Fayetteville's Jim Pokel hit 38 homers to Morton's 32.

One of the most spectacular triple-crown attempts was that of Danville outfielder Leon Wagner. In 1956, Wagner hit 51 home runs and drove in a still-standing league-record 166 runs. However, his fine .330 batting average was short of High Point-Thomasville outfielder Curt Flood's .340.

Raleigh-Durham catcher Cliff Johnson was the next player to come up just short. Johnson failed to win the triple crown in a most unusual manner. He ended the 1970 season with league-leading totals of 27 home runs and 91 runs batted in. His .332 batting average was also the league's best mark. However, Houston promoted him to Oklahoma City late in the season. Johnson finished his Carolina League season with 422 at-bats, 12 short of the minimum necessary for the batting title. Salem's Rennie Stennett captured the title at .326.

Two years later, Salem's highly touted outfield prospect, Dave Parker, led the league in two of the three triple-crown categories. His .310 average beat Kinston's Mike Krizmanich by one percentage point and Lynchburg's Jerry Maloff by two. His 101 runs batted in led the league comfortably. However, his 22 home runs were one short of the league-leading total of Lynchburg's Bob Gorinski.

The 1981 season stands as the only season in which two players made a serious effort at the triple crown. Durham outfielder Brad Komminsk led the league with a .322 batting average. Salem outfielder Gerald Davis was the runner-up at .306. Komminsk drove in 104 runs, one more than Davis. However, the Salem star hit 34 home runs, while Komminsk hit 33. A midseason bout of mononucleosis almost certainly cost Komminsk the home-run title.

The most recent contender was Lynchburg outfielder Phil Plantier. In 1989, Plantier led the league with 27 home runs and 105 RBIs. However, his mark of .300 left him third in the batting race, nine percentage points behind Frederick's Luis Mercedes.

These near-misses serve to indicate how rare Ray Jablonski's feat was and how special 1951 was for the Winston-Salem star.

opened the playoffs at home. Ben Rossman rewarded Brett with a superb mound performance, which Reidsville's Mike Forline matched. The two pitching aces exchanged scoreless innings until the eighth, when Souter doubled in Hodgin with the game's only run. Reidsville won the second game 3-2, scoring single runs in each of the last two innings. When Souter won game three 5-3 with a two-run homer in the 10th inning, Reidsville had won three straight nail-biters, and another regular-season champion had bit the dust.

The other first-round series pitted the Bulls against Winston-Salem. The Cards had some fine players, including first baseman Paul Owens (.338, 11, 105), outfielder Karol Kwak (.306), and pitcher Lee Peterson (19–6, 1.94). They were no match for the Bulls, however, who swept the series in three straight. In the opener, crafty southpaw Eddie Neville (17–9, 1.72) threw a five-hit shutout, got three hits, and drove in five runs. This was reminiscent of a Neville performance of August 29, when he blanked Greensboro for 18 innings before doubling and scoring the only run in a 1–0 victory.

Though the Bulls had the league's leading hitter, outfielder Emil Karlik (.347, 17, 93, 35 doubles, 31 stolen bases), along with outfielder Charles "Chick" King (.315), they never had much of a chance against the rampaging Reidsville Luckies, who swept Durham and ran their postseason record to a perfect seven for seven. Forline got Reidsville off on the right foot by beating Neville 7–0 in the opener. Ken Deal then threw a three-hitter to win the second game 2–0. Jack Sanford went three for four to lead Reidsville to a 6–5 win in the third game. Forline beat Neville again in the final contest to give Reidsville its only Carolina League title. Reidsville overcame a 3–2 deficit in the final game by scoring single runs in the eighth and ninth for a 4–3 victory; Souter doubled in the game-winner.

Although neither Greensboro nor Danville won a playoff spot, both boasted some solid individual performances. Greensboro infielder Emidio Riga batted .322, while Robert Hartig (16–11, 2.52) anchored the pitching staff. Danville first baseman Dale Powell batted .280, with 25 home runs and 105 RBIs.

The league's two worst teams, Fayetteville and Burlington, provided a good deal of excitement.

Twenty-three-year-old Fayetteville right-hander Leonard Matarazzo went 22–8, with a 2.21 earned-run average and a still-standing league-record nine shutouts. He finished the season with the Philadelphia Athletics, where his big-league career consisted of exactly one inning.

Burlington finished the 1952 Carolina League season with a horrid record. Yet the Pirates' farm team boasted perhaps the most highly publicized prospect in Carolina League history. On May 13, "Rocket" Ron Necciai, a six-foot-five 19-year-old right-hander, struck out 27 batters for Bristol, Tennessee, of the

Appalachian League in a 7–0 no-hit victory over a team from Welch; two strikeouts resulted in passed balls, giving Welch 29 outs. Overnight, Necciai became a national phenomenon. The Pirates promoted him to Burlington on May 23. He pitched 18 games for the Pirates, compiling a 7–9 record for a last-place team that was at the bottom of the league in batting average, runs scored, and fielding average. His earned-run average of 1.37 provides a better indication of his dominance, along with his 172 strikeouts in 126 innings. Stunned observers compared him favorably to Dizzy Dean, Bob Feller, and other fireballing greats, and Carolina League fans flocked to see him pitch. Burlington attempted to limit his appearances to home games, but Ted Mann ordered them to pitch him in a regular rotation. Necciai became so popular around the league that the other teams complained when he didn't pitch in their park.

Necciai finished the 1952 season with the Pirates. Unfortunately, a combination of stomach ulcers, a brief tenure in the United States Army, and a sore arm ended his career prematurely. The can't-miss Necciai won one game in the majors. Ironically, his unheralded Burlington teammate Ron Kline, who went 3–6 in 1952, won 114 major league games.

1952 Final Standings

Raleigh	79–57	
Durham	76–59	
Winston-Salem	74–63	
* Reidsville	74–64	playoff winner
Greensboro	70–64	
Danville	65–74	
Fayetteville	63–73	
Burlington	45–92	

———◆———

There was one major change for the 1953 season. Danville became a farm team of the New York Giants. New York was one of the first major league teams to sign black players and by 1953 had already fielded lineups which included such prominent black players as Monte Irvin, Hank Thompson, and Willie Mays. Over the next six years, the Giants funneled some of the finest young black talent in baseball through Danville. One of the best was 1953 prospect Bill White, a 19-year-old first baseman. The other league teams eventually followed the Giants' lead.

While the Carolina League was negotiating the tricky shoals of a new racial order, Raleigh and Reidsville were demonstrating that veteran-laden independent teams could be more than competitive against major league farm teams. The Raleigh Capitals, again managed by Herb Brett, jumped to another fast start, winning 16 of their first 20. Early competition, surprisingly, came from Burlington, picked by most league observers to duplicate its last-place finish of the previous two seasons. Yet the Pirates had given Burlington a fine pitching staff, as was demonstrated on April 27, when Bill Beane no-hit the formidable Caps.

Burlington absorbed the shock of Raleigh's fast start and caught the Caps on May 21. The teams were tied at the end of the month. Burlington beat Raleigh on June 1 and slowly began to open up a working margin. By June 26, Burlington led Raleigh and Danville by 5½ games. The Pirates' surge was led by outfielder Bob Honor (.328, 15, 96), first baseman George Hott (.308), outfielder Joe Burgess (20 home runs), and pitchers Don Urquhart (12–7) and Joe Perrota (14–6). One of Burlington's less formidable players was local boy Jack McKeon, who batted a mere .181. McKeon went on to better things as a manager in both the Carolina and National leagues. As San Diego general manager in the 1980s, the trade-happy McKeon came to be known as "Trader Jack."

The slumping Capitals were perhaps distracted by disappointing attendance and rumors that the club's five owners were considering selling the team. Concerned league directors were convinced that fans were turned off by long games and ordered teams to make every effort to keep contests under two hours.

Raleigh began eating into the Burlington lead in early July. On July 7, the Caps blasted the Pirates 14–5 to pull within one game. Outfielder Rudy Tanner got four of Raleigh's 18 hits and drove in three runs. The next day, Urquhart beat the Caps 4–2 to push the lead back to two.

Burlington remained on top as late as July 17, when it was tied with Raleigh and Danville at 52–34. An eight-game losing streak followed. Much of this collapse can be blamed on a dramatic turnaround in the fortunes of Urquhart, who won his first 12 decisions before developing a sore arm and finishing the season with seven straight losses. Pittsburgh sent Necciai back to Burlington for a brief period, but the former phenom was unable to pitch because of his stomach problems.

Raleigh's surge was led by pitchers Ben Rossman (20–5, 2.45) and Dizzy Voiselle (13–3, 2.51). Voiselle won 10 straight decisions before a 2–1 loss to Fayetteville on July 28. Raleigh was also helped by the midseason addition of outfielder Bill Fowler, a former North Carolina State star and Korean War veteran. Fowler joined a lineup which included Tanner and outfielder Jack Hussey (.292, 29, 112).

Raleigh's main competition down the stretch came from Danville's young prospects. In addition to White (.298, 20, 84), the Leafs featured third baseman

Bob Caldwell (104 RBIs) and outfielder John Hafenecker (.303). Their undisputed star, however, was 20-year-old Venezuelan-born right-hander Ramon Monzant (23-6, 2.73), the league's dominant pitcher.

Danville caught the Caps on August 20 but then dropped back. When Rossman beat Fayetteville 17–3 on August 31 for his 19th win, Raleigh opened its lead back to 3½ games. The Caps built the lead to 4½ before beginning a crucial four-game series at second-place Danville; the series consisted of consecutive doubleheaders. Danville took the first twin bill on September 2 to cut the lead to 2½; Bill White went four for five in the nightcap with two home runs, five runs scored, and five runs driven in. Rossman ended the slide in the next day's opener with a 9–3 victory, his 20th of the season; Danville won the nightcap to keep the margin at 2½ games with five to play. When Danville lost all five, Raleigh backed into the pennant even though it lost seven of its last 10 games. Burlington held on for third place, while Reidsville was a solid fourth.

Raleigh and Danville entered the playoffs on a down note, while Reidsville hoped to duplicate its playoff title of the previous season.

The first round again matched Reidsville with the regular-season champions from Raleigh, and again Reidsville pulled the upset. The Luckies had some familiar names, including player-manager Ralph Hodgin (.303), outfielder Jack Mitchell (.316, 52 stolen bases), first baseman Jack Sanford (.324), and pitchers Joe Micich and Mike Forline. Micich beat Raleigh 4–2 in the opener, as Al Spaziano's two-out, two-run double in the top of the eighth provided the winning runs. Raleigh won the second game 1–0, with Lunsford Lewis outdueling Forline. Rossman won game three for the Caps, but Reidsville evened the series in game four, as Micich pitched a six-hitter and hit an eighth-inning grand-slam home run. The fifth game was anticlimactic. Raleigh shortstop Jimmy Edwards booted a double play in the fourth inning, leading to 10 Reidsville runs. When the Luckies held on for a 12–6 win, it marked the seventh time in eight years that the regular-season champion had not won the playoffs.

In the other first-round series,

Ramon Monzant
Greensboro News & Record

Danville had little trouble with Burlington, whose bullpen blew late leads in the first and fifth games. The Pirates did win game three behind Joe Perrota, but that was their only victory. Danville's best performance came in the second game, a 14–1 rout, when pitcher Lloyd Lundeen supported himself with four hits, four runs scored, and four runs batted in.

Danville jumped on top of Reidsville in the opener of the championship series as Monzant threw a 1–0 shutout. Reidsville evened the series in game two behind Ken Deal, setting the stage for a memorable third game. Reidsville manager Ralph Hodgin hit a three-run homer in the top of the ninth to give the visitors a 6–5 lead. His Danville counterpart, Andy Gilbert, tied the game in the bottom of the ninth before Chuck Allen homered for a 7–6 Danville victory. Ironically, Gilbert, who had homered earlier, was playing only because White had jumped ship, citing a need to begin college classes in Ohio. Forline defeated Monzant to even the series at 2–2. Danville won the fifth game 3–2, scoring the winning run in the bottom of the ninth on doubles by catcher George Lefelar and center fielder John Hafenecker. The Leafs captured their first Carolina League title since 1945 with a 14-hit 10–6 win in game six.

Danville's title demonstrated the talent of the farm-team prospects flooding into the league. Further proof was the large number of 1953 players who graduated to solid big-league careers. The best was White, who was traded from the Giants to the St. Louis Cardinals. A perennial All-Star first baseman for the Cards, White finished his big-league career with a .286 batting average, 202 home runs, and 1,706 hits. In 1988, he became president of the National League. His Danville teammate Monzant won 16 games in the majors.

Additional 1953 players who graduated to the majors included Greensboro shortstop Don Buddin (league-leading 123 RBIs), Greensboro catcher Ed

Don Buddin
N.C. Division of
Archives and History

Sadowski, Winston-Salem shortstop Don Blasingame, Durham outfielder George Alusik (.331 in 31 games), and Durham pitcher Duane "Duke" Maas. Other standouts included earned-run-average leader Duane Wilson of Greensboro, batting leader Bill Radulovich of Durham (.349, 19, 90), and Bulls veteran Eddie Neville (21–8, 2.28).

After the season, Reidsville shortstop Walter Frye retired to take a position at Oak Ridge Military Institute. In his seven Carolina League seasons, Frye set still-standing career league records with 953 games played, 3,629 at bats, and 929 hits.

1953 Final Standings

Raleigh	83–57	
* Danville	79–59	playoff winner
Burlington	75–65	
Reidsville	73–66	
Greensboro	70–70	
Winston-Salem	69–70	
Durham	64–75	
Fayetteville	44–95	

———◆———

There were several changes in the league for the 1954 season. The Raleigh franchise moved to High Point-Thomasville, which played as a Cincinnati farm team. Philadelphia and Fayetteville ended their unproductive relationship. Fayetteville went independent and grabbed key former Raleigh players such as Al Cleary (18–6), Dizzy Voiselle (12–5), Jack Hussey (.322, 32, 115), Bucky Jacobs, and Rudy Tanner. Winston-Salem lost its working agreement with St. Louis and went independent.

The independent Fayetteville Highlanders and the Greensboro Patriots, a Boston Red Sox farm team, were both undefeated at the end of April, the former at 10–0, the latter at 8–0. Fayetteville beat Greensboro 8–1 on May 1 behind Cleary. The next day, Greensboro handed the Highlanders their first loss, 10–9.

Early league play was highlighted by some exceptional pitching. On May 9, Reidsville's George Starette outdueled Danville's John Brady 1–0. Starette threw a no-hitter, while his counterpart allowed only one hit in eight innings; a reliever gave up another hit in the ninth. The game's sole run was unearned. The next day, Winston-Salem's Bill Washburn no-hit the Hi-Toms 4–0 before a sparse home crowd of 163.

Greensboro and Fayetteville continued to lead through May, with Burlington a solid third. Greensboro was paced by the league's leading batter, catcher Guy

Morton (.348, 32, 120), shortstop John Pfeiffer, John Patula (12–7, 1.58), and Ed Mayer (17–8).

On June 4, Fayetteville moved into first when second baseman Bobby Lyons hit a two-run homer in the ninth to pace the Highlanders to a 5–3 win over Greensboro. The game was marred by a beanball duel between Cleary, who had a reputation as a headhunter, and Greensboro's John Patula. President Mann fined both $25 and suspended them for five days. He also criticized umpires Paul Pryor and Junie Reed for losing control of the game, an unusual public criticism of umpires. The two teams exchanged barbs on the field and in the newspapers the rest of the season.

Bad blood wasn't the only problem concerning league officials. The continuing deterioration in attendance was raising eyebrows across the circuit. By midseason, Burlington was talking about moving to Kinston, Reidsville was talking about moving to Lexington, and a terrible Winston-Salem team wasn't drawing anyone. Winston-Salem tried an unusual approach to revive its season. After hiring Herb Brett away from Wichita to manage its last-place team, it tried to convince the league directors to declare a split season. Winston-Salem lost by a 6–2 vote, getting support, not surprisingly, only from seventh-place Reidsville.

These concerns notwithstanding, the league still offered an exciting pennant race. On June 10, the Highlanders won a most unusual doubleheader against High Point-Thomasville. After Voiselle won the first game 2–1, Fayetteville erupted for a 34–8 win in the nightcap. In that game, first baseman Jim Pokel (.296, 38, 103) hit three homers and a double and drove in seven runs to spark the Highlanders, who scored 13 runs in the third inning to overcome a 6–5 deficit.

Despite this impressive performance, Fayetteville wasn't even the league's hottest team in June. Burlington moved into first place on June 21 with a 5–3 win over the Highlanders. The Pirates went 22–10 in June, keyed by third baseman Gene Hassell (.337), outfielder Bill Wiltrout (.325), player-manager Stan Wentzel (.318, 20, 108), first baseman R. C. Stevens (.293, 25, 115), Harry Gilbert (17–6), and Don Schultz. Stevens and outfielder Herb Bush were Burlington's first two black players.

Also hot were the Durham Bulls, who won 10 straight, paced by pitcher Bob Bruce, who threw three consecutive shutouts. On July 1, the Bulls hit seven home runs in a 16–3 win over Greensboro. They were paced by outfielder George Bullard (.341), outfielder Bill Hoffer (.319), third baseman Steve Demeter (.307, 23, 111, 48 doubles), first baseman Larry "Bo" Osborne, pitcher Bob Cruze (19–7), and Eddie Neville. Demeter, a 19-year-old from Pennsylvania, was in the second year of a 12-team, 20-year minor league career. He eventually played over 2,300 games in the minor leagues but only 15 in the majors.

Fayetteville received a scare in late June, when Voiselle was diagnosed as having polio. It was evidently a mild case; Voiselle made a complete recovery and missed only six weeks. In the meantime, Fayetteville acquired Ken Deal from Reidsville to fill the void.

Burlington stretched its lead during the early part of July. It led Fayetteville by three games on June 30 and six games on July 3. Greensboro fell back even farther. Burlington's surge was sparked by third baseman Gene Hassell, who had a 23-game hitting streak before injuring a shoulder while sliding. The Highlanders responded to this sudden change of fortune by dismissing manager Hugh Taylor in mid-July, replacing him with former New York Yankees first baseman Aaron Robinson.

Burlington pulled out to a seven-game advantage on July 23 before losing its offensive punch. On July 24, Fayetteville's Pokel hit a homer to give his team a 1-0 win over Burlington. At the end of July, Burlington led Fayetteville by four. This margin slipped away quickly in August. On August 5, Burlington lost to the Hi-Toms 10–5 in a game marred by a beanball-precipitated near-riot. The following day, Fayetteville beat Burlington 9–3 to cut the lead to half a game. On August 7, Cleary threw a one-hitter at the Pirates, putting Fayetteville in first place. Burlington briefly regained the top spot before falling back.

The two teams were tied when Fayetteville journeyed to Graham, where Burlington played its home games, on August 12. Fayetteville won

Don Schultz's No-Hitter

It's a baseball axiom that a good umpire is one who is never noticed. The same is true of an official scorer. Usually a local sportswriter, the official scorer is assigned by the home team to determine such things as whether a particular play is scored a hit or an error, whether a pitch that gets past the catcher is scored a wild pitch or a passed ball, and, sometimes, whether a save is awarded or not. Players paying close attention to their statistics often argue with a scorer's decision, but the casual fan hardly ever gives it any notice.

Of course, there is an exception to every rule. In the Carolina League, that exception came in Durham on June 4, 1954, when Burlington's Don Schultz beat the Bulls 4–0. In the bottom of the first inning, Durham second baseman Bobby Taylor hit a pop fly into shallow center field. Burlington shortstop Johnny Richardson reached the ball but was unable to hold it. Official scorer Jack Horner, a respected sportswriter for the *Durham Morning Herald*, ruled the play a hit but announced to others in the press box that it was a "tentative hit" and would be changed to an error if the Bulls didn't get any more hits. When this unlikely scenario came to pass, Horner did indeed change the call to an error, giving Schultz a no-hitter.

Horner came in for some criticism, especially from *Durham Sun* writer Hugh Germino, who called the decision a "boner" and reminded his colleague that there "was no place in baseball for sentimentality." The two feuded in print for a few weeks, although Horner later admitted that the dispute was largely manufactured to sell some extra papers. Controversial or not, Schultz's no-hitter stood.

the first game by a 12–0 score, as Cleary again shut out the Pirates and third baseman Bucky Jacobs drove in four runs on five hits. The next day, Burlington blew a chance to tie the race, as Fayetteville scored three times in the top of the ninth for a dramatic 8–7 win. The Highlanders went on to win seven straight and never trailed again. One unfortunate note in their title run came in the middle of the month, when outfielder Dewey Benson separated his shoulder. At the time, he was batting .385 and leading the league by a wide margin; because of the injury, he finished the season without enough at-bats to qualify for the batting title.

The fight for fourth place and the final playoff spot went down to the wire between Danville and Durham. The Leafs had a 3½-game lead over Durham as the season entered its final week but lost their hold on fourth as the Bulls won their final seven contests. The Bulls clinched fourth on September 6, the season's last day, in a most unusual doubleheader. In the blazing heat of a 103-degree Durham afternoon, the Bulls beat the Highlanders, who had already clinched first place, in 12 innings. The two teams then traveled to Fayetteville, where the Bulls won the nightcap 11–4 to edge Danville for fourth by half a game.

The Bulls ran their winning streak to eight when they beat Fayetteville 12–9 in the playoff opener. However, the regular-season champs took the best-of-five series with three straight wins.

The other series, matching second-place Burlington and third-place Greensboro, went the full five games. The Patriots won the first two but were unable to finish off the Pirates. Burlington won game three 6–5 on an RBI single by shortstop Jack Richardson in the eighth inning. The Pirates took game four to even the series, then closed it out by winning game five by an 8-5 score. Herb Bush hit a grand slam for the winners in the bottom of a five-run first.

Surprisingly, the Fayetteville-Burlington series marked the first time since 1945 that the regular-season champion and runner-up met in the playoff championship. Burlington won the opener 6–4, keyed by a two-run pinch-hit homer by manager Stan Wentzel. The hard-hitting Highlanders then proceeded to pummel the Pirates, winning the last four games of the series 15–8, 11–4, 11–1, and 12–2. Hussey and Jacobs were especially potent for Fayetteville.

Danville finished with a winning record despite missing the playoffs. Future Giants outfielder Willie Kirkland played briefly for the Leafs, while outfielder Robert Smith (.293, 14, 94), first baseman Andy Gilbert (.367, 11, 35), third baseman Ozzie Virgil, and pitcher Curt Barclay (19–11, 3.16) had productive longer stays.

The efforts of outfielder Noah Goode (.335), first baseman Don Stafford (.305), outfielder John Lybrand (.301), and pitcher Woody Rich (13–6) helped make High Point-Thomasville competitive.

Reidsville suffered its worst season since 1948. The Luckies had some decent hitters but poor pitching. Mike Forline ended his Carolina League career with a league-record 89 wins.

Winston-Salem's short-lived experiment with independence was an unmitigated disaster. An inability to obtain talent led to the worst Twin City team in league history.

None of the 1954 Carolina League players became major league stars. However, Kirkland, Virgil, and Bruce had decent big-league careers. Bob Shaw, who was an unimpressive 6–13 for the Bulls, won 108 major league contests, including an 18–6 season for the 1959 American League–champion Chicago White Sox.

1954 Final Standings

*Fayetteville	86–51	playoff winner
Burlington	82–56	
Greensboro	79–59	
Durham	70–68	
Danville	70–69	
High Point-Thomasville	66–73	
Reidsville	56–83	
Winston-Salem	44–94	

—♦—

The three 1954 independents all became farm teams for major league clubs in 1955, leaving the league with no unaffiliated teams. Fayetteville signed with the Baltimore Orioles, Reidsville with the Philadelphia Phillies, and Winston-Salem with the New York Yankees.

Reidsville got off to a hot start, winning seven of its first eight games and nine of its first 12. It was sparked by slugging first baseman Ken Menkel, who hit seven home runs in his first 11 games, evoking comparisons with Muscle Shoals. The pitching staff was too weak to sustain the pace, however. In a tumultuous May 5 doubleheader, Reidsville lost a pair to Danville by 9–3 and 7–5 scores. In the nightcap, umpire Harry Morgan ejected manager Charlie Gassaway and all seven benchwarmers for arguing. The Phillies promoted Menkel to Albuquerque in early June, replacing him with a Shoals look-alike, 240-pound John Moskus.

Reidsville, High Point-Thomasville, Greensboro, Danville, and Fayetteville all took turns in first place during May and June. On June 7, only 2½ games separated the top six teams. The Hi-Toms took command in July, when they went 22–10. On July 21, they pounded Reidsville 17–4 to move into a virtual tie with Fayetteville. They pulled away down the stretch. Several Hi-Toms pitching performances stood out during this period. Rene Solis one-hit Danville on July 31, while 39-year-old Woody Rich duplicated that feat against Durham on August 9.

Several other performances stood out. On June 12, Fayetteville's Bill Fowler hit four doubles in a game. Winston-Salem outfielder Frank Wehner hit three home runs and a triple on July 9 at Durham to become the third player in league history to total 15 bases in a game. John Fitzgerald of Danville struck out 19 Winston-Salem batters on June 28. On July 15, Durham beat Reidsville 5–1 in 18 innings on a grand-slam homer by Jim McManus.

Unfortunately, increasingly smaller crowds were seeing these standout performances. Fayetteville became worried about poor attendance and even floated the trial balloon of not finishing the season. Late in the campaign, it played a home game in Raleigh. Winston-Salem, Durham, Reidsville, and Burlington were all worried about dwindling crowds.

High Point-Thomasville had little trouble holding on to its lead during August. The Hi-Toms had an interesting blend of prospects and veterans. The best prospect was 22-year-old Cuban outfielder Danny Morejon (.324, 13, 86). His teammates included catcher Ed Cannon (.317), Jack Taylor (17–11, 1.78), Rich (19–4, 2.84), and Solis. At one point, Rich won 14 straight games to go to 19–2, but he was unable to reach the magic 20-win total.

Fayetteville and Danville engaged in a close race for second place, while Durham, Reidsville, Greensboro, and Winston-Salem went down to the wire for fourth.

Fayetteville held onto second most of the season despite changing managers twice. Jack McKeon replaced Aaron Robinson in mid-June as player-manager but was forced to step down when he became injured. Longtime Carolina League player Jack Sanford replaced McKeon. Despite Fayetteville's farm-club status, its roster included such familiar names as Bucky Jacobs, Jim Pokel (.321, 22, 77), and Jim Foxworth. Outfielders Al Viotto (.309, 22, 80) and Joe Cristello (.303, 22, 97) added punch to the lineup.

Fayetteville collapsed in the last two weeks of the season and lost second place to the Danville Leafs, a farm team of the Giants. Danville had some outstanding prospects, including power-hitting first baseman Hal Holland (.290, 31, 121), shortstop Mel Collins (.304), outfielder Joe Moran, catcher Bob Schmidt, and pitchers John Fitzgerald, Hal Woodeshick, and Sherman Jones.

The Durham Bulls filled the playoff roster by narrowly capturing fourth place. The Bulls clinched the final spot on the next-to-last day of the season when they took a pair of one-run decisions over Fayetteville, while Reidsville lost two to Danville and Greensboro lost a pair to Burlington. Second-year Bull Bob Bruce won several key games down the stretch. Other top Bulls included catcher Charlie Lau (.293), McManus, and relief pitcher Max Simmons (17–9).

The league decided to expand the first round of the playoffs back to a best-of-seven format, a move reversed the following season.

Fayetteville, which had finished the regular season in a slump, beat Danville in their opener on a Jim Foxworth three-hitter. Danville won the next four games, however, to easily capture the series.

The other semifinal series was much more competitive. The Hi-Toms beat Durham in game one, as league Player of the Year Morejon drove in three runs. Rich won the second game, but the Bulls captured game three 7–5 when Lau hit a two-run homer in the top of the 12th. The Hi-Toms scored six runs in the top of the first in game four and cruised to an easy win. Facing elimination, the determined Bulls won the next two contests; Lau went three for four with a home run and five runs batted in during game six. In the seventh game, Durham took a 3–1 lead into the bottom of the fourth before a three-run Morejon homer gave High Point-Thomasville the lead. Rich saved the 7–6 win for Taylor, who captured his third win of the series.

Unfortunately, this unexpectedly tough seven-game series depleted the Hi-Toms' pitching staff, while Danville continued proving it could win close games. The opener was tied 3–3 when Moran and Schmidt hit back-to-back home runs in the top of the eighth for a 5–3 Danville victory; Sherman Jones pitched one-hit ball in relief over 4⅓ innings for the win. The Hi-Toms captured game two behind Woodeshick, while Danville won the third game 8–7 in 12 innings, hitting Rich hard. Danville's Fitzgerald gave his team a 3–1 lead when he outdueled Taylor 1–0 in game four; Moran's eighth-inning sacrifice fly drove in the game's lone run. After losing the fifth game, Danville won the series with a 3–1 triumph in game six. Larry Devitta pitched a three-hitter and had a two-run single. Again, the regular-season champion had come up short in the playoffs.

The 1955 Carolina League season was characterized by its balance. Only 20 games separated the top and bottom teams of the league, and for the first time ever, there was no genuinely bad team.

Fifth-place Reidsville missed the playoffs by only one game. Its two first basemen, Menkel and Moskus, combined for 31 homers and 116 runs batted in.

Rivals Greensboro and Winston-Salem also narrowly missed the postseason. The former was paced by infielder Joe "Peppy" La Monica (.312) and catcher Jerry Zimmerman. Winston-Salem had a potent batting attack which included outfielders Jim Engleman and Tommy McDonald (27 home runs). Frank Wehner batted .271 and hit 19 homers in 62 games before being promoted.

Burlington gained the dubious distinction of being one of the best last-place teams in league history. Bucky Jacobs batted .309 for the Pirates.

Around the league that year, rookie Dave Wickersham won only a single contest but developed into a solid major league player, as did Bruce, Woodeshick, Schmidt, and Zimmerman. Charlie Lau had a forgettable major league career but became a highly successful major league batting coach in the 1970s and 1980s, particularly with the Kansas City Royals. Morejon enjoyed only a very brief appearance in the big leagues, while neither Menkel nor Moskus ever made the majors.

1955 Final Standings

High Point-Thomasville	80–58
* Danville	73–64 playoff winner
Fayetteville	70–67
Durham	69–69
Reidsville	68–70
Greensboro	66-72
Winston-Salem	65–73
Burlington	60–78

—◆—

Reidsville and Burlington, the two bottom teams in attendance in 1955, moved after the season, the former to Wilson and the latter to Kinston. Reidsville's departure marked the apparently permanent disappearance of professional baseball in that city. Although neither Wilson nor Kinston had ever been in the Carolina League, both had hosted minor league ball in circuits like the Virginia and Coastal Plain leagues.

Also in 1956, Fayetteville became a Cleveland Indians farm team, but it still retained an unusually high number of older players. Danville remained the only Virginia team in the league.

The Durham Bulls jumped off to an early lead, closely followed by Danville, High Point-Thomasville, and Greensboro. On May 1, Kinston toasted its induction into the Carolina League with a 27–1 drubbing of Greensboro. Fayetteville's Jim Pokel hit eight homers in his first 22 games. On May 10, his teammate Ed Cook drove in nine runs in a 13–11 win over the Hi-Toms. Cook had a streak of eight home runs in seven games during May. Led by Pokel and Cook, Fayetteville headed a close race at the end of May, half a game ahead of High Point-Thomasville.

By that time, it was apparent that the league had some exceptional prospects. Two stood out in particular. Eighteen-year-old Hi-Toms outfielder Curt Flood and 22-year-old Danville outfielder Leon Wagner compiled dazzling statistics and set tongues wagging. Both were black, as were several other top prospects, including Flood's teammate Orlando Pena and Wagner's teammates Willie McCovey, Tony Taylor, and Jose Pagan. Flood later wrote scathingly on the unfriendly reception he received from many fans, opponents, and even teammates.

Flood hit a pair of homers on June 4 in a 19–1 win over Kinston to put the

Hi-Toms in first place. Danville kept pace until the middle of the month, when they lost 10 of 11. This slump occurred despite Wagner's demolition of league pitching; on June 15, he hit his 20th home run in Danville's 65th game.

Fayetteville's veterans squared off against the youngsters of High Point-Thomasville, Danville, and Wilson. At the end of June, Fayetteville and the Hi-Toms were in a virtual tie, one game ahead of Wilson and Danville. The veteran Fayetteville team made its share of enemies, exemplifying the tension between the old Carolina League and the new Carolina League. Durham manager Johnny Pesky, the former Red Sox star, complained that the Highlanders "get six or seven runs on you and then try to rub your nose in the ground. . . . [They are a] bunch of veterans who play that way mainly because most of them figure that they never will get to the big leagues any way."

Leon Wagner finished June with 24 home runs and 82 runs batted in, figures which put him in position to challenge the league marks held, respectively, by Muscle Shoals and Woody Fair. These challenges provided a backdrop to the pennant race in July and August.

Danville, the Hi-Toms, Fayetteville, and Wilson all led during July. On July 14, McCovey and Wagner hit back-to-back homers in the bottom of the eighth inning to give Danville a 5–4 win over Fayetteville and drop the Highlanders into a tie for first with Wilson. Fayetteville surged back and opened up a three-game lead over High Point-Thomasville on July 26. On July 30, the Highlanders beat Kinston 18–2, as Larry Spinner hit two homers and drove in seven runs. Fayetteville led the Hi-Toms by two games at the end of July, with Wilson four games back and Danville 4½ behind.

The Durham Bulls were only five games behind Fayetteville at the end of July. The Detroit farm team illustrated the ways in which a major league affiliate could change a team's roster during a season. In the middle of the campaign, the Bulls acquired outfielder Emil Karlik after his release from the United States Army. They also acquired former Texas Christian University catcher Bob White, relief ace Max Simmons from Augusta, and shortstop Richard Camilli and second baseman Jim Hughes from Terre Haute. The refurbished Bulls won 10 of their last 13 games in July, closing the month with a doubleheader sweep of Danville, despite Wagner's 36th homer. Camilli, son of former Brooklyn Dodgers star Dolph Camilli, ended the season with a .339 batting average, while Bob Cruze and Max Simmons combined for 31 wins.

The race had some dramatic reversals in August. The Wilson Tobacconists, usually called the "Tobs," fell apart completely, finishing in fifth place; they lost 24 of their last 34 games. On August 6, the Hi-Toms beat Fayetteville 11–1 to take a one-game lead over the Highlanders. Fayetteville regained the lead two days later, when Pokel's bottom-of-the-ninth grand slam beat High Point-Thomasville. Meanwhile, the streaking Bulls won eight straight and 19 of 24,

Carolina Leaguers in the Hall of Fame

Only a small percentage of Carolina League players make the major leagues. An even smaller number become big-league regulars, fewer still All-Stars. The highest honor a major league player can attain—election to the Hall of Fame—is reserved for only a handful.

As of this writing, 10 former Carolina League players are members of the Hall of Fame. Half of them played in the Carolina League as young minor leaguers on their way up the chain of organized baseball. Three were former major league stars who managed in the Carolina League and couldn't resist the temptation to see if they could still hit the old horsehide. Two are special cases who qualify only with a great big asterisk. Following are brief sketches of these men's Carolina League seasons.

The five Hall of Famers who played in the league during the early portion of their careers were Willie McCovey, Carl Yastrzemski, Joe Morgan, Johnny Bench, and Rod Carew. All had outstanding seasons in the Carolina League, but none was more outstanding than Yaz, who not only won the league's Rookie of the Year award (since discontinued), but also was named league Player of the Year, the only Carolina League Hall of Famer to be so honored.

It's easy to see why Yastrzemski set tongues wagging. The 19-year-old Long Islander had never played pro ball before showing up in Raleigh in the spring of 1959. He had briefly attended Notre Dame University but had never played for the Fighting Irish. Early in the season, his manager, Ken Deal, a former pitcher for several teams in the Carolina League, compared Yaz favorably to Ted Williams. Bill Jessup, president of the league in 1959, recently recalled that Yaz was "the best young hitter I've ever seen."

Yastrzemski got off to a slow start before Deal made a slight adjustment in his stance. From that point, there was no stopping the pride of Southampton. Yaz led Raleigh to a 15-game winning streak, the second-longest in league history. He also led his team to the regular-season pennant, something none of the other Hall of Famers was able to do. Raleigh was swept in the playoff finals, however, by a Wilson team led by future Pirates star Bob Veale and current Duke University athletic director Tom Butters. Yaz flirted with a .400 batting average before a late-season ankle injury helped drop him to a league-leading .377. No Carolina League batter has since equaled that mark. He also led the league with 34 doubles and 170 hits, slugged 15 homers, and drove in 100 runs. Less impressive was his fielding, mostly at second base. His wild throwing arm contributed to a league-leading 45 errors. In 12 games at shortstop, he fielded .790. Small wonder that he was switched to the outfield in 1960.

Yastrzemski liked Raleigh so much that he and his girlfriend, Carol Casper, were married there in January 1960. He made it to the majors the following year and went on to play 23 years for the Boston Red Sox, where he hit safely 3,419 times, including 452 home runs. He won the triple crown and the American League Most Valuable Player award in 1967.

The same year Yastrzemski was tearing up the Carolina League, San Francisco Giants rookie Willie McCovey was tearing up the National League. Three years earlier, McCovey had been named the Carolina League's All-Star first baseman as a member of the Danville Leafs. The 18-year-old McCovey was in his second pro season, having started in 1955 in the Georgia State League.

He showed considerable promise in Danville, leading the league with 38 doubles and collecting a .310 batting average, 29 home runs, and 89 runs batted in. He also showed some areas that needed

Willie McCovey
Greensboro News & Record

work, striking out 113 times and committing 34 errors. McCovey went on to hit 521 home runs in the major leagues.

As good as McCovey was, no one would have named him the Leaf most likely to make the Hall of Fame. That honor belonged to Leon Wagner, a hard-hitting outfielder who blasted 51 homers for Danville and drove in an astonishing 166 runs, a league record that has never been seriously challenged. Even with Wagner and McCovey, Danville failed to win either the regular-season or the playoff championship.

Two future Hall of Famers were on their way up in the Carolina League in 1966. Panamanian-born second baseman Rod Carew played for the Wilson Tobs, while Peninsula featured young catcher Johnny Bench.

Carew batted .292, a respectable average but far below the standard he set during his distinguished major league career. However, he was well over .300 for most of the season before a series of minor injuries slowed him down. Carew added 28 stolen bases. The speedy third-year pro was named a league All-Star. At age 20, Carew was older than were Yastrzemski, McCovey, Bench, and Morgan during their stays in the Carolina League. He jumped

to the majors in 1967 for Minnesota and was named American League Rookie of the Year. Carew led the American League in batting seven times and retired after the 1985 season with a lifetime .328 batting average and 3,053 base hits. He credited Tobs' manager Vern Morgan with improving his shaky defense enough to help him make the majors.

Carew's memories of his year in Wilson are not entirely positive. He had played well the previous season in the Florida State League and was disappointed at not being promoted to a higher league in 1966. There were also some racial incidents. In his 1979 autobiography, Carew, he tells of receiving threatening letters in the mail signed by the KKK.

Eighteen-year-old Johnny Bench was in his second year of pro ball in 1966. The Oklahoma phenom batted .294 for the Peninsula Grays, with 22 home runs and 68 RBIs in only 98 games. Even casual observers were impressed with his powerful throwing arm and first-rate catching skills. He also impressed observers with his world-class temper. Bench later wrote, "I had such a temper when things went bad. I used to throw my batter's helmet, just smoke it and crack it, bounce it off the ground, the dugout, anything in the way." Once, Bench broke a bat so badly that a piece of it lodged in his neck. Fortunately, it did not cause a serious injury.

Once Bench began controlling his temper, he began dominating the league. Late in the season, he was promoted to Buffalo of the International League. He made the big leagues the following year. His entire 17-year career in the majors was spent in Cincinnati, where his many skills led numerous observers to declare him the best catcher in major league history.

Bench shared Carolina League All-Star honors with another promising catcher, Raleigh's Manny Sanguillen, who batted .328 for the Caps and went on to an outstanding big-league career. Bench's Cincinnati Reds and Sanguillen's Pittsburgh Pirates struggled for National League supremacy throughout much of the 1970s.

The only one of the five Hall of Famers not to make the Carolina League All-Star team was Joe Morgan, who played second base for the Durham Bulls in 1963. The All-Star second baseman that year was Roy White of Greensboro, who, like Yaz, went on to make his major league mark as an outfielder. Morgan's absence from the All-Star roster can be attributed to the fact that he started the 1963 season—his rookie season in the pros—at Modesto in the California League before being promoted to the Bulls. Once in Durham, he found Carolina League pitching to his liking. He batted .332, with 13 homers and 43 runs batted in.

When the diminutive Morgan arrived in the Bull City, he was given a uniform several sizes too small. When he complained to his skipper, Billy Goodman, he was told, "You're here to make good, not look good." More practically, Goodman, a former American League batting champ, impressed upon Morgan the advantages of patience at the plate.

The left-handed-hitting Morgan took immediate aim at Durham Athletic Park's short right-field fence. He recalled in 1984, "Sure I remember that park. No left-handed hitter forgets that short right field

fence." Morgan homered in his first at-bat at Durham Athletic Park, a two-run pinch-hit blast against Winston-Salem on June 8. The blow helped Durham overcome an 8–0 deficit en route to a 13–9 win, an auspicious beginning for the rookie.

Surprisingly, Morgan, who stole 689 bases in the majors, wasn't much of a threat to run in Durham. He picked up only seven steals in 95 games. Perhaps that was a reflection of Goodman's many years with the Boston Red Sox, a team that rarely used the stolen base.

After the conclusion of the 1963 minor league season, the 19-year-old Morgan was promoted to Houston. Houston unwisely traded him to Cincinnati after the 1971 season, receiving as part of the deal another former Carolina Leaguer, Lee May, who had played at Rocky Mount. The Reds felt comfortable in trading the promising first baseman because of the presence of another former Rocky Mount player, Tony Perez. Morgan teamed with Bench, Perez, and Pete Rose to lead the "Big Red Machine" to 1975 and 1976 World Series titles. Morgan won the National League Most Valuable Player award both of those seasons, becoming only the second player (along with Ernie Banks) to win that honor in consecutive seasons.

It's probably coincidental that three of these five men played second base in the Carolina League, but you might want to keep your eye on the latest crop of second basemen.

The three Hall of Fame player-managers in the league's past are Heinie Manush, Joe "Ducky" Medwick, and Enos "Country" Slaughter. All played primarily as pinch hitters.

Manush was an outfielder in the major leagues from 1923 through 1939, mostly for Detroit and Washington. He had a lifetime batting average of .330. He was a player-manager for Rocky Mount, Greensboro, and Roanoke in the Piedmont League from 1940 through 1943, so he knew his way around Carolina League country prior to becoming manager of the

Martinsville Athletics in 1945, the league's inaugural campaign. Statistics for 1945 list him only in the "10 Games and Under" category.

More active was Medwick, a hard-hitting National League outfielder from 1932 through 1948. Medwick won the triple crown for St. Louis in 1937, the last National League player to accomplish that feat. He finished his big-league career with a .324 average and 205 home runs. He also gained a reputation as a hard-headed, hot-tempered ballplayer who made few friends. Medwick managed the independent Raleigh Caps to a third-place finish in 1951. In addition to batting .285 in 158 at-bats, he was in constant hot water with the league office for abusive language, much of it employed toward umpires.

North Carolina native Enos Slaughter moved into the Carolina League in 1961, only two years after the conclusion of a distinguished 19-year big-league career which saw him bat .300 and hit 169 home runs. Slaughter played most of his career with the St. Louis Cardinals. He gained notoriety for his take-no-prisoners style of baseball and is best remembered for his performance in the 1946 World Series against the Boston Red Sox, when he scored the winning run in the seventh game on a mad scamper from first base. He and Medwick were teammates briefly at St. Louis, but the Cardinals traded Medwick to Brooklyn in 1940 in order to give the younger Slaughter a chance to play full-time.

Slaughter was hired shortly before the 1961 season by Raleigh general manager Herb Brett. The Caps were a farm team of the expansion New York Mets, who hadn't even begun play in 1961. The Mets didn't give Slaughter much to work with. Even in spring training, he recognized that "the kids I had would be severely overmatched in the Carolina League." The Mets paid little attention to Slaughter's suggestions for signing players and his generally negative assessments of his players' talent. The Caps finished in last place in both halves of the league's split season, and Slaughter was fired. However, he showed that he still knew his way around the plate, batting .341 in 41 at-bats, with no home runs and nine runs batted in.

The other two members of the Hall of Fame who played at least one official Carolina League game are Satchel Paige and Jim Palmer. Honorable mention in the Hall of Fame category goes to Clarence "Ace" Parker, player-manager for the Durham Bulls from 1949 through 1952. The former Duke University football and baseball star is a member of both the professional and college football halls of fame.

This list of 10 Carolina Leaguers in the Hall of Fame will certainly increase in the near future, with former Rocky Mount player Tony Perez and active major leaguer and former Winston-Salem star Wade Boggs the most likely to be inducted. If so, they will join a select club of baseball's elite.

including a devastating sweep of the Hi-Toms on August 9. That same day, Wagner's 43rd home run helped Danville beat Winston-Salem. The Hi-Toms took over first place on August 12 but relinquished it to Fayetteville two days later. The Bulls stayed close with a five-homer 20-4 rout of Winston-Salem that same day.

At that point, it looked like the top three teams would go down to the wire. However, the Hi-Toms went on a 19–4 run to blow the race wide open. Flood got some big hits, including a ninth-inning home run to beat Wilson on August 22. Old-timers Rich and Taylor combined with the 22-year-old Pena to win one big game after another.

The competition collapsed. The Bulls lost six straight late in August to fall out of contention. One of these losses took place on August 27 at Greensboro. Patriot fans heckled the Bulls throughout the game and attacked them afterwards. In the postgame brawl, pitcher Harry Coe was hit in the head by a bottle, sustaining a cut that required six stitches, and Jim McManus broke his left hand. McManus missed the rest of the season, a crucial loss with the playoffs approaching.

Fayetteville unraveled completely. The Highlanders went 10–19 in the month and were no-hit by 21-year-old Greensboro pitcher Ken McBride on the 30th. Fayetteville ended the season in fourth place.

Wagner closed out his spectacular season with 51 home runs, four short of Shoals's league record. He did break Woody Fair's RBI mark with a still-standing league-record 166. He also batted a healthy .330. Flood won the batting title, keeping Wagner from the elusive triple crown. Some excitement was generated late in the season by Kinston, which replaced manager Jack Paepke with 23-year-old Tex Taylor, the youngest manager in league history.

High Point-Thomasville entered the playoffs on a hot streak as the clear choice for the title. Curt Flood, who edged Wagner for the Player of the Year award, had put together an outstanding season, with a .340 batting average, 29 home runs, 128 runs batted in, and 19 stolen bases. He also led the league with 133 runs scored, 154 games played, and 388 put-outs. Flood was supported by first baseman Karl Kuehl, second baseman Billy Joe Ford, outfielder Bert Haas (.326), and pitchers Orlando Pena (19–12), Jack Taylor (22–11), and Woody Rich. Naturally, the Hi-Toms ended their season in the playoffs with three straight losses to a Fayetteville team that had collapsed at the end of the regular season. Jim Pokel was the key to the Highlanders' victory. His sixth-inning grand slam off Taylor keyed a 6–3 win in the opener, while his three-run double in the 14th inning won game three.

McCovey and Wagner led Danville to a four-game victory over the Bulls in the other first-round matchup. McCovey's three-run homer and Al "Pinky" Wilson's three-hitter beat Durham 5–0 in the opener. After a Durham win, Wagner drove in six runs as Danville won game three 8–3. McCovey hit two solo homers and Wagner one to propel Danville to a series-ending 5–4 win in the fourth game.

Danville and Fayetteville brought plenty of firepower to an exciting championship series. In addition to Wagner, Danville had McCovey (.310, 29, 89, league-leading 38 doubles). Pinky Wilson and Charles Davis each won 18 games to anchor the pitching staff. The Highlanders countered with Pokel (.267, 25, 71), Ed Cook (.272, 28, 87), outfielder Richard Hofleit (.299, 20, 78), and future big-league pitchers Wynn Hawkins and Dan Osinki.

Jack Lewis hit two homers to lead Danville to a 6–3 win in the opener, but

Fayetteville evened the series the following day despite two McCovey home runs. Ted Fowler threw a four-hit shutout for Fayetteville in game three to give the Highlanders a one-game lead, but Danville evened the series in game four by scoring eight runs in the last three innings for an 11–7 victory; Wagner hit a grand slam in the five-run eighth inning. The fifth game was one of the most exciting in league playoff history. Danville took a 7–3 lead into the bottom of the eighth, when the Highlanders sent 13 men to the plate and scored seven runs. McCovey and Wagner hit solo homers in the top of the ninth, but the Leafs fell short by a 10–9 score. Fayetteville put game six away with an eight-run first inning and cruised to the title 11–1; Danville starter Vic Davis walked three batters, hit another, and threw a wild pitch in the fateful first. Altogether, in the eighth inning of the fifth game and the first inning of the sixth game, Fayetteville scored 15 runs in consecutive innings.

Flood, Wagner, and McCovey went on to outstanding major league careers. Flood batted .293 over 15 seasons and gained notoriety for his unsuccessful fight against baseball's reserve clause. Wagner hit 211 big-league home runs, while McCovey became a member of the Hall of Fame. Pagan, Taylor, and Pena also became solid major leaguers, as did Greensboro outfielder Lu Clinton and pitcher Ken McBride. Their teammates Ted Wills and Arnold Early had undistinguished stops in the big time, as did Kinston's Jim Duffalo and Winston-Salem's Jim Bronstad.

1956 Final Standings

High Point-Thomasville	91–63	
Durham	84–69	
Danville	83–69	
* Fayetteville	78–71	playoff winner
Greensboro	75–79	
Wilson	72–79	
Kinston	66–87	
Winston-Salem	59–91	

✦ ✦ ✦

Bubba Morton, Durham Bulls
Greensboro News & Record

CHAPTER THREE
1957 — 62

♦ ♦ ♦

Ted Mann resigned as league president prior to the 1957 season. He was replaced by Julian Clyde "Bill" Jessup, invariably described as a "baseball man." Jessup had played baseball at Duke University and been a scout for the Detroit Tigers and a salesman for the Rawlings Sporting Goods Company. Most important, he had numerous contacts in the baseball world. Jessup took over during an unsettled period when the minor leagues were continuing their decline. Twenty-eight minor leagues started the 1957 season, 24 the 1958 season, and 21 the 1959 season.

The Carolina League shared in this decline. Fayetteville and Wilson dropped out after the 1956 season, leaving only a six-team circuit. The league's problems continued in the early part of the 1957 season. Financial troubles forced the Kinston team to move to Wilson early in the season. As a result of this unexpected development, the league decided to have a split season, the first time this format was used.

Durham and Winston-Salem fought for first place early, each capturing 14 of its first 21 games. The Bulls were led by outfielder Bubba Morton (.310, 18, 82), their first black player, along with shortstop Frank Kostro, first baseman

Dick Colone (103 RBIs), and pitchers David Reed and Joe Grzenda. Future major league relief ace Phil Regan struggled through a 9–14 season as a starter. Winston-Salem countered with outfielder Pedro Cardenal, shortstop Jack Krol, powerful catcher Gene Oliver (.285, 30, 94), George Moton (18–10), and Jack Swift. The Bulls opened up a 1½-game lead by the end of May and held on despite the loss of pitching ace Al Pehanick (10–3, 2.29), who was promoted to Augusta of the Sally League.

High Point-Thomasville dominated the second half of the split season, winning seven of its first eight games to jump out on top. Its best moment may have come on July 17, when it scored eight runs in the top of the ninth to nip Danville 12–11.

The Bulls were never a factor in the second half, losing 13 of their first 20 starts. They did get the season's best pitching performance when Grzenda threw a one-hitter and struck out 17 Wilson Tobs in an 8–1 victory. Tex Taylor's infield single in the first was the only Wilson hit.

The veteran Hi-Toms had more experience than their rivals. For example, infielder Fred Harrington was 35, while pitching ace Jack Taylor was 30. First baseman Eddie Logan (.327), outfielder Fred Van Dusen (.310, 25, 93), and second baseman Billy Joe Ford (.290, 20, 85) provided the power for Taylor, Art Hirst, Dallas Green, and Jerry Kettle.

Greensboro got hot in late July. The Patriots had a strong pitching staff which included future Boston Red Sox star Bill Monbouquette (11–6), Chuck Smith, Herb Benner, and Bill Lore (13–3, 1.31). Outfielder Leroy Bradley hit .300. On August 2, Greensboro beat Wilson 14–0 to take over first place from the Hi-Toms. Its lack of hitting did it in down the stretch, however. Paced by Eddie Logan's 12-game hitting streak, the Hi-Toms surged back into the lead and pulled away for a 5½-game win over Greensboro.

Durham won a coin toss to give it home-field advantage for the playoffs. This turned out to be an important coin toss, as the home team won all seven games in the postseason.

The Bulls captured the first two. David Reed, a submarine-throwing right-hander, struck out 13 in a 4–2 opening-game win, while Jerry Thomas threw a one-hit shutout to win game two. The Hi-Toms scored three unearned runs in the eighth inning to win game three 5–2. Game four matched two future major league pitching standouts. Hi-Toms star Dallas Green beat Durham's Phil Regan 9–2, as the home team scored eight runs in the bottom of the eighth on six singles, two walks, and an error. Durham scored five runs in the bottom of the first inning and held on for an 8–4 win in game five. Bubba Morton hit a two-run homer in the first, while Frank Kostro had two triples, a double, and three runs batted in; umpire Charles Butler ejected six Hi-Toms and one Bull for excessive arguing and bad language. Jack Taylor evened the series at three when

The Kinston Eagles Fall Apart

Off-season franchise shifts are common in the Carolina League, as they are in most minor leagues. Only once, however, has the league been forced to accept a franchise move in the middle of a season.

That unfortunate circumstance came to pass in 1957. The trouble spot that year was Kinston. The Eagles, in their first year as a Washington Senators farm club, lost their first seven contests, and frustrations mounted among players, management, and fans. Those frustrations boiled over on April 25, when Kinston pitcher Dwight Feimster hit umpire Charles Butler with the ball when Butler approached the mound to warn him about cursing.

The Senators tried to help their floundering farm team. On May 3, they sent five new pitchers to Kinston, but they were no improvement. On May 9, Kinston blew an 11–4 lead and lost to the Hi-Toms 16–15. The following day, beleaguered Kinston owner L. C. "Red" Fowler announced that his club was moving immediately to Wilson. Fowler cited poor attendance—fewer than 3,000 in seven home dates—as the reason for the move.

Unfortunately, Fowler neglected to refund $7,000 owed mostly to season ticket holders and advertisers. Wilson fans came up with some money to repay ticket holders, but it apparently never made it back to Kinston. National Association president George Trautman ordered Fowler to relinquish control of the team. Raleigh, Wilmington, Lynchburg, and Burlington were all mentioned as possible sites for the team. Finally, Wilson radio executive and tobacco man Penn Watson took over the franchise and sold stock in the club. The league agreed to pay $5,035 to Kinston ticket holders. Kinston eventually got back in the league in 1962.

The midseason shift in 1957 had one important consequence. Because of the unusual circumstances, league directors voted in favor of the league's first split season. Eventually, the split season became the league's format of choice.

he beat Durham 6–1. A modest crowd of 1,250 saw a closely contested seventh game played on a wet field after an afternoon shower. The Bulls won 3–1 behind an unlikely hero. Leading 3–0 with one out in the fourth, starter Joe Grzenda lost his control and walked the bases loaded. Alan Dwyer, only 2–11 in the regular season, came in and put out the fire without allowing a run. Center fielder Morton made three outstanding catches to preserve the win, while the frustrated Hi-Toms stranded a dozen baserunners.

Danville and Kinston-Wilson were also-rans. The Leafs had some good hitters, including outfielder Robert Perry (.312, 30, 90), first baseman Inocencio Rodriguez (.289, 25, 114), and Sal Ferrara (.307). Allen Milley (.338, 14, 47) was leading the league in batting when he was promoted to Springfield, Massachusetts, in midseason. Reggie Lee (15–6) paced a mediocre pitching staff. Kinston-Wilson's best players were outfielder Dan Porter and pitchers Ron Bloodworth and Alex Gordey. Jim Hall, who went on to success as an outfielder for Minnesota in the early 1960s, batted only .233, with six home runs.

1957 First-Half Final Standings

*Durham	43–25	playoff winner
Winston-Salem	40–27	
Greensboro	36–31	
High Point-Thomasville	38–33	
Danville	28–39	
Kinston-Wilson	21–46	

Second-Half Final Standings

High Point-Thomasville	46–28
Greensboro	40–33
Durham	36–36
Danville	35–38
Winston-Salem	32–41
Wilson	30–43

—◆—

Raleigh and Burlington rejoined the Carolina League for the 1958 season, although Burlington changed its name to Alamance, the name of its home county. The league was an eight-team circuit again. Greensboro became a New York Yankees farm team, while the Raleigh Caps picked up a working agreement with Boston. Alamance reached an agreement with the Cleveland Indians. The split season was dropped in favor of the traditional four-team playoffs, although the series were reduced to three games.

Attendance continued to decline. The fans who did come out were able to focus on several highly publicized bonus babies. Chief among them was 18-year-old Wilson outfielder Dave Nicholson. Wilson general manager Jim Mills told one newspaper that Nicholson was the "finest looking prospect I have ever seen." Winston-Salem pitcher Von McDaniel had appeared in the majors in 1957 but was in the minors for more seasoning in 1958. Alamance's Ken Kuhn and Wilson's Frank Zupo had also received large signing bonuses from their major league organizations.

The Danville Leafs led much of May but never by a large margin. The Hi-Toms took over first place in early June, and the two flip-flopped the remainder of the month, with Raleigh and Winston-Salem hanging close. Raleigh faded out of contention in late May, while Wilson lost nine straight in late June to drop into the second division. Danville trailed the Hi-Toms by only one game at the end of June but hit a dry spell and dropped to fourth place by the middle of July. A 10-game winning streak put Greensboro in the race, and the Yankees took a one-game lead over High Point-Thomasville as the season headed into August.

The middle of the season was highlighted by some exceptional hitting performances. Greensboro's Jim Johnston hit three homers on June 24 in an 11–8 win over the Hi-Toms. Alamance's Ken Kuhn hit safely in 12 consecutive at-bats, including going eight for eight in a doubleheader sweep of Durham. On July 21, Greensboro hit eight home runs in a 21–9 thrashing of Danville. Six days later, Wilson hit seven homers in a 12–4 win over Raleigh. On July 28, the Hi-Toms scored 11 runs in the top of the first against Winston-Salem and held on for 17–11 victory; Jackie Davis drove in six runs in the first inning on a grand slam and a two-run double.

The Danville Leafs put together a 13-game winning streak which enabled them to overtake Greensboro and High Point-Thomasville during August. They compiled a 24–8 record for the month to finish four games ahead of the Hi-Toms and five ahead of Greensboro. Robin Coffman, Allen Milley, and future big-league pinch-hitting standout Manny Mota gave the Leafs a trio of .300 hitters, while Don Hyman and Andy Yetsko combined for 34 victories. Alamance, in last place as late as July 11, rode a late nine-game winning streak to a fourth-place finish, only a game ahead of Winston-Salem.

The game of the season took place on August 27, when hard-throwing Ra-

Manny Mota
Greensboro News & Record

leigh right-hander Ben Tench, a former Wake Forest standout, no-hit Alamance and defeated its star pitcher, Steve Hamilton, by a 2–0 score. The habitually wild Tench walked nine batters in the seven-inning game.

Alamance continued its surge to an unlikely postseason championship in the new two-out-of-three format. After losing its first-round opener to Danville, Alamance captured the final two contests 4–2 and 7–2. Steve Hamilton won the series finale, while Walter Bond had a triple and a home run and collected four runs batted in.

In the other first-round matchup, Greensboro eliminated the Hi-Toms with two convincing victories.

Alamance and Greensboro played an exciting championship series. Alamance won the opener 7–5, as Whitey Williamson had a pair of solo homers and Bond drove in three runs. The Yankees won the second game 6–3, with third baseman Bob Bauer accounting for two home runs and five runs batted in. In the final game, Alamance scored five times in the top of the first, only to see the Yankees come back to tie the game. An RBI single by Lou Holdener in the eighth and a relief appearance by Hamilton resulted in a 6–5 Alamance win and a league title.

The champions presented one of the most physically imposing teams around. Both outfielder Walter Bond (.296, 13, 70) and pitcher Steve Hamilton (15–14) stood six-foot-seven. The latter, a basketball star at Morehead State in the 1950s, eventually became a standout major league relief pitcher. Bond's big-league career and life were cut tragically short in 1967 by leukemia. Ken Kuhn ended up with a .309 batting average.

The Hi-Toms' best players included outfielder Jackie Davis (.302, 25, 88), Tony Curry (.293, 20, 83), veteran infielder Billy Joe Ford, and pitchers Jack Taylor (19–9) and Gene Snyder. Chris Short and Art Mahaffey were average Carolina League pitchers but became aces for the Philadelphia Phillies during the mid-1960s.

Playoff runner-up Greensboro featured Jim Johnston (.284, 14, 79), Bill Carr, and Frank Wehner. Pitchers Harry "Duke" Addis and Don Thompson each won 15 games.

The better players on the second-division teams included Winston-Salem's .300 hitters, Phil Jantze and Pedro Cardenal; catcher Bob Tillman (.282, 18, 76) and pitcher Tracy Stallard (9-6) of Raleigh; outfielders Fred Valentine (.319) and Hal Holland (.286, 18, 79) and pitcher Jack Fisher (14–11) of Wilson; and Durham pitcher Don Aehl (11–7, 1.87). The highly touted Nicholson (.225, 10, 29) demonstrated a knack for striking out that plagued his major league career. His teammate Cal Ripken (.216) was even less effective; Ripken's big-league success came as a coach, but his namesake son became a star in the majors. Another highly regarded prospect, Winston-Salem outfielder Jim Hickman, struggled before being demoted to Billings of the Pioneer League; Hickman

Art Mahaffey and Chris Short   Greensboro News & Record

eventually spent 13 years in the majors. Jack Fisher and Tracy Stallard went on to enjoy their 15 minutes of fame in 1961 when they gave up, respectively, Roger Maris's 60th and 61st home runs.

1958 Final Standings

Danville	80–59	
High Point-Thomasville	76–63	
Greensboro	75–64	
* Burlington	70–67	*playoff winner*
Winston-Salem	69–68	
Raleigh	63–73	
Wilson	60–78	
Durham	58–79	

—◆—

The league dropped back to six teams in 1959, losing both Danville and High Point-Thomasville, neither of which could maintain its major league working agreement. Danville's fruitful relationship with the New York Giants ended when the parent club moved to San Francisco and elected to affiliate with Eugene, Oregon, of the Class B Northwest League. The Phillies dropped the Hi-Toms for Des Moines of the Three-I League. The departure of Danville, a charter member of the circuit, made the league an all–North Carolina organization for the first time.

The Wilson Tobs jumped out to an early lead, paced by outfielders Larry Elliott (.265, 25, 85) and George Watts (.323) and pitchers Don Dobrino (15–7), Tom Butters, and Bob Veale. They finished May with a sterling 27–14 record and a three-game lead over the Durham Bulls.

The Raleigh Caps started slowly but got hot in late May. The Caps had one of the most intriguing collections of players in league history. Pitcher Warren Hodgdon won his first nine decisions to carry the pitching staff early. He ended up 13–5. Future major leaguer Bill Spanswick (15–4) missed the first month with an injury but pitched effectively once he got under way. At midseason, fireballing right-hander Dick Radatz, fresh from a stellar career at Michigan State University, joined the staff. So fearsome was the six-foot-five 230-pounder that he eventually acquired the nickname "the Monster." Yet Radatz might not have been the hardest thrower on the club. Ben Tench, a six-foot-three 205-pounder from Wake Forest, had pitched for Raleigh in 1958. He started the 1959 season at Allentown in the Eastern League but was demoted to Raleigh because of control problems. Tench struck out 34 in his first two starts back in the Carolina League. On June 3, he fanned 19 Tobs in a four-hit 3–0 win; he also walked nine, graphic evidence of his erratic control. The pitching staff also included Galen Cisco, a former Ohio State University football player. Third baseman Tom Agosta (.314), first baseman Hal Holland, and outfielder George Lewis (.302) supplied plenty of offense.

Despite their considerable skills, Hodgdon, Radatz, Spanswick, Tench, and the rest played second fiddle to Raleigh's spectacular second baseman, Carl Yastrzemski. The Red Sox had signed the Long Island native after he had made a brief stop at Notre Dame. They touted him as their best prospect in years, even comparing him to the peerless Ted Williams. For once, the hype was not exaggerated. Yaz dominated the 1959 Carolina League season, his first professional campaign. By the time the last pitch of the season was thrown, he had compiled a league-leading .377 batting average, with 15 home runs, 100 runs batted in, and 34 doubles; he also made 45 errors, which suggests that his switch to the outfield the following season was a wise move.

Paced by Yastrzemski and an unusually deep pitching staff, the Caps put together a 14-game winning streak to move into the race. The last win of the streak was an 8–7 victory over Wilson on June 12, which cut the Tobs' lead to two games; Yastrzemski keyed the win with a five-for-five performance. Raleigh finally caught Wilson on June 26. When Bill Spanswick one-hit Greensboro on June 30, the Caps had a two-game lead.

The Greensboro Yankees, a club with poor pitching but good hitting, became Raleigh's nemesis in early July. On July 1, an eighth-inning inside-the-park grand slam by Don Lock beat Raleigh 9–7. The loss ended an 18-game Raleigh home winning streak and was Warren Hodgdon's first setback after nine wins; the

Carl Yastrzemski
N.C. Division of
Archives and History

Yanks also terminated a 17-game Yastrzemski hitting streak. On July 10, the Yanks took a pair from Raleigh to drop the Caps one game behind Wilson. A Raleigh bullpen collapse resulted in a five-game losing streak and forced manager Ken Deal to activate himself. Yastrzemski and outfielder Tom Agosta suffered minor injuries, while knuckleball ace Merlin Nippert went down with an arm injury. Raleigh and Wilson took turns in first place throughout July. The Durham Bulls kept threatening to climb into the race but could get no closer than four games.

Bob Veale, a hard-throwing but wild six-foot-seven left-hander, made a dramatic comeback for the revitalized Tobs. Veale spent the middle part of the season on the disabled list with a sore arm and was told by at least one doctor that he would never pitch again. He came off the disabled list on July 15 and beat Greensboro 5–1 in his first start, allowing only two hits and striking out 16 Yankees. Veale no-hit Raleigh on July 23, striking out 14 and walking nine. In the second inning, he walked the bases loaded and then struck out the side. He also fanned Yastrzemski three times. Veale finished the season with a 12–5 record, a 3.49 earned-run average, and 187 strikeouts in 147 innings. His size, speed, and lack of control—he walked 126 batters—suggest how intimidating he must have been.

Veale beat Raleigh on August 2 to put Wilson in front for the last time. The Caps surged again, winning eight straight to pull away. When the Caps beat Veale 8–4 on August 12 to go up by five games, Wilson general manager Jim Mills conceded that Raleigh had wrapped up first place, but he presciently reminded the Caps that anything could happen in a short postseason series. Mills knew that the late-season acquisition of second baseman Maurice Lerner (.372) and first baseman Donn Clendennon (.370) had made his club dangerous.

Raleigh pulled away to win by a deceptive 6½ games over Wilson. Durham finished third, while Winston-Salem took the last playoff spot.

The postseason was characterized by almost constant rain. While Wilson swept Durham in three games, the Raleigh–Winston-Salem opener was rained out for three consecutive days. In response, league president Bill Jessup reduced the series to three games. Raleigh won a pair of one-run contests to move into the championship round.

Wilson won the opener 4–3 in 10 innings on a two-out RBI triple by Larry Elliott; Tom Butters was the winning pitcher. Game two was rained out three times before Wilson won 5–4. Ben Tench's characteristic wildness sunk the Caps. He walked five batters in the first 2²⁄₃ innings. Raleigh fell behind 3–0 and never caught up.

The third game of the series, played in Raleigh's Devereaux Meadow, was one of the rowdiest in league history. Radatz and Dobrino engaged in a tense pitching duel. In the sixth inning of a scoreless game, Radatz came to bat with men on first and second and nobody out and attempted a sacrifice bunt. Wilson let the pop bunt drop and turned it into a double play. Raleigh manager Ken Deal stormed out of the dugout and argued, incorrectly, that the infield fly rule should have been invoked. Umpire Richard Powers ejected Deal, at which point Raleigh first baseman Hal Holland jumped into the discussion. Holland had an unfortunate knack for losing his temper, a habit that probably kept him out of the major leagues. Powers ejected Holland, who, incredibly, went into the stands and began berating Bill Jessup. The stands erupted into fistfights between rival fans. Several were arrested, one of whom was a friend of Jessup's trying to protect the league president. This fighting continued sporadically throughout the game. One fight involved Wilson second baseman Maurice Lerner, who threw a ball into the stands while warming up, presumably by accident. When he went into the stands to retrieve it, he got into a fracas with a fan.

Players from both teams disputed virtually every call as the scoreless game went into the ninth inning. The Tobs broke the game open in the top of the ninth, scoring five times. A two-run throwing error by first baseman Dean Robbins, in the game because Holland had been ejected, opened the floodgates. After the 5–0 Wilson win, an enraged fan attacked umpire Powers, drawing blood; a police escort was necessary for Powers to leave the stadium.

Jessup fined Deal and Holland $50 the following day, as Wilson completed a four-game sweep by a 1–0 score. Butters, who later became a successful athletic director at Duke University, threw a one-hitter at the Caps. A second-inning home run by Gil Watts provided the game's only run.

Although Durham and Winston-Salem lacked the overall talent to compete with Raleigh and Wilson, both featured several players whose baseball careers thrived well into the 1960s.

Durham shortstop Dick McAuliffe and third baseman Don Wert both started for Detroit's 1968 World Series champs. The star of that series, Mickey Lolich, walked 45 batters in 37 innings for the Bulls in 1959, clear evidence that he needed more polish. Outfielder Dan Briner and Dick Sheldon had good seasons for the Bulls, though they never reached the heights attained by some of their teammates.

Winston-Salem outfielder Mike Shannon, first baseman Fred Whitfield (.293, 25, 103), and Gordy Richardson all made the majors. In fact, St. Louis's Shannon was on the losing side in the aforementioned 1968 World Series.

Greensboro led the league in runs scored but still finished 22 games below .500 because of a woeful pitching staff. Don Lock (.283, 30, 122) led the league in home runs despite striking out 167 times. Glen Merklen (.266, 23, 86) helped the Pats' run production, as did 1962 American League Rookie of the Year Tom Tresh, who batted .281 before being promoted to Binghamton of the Eastern League. With some competent pitchers, Greensboro would no doubt have been a contender.

Nothing could have made a contender of hapless Alamance.

Despite an exciting pennant race and the presence of some genuinely talented young players, attendance for 1959 barely surpassed 50,000 per team.

Carl Yastrzemski's postseason travels provided an unusual coda to the 1959 season. After the conclusion of the Carolina League campaign, Yaz was promoted to Boston's AAA affiliate in Minneapolis, where he was ruled eligible for the postseason. Minneapolis won the American Association championship and advanced to the Little World Series against the International League champion Havana Sugar Kings. Because of unusually cold autumn weather in Minneapolis, most of this series was played in Havana. The series took place not long after the successful conclusion of Fidel Castro's revolution, and the dictator—an avid baseball fan—attended every game, accompanied by armed soldiers. Havana took advantage of one of the more imposing home-field advantages in baseball history to win the series in seven games.

1959 Final Standings

Raleigh	78–52	
*Wilson	71–58	playoff winner

Durham	70–60
Winston-Salem	67–62
Greensboro	54–76
Burlington	49–81

—◆—

League officials decided to experiment again in 1960 with a split-season format in which the first-half and second-half champions would meet in a best-of-seven championship.

Attention was wrenched away from such concerns on April 23 when Durham Bulls owner Charles Allen, a local banker and insurance executive, was killed by an intruder outside his home. Allen was the last of the original owners left in the league.

The 1960 season belonged to the Greensboro Yankees, a farm team of baseball's most famous franchise. The New York Yankees were in their heyday during the early years of the Carolina League, but this was the first time one of their farm teams had ever won a Carolina League title.

Greensboro's early competition came from Raleigh. The Capitals won 14 of their first 18 games, paced by Radatz, who struck out 18 Winston-Salem batters on April 26. On May 20, "the Monster" beat Wilson 7–3, with 16 strikeouts, to run Raleigh's record to 21–7. Much of Radatz's support came from outfielder Mike Page, who batted over .400 well into May.

Also worthy of mention was 18-year-old Durham bonus baby Pat Dobson, who beat Greensboro 12–1 on May 14 for the first professional win in what became a distinguished career.

Greensboro stayed close to the Caps with an aggressive running game. On May 20, the Yanks beat Winston-Salem when Jim Orton stole home in the last inning with the bases loaded and no one out. On May 28, Greensboro cut Raleigh's lead to two games by nipping the Caps 1–0 in 12 innings. Greensboro's Jack Cullen struck out 19, while a bases-loaded walk to George Banks scored the game's sole run. At the end of May, Raleigh was 28–11, Greensboro 29–14, and everybody else below .500.

On June 1, Alamance dedicated Fairchild Stadium with a win over Durham, its seventh straight victory; the streak reached eight before ending with a 2–0 loss to Greensboro. The Yanks took over first place on June 5 with a win over Alamance but fell back two days later when Raleigh beat Greensboro aces Jim Bouton and Jack Cullen in a doubleheader. At that point, Raleigh was 31–14 and Greensboro 33–17. On June 12, Greensboro regained first with an 11–1 win over the Bulls. Raleigh won back the top spot for one day before falling behind Greensboro for good on June 15. Greensboro then put Raleigh away with a three-game sweep on June 16, 17, and 18. Two days later, the surging Yanks pounded Alamance 19–6, as Jim Johnston hit a pair of homers and drove in five runs and Phil Linz went four for six with four RBIs. Greensboro pulled away to a 5½-game first-half title.

The second half was much different, pleasing proponents of the split-season concept.

Greensboro's star shortstop, Phil Linz, cut his foot on a piece of glass at a team picnic and missed the first dozen games of the second half. Meanwhile, first-half aces Bouton and Cullen (9–2 at midseason) slumped in the second half. The Wilson Tobs, in the first year of a contract with the Washington Senators, had finished the first half with a 10-game winning streak; they carried that momentum into the second half. Alamance likewise showed dramatic improvement. The Caps lost Radatz to Minneapolis of the American Association and four other starters to Allentown of the Eastern League. However, they did get Bill Spanswick and Warren Hodgdon back. After jumping off to a 9–3 start, they slumped and dropped out of contention.

Wilson moved into first place in late July and finished the month at 20–12, 2½ games ahead of Alamance. The Tobs were led by veteran Gene Davis, who was on his way down from higher leagues, and pitchers Lee Stange (20–13), Joe Bonikowski, and Joe Kaiser. They won 10 of 11 to take a solid three-game lead over Alamance on August 13. Stange started the season at 6–10 before turning things around. The right-hander, touched for a league-record 30 home runs, became the only pitcher ever to lead the league in wins and losses in the same season. Wilson was aided considerably by pitcher Max Sherrill, picked up after he was released early in the season by Raleigh; Sherrill started 6–1 for the Tobs. Third baseman Rich Rollins batted .341 after joining the team in midseason from Kent State University. Cuban shortstop Juan Visteur and second baseman Jim Burton augmented the Wilson attack.

The first-half champs were never able to get close to the top in the second half. They did have one triumph, however, drawing a record crowd of 12,049 on August 23 for a twin bill against Durham.

Wilson maintained its lead into late August. The Tobs led Alamance by three games as late as the 27th before losing five of six and seeing their cushion dwindle to a mere half game at the end of August. On September 1, the suddenly punchless Tobs lost to Alamance to drop into second. The following day, Alamance took two close games from Raleigh. The Indians then pulled away for a three-game victory over Wilson.

On the season's concluding day, Raleigh's Hodgdon no-hit Greensboro 6–0 in the first game of a doubleheader. Raleigh then won the nightcap 13–9, not an auspicious sign for a Greensboro team entering the playoffs.

Greensboro recovered to defeat Alamance with relative ease. Bouton won the opener 5–4 despite a three-run double by Indians catcher Howard "Doc"

Edwards. Jim Johnston drove in the winning run with a sacrifice fly. Cullen outdueled Jerry Lis to win game two 1–0, as Greensboro scored an unearned run in the bottom of the ninth. The Yankees won game three 5–3, scoring all five runs in the third; Edwards hit a three-run homer in the bottom of the ninth to end a 22-inning Alamance scoreless streak. The Indians stayed alive with a win in the fourth game, but Bouton closed the series out with a 6–2 win in game five.

Greensboro's Linz (.3207, 4, 74) won the league batting title by .0002. Third baseman George Banks and Jim Johnston each hit 26 homers, while Ed Gary and Fred Carpenter batted over .300. Bouton, Cullen, and Larry Del Margo combined for 41 wins.

Alamance outfielder Mitchell June (.3205, 24, 90) narrowly missed the batting title. Edwards led the league with 24 errors behind the plate but overcame his shortcomings well enough to play five years in the majors. Alamance pitcher Sonny Siebert was a converted first baseman, a position change that eventually paid off handsomely for the former University of Missouri baseball and basketball All-American; he went on to win 140 games in the majors.

Winston-Salem and Durham were also-rans. The Red Sox had third baseman Ed Olivares (.317, 35, 125) and outfielder Rogers Robinson (.298, 16, 86), while Durham featured bonus baby Andy Kosco (.273, 22, 75). Wert (.276, 18, 88) returned for another year in the Bull City, as did Lolich, who still had serious control problems. Dobson finished with a 7–9 mark.

Break the Record Night

Attendance at minor league baseball games has always been heavily dependent on promotions. That was certainly the case in the early 1960s, when the Carolina League and other minor leagues were having a hard time attracting fans. Yet creative promotions sometimes worked, as was demonstrated in 1960 by Greensboro general manager Jon Ferraris.

Ferraris's first triumph was on June 11, when a crowd of 6,756 saw the Greensboro Yankees beat Winston-Salem 9–3 on All Kids Night; most seats were purchased by local merchants and distributed free to area youths. One week later, a promotion with Cone Mills attracted 8,573 to watch the G-Yanks beat Raleigh 4–1.

Ferraris's masterpiece, however, took form on August 23 on Break the Record Night. The grocery chain Bi-Rite Super Market bought out the entire stadium and distributed free tickets for the asking. The result was an official crowd of 12,049, although Ferraris claimed the actual number may have been thousands more. The announced crowd remains the largest in a Carolina League ballpark by a substantial margin. The massive crowd was treated to two fine pitching duels. In the opener, Pat Dobson and the visiting Durham Bulls beat Greensboro 3–1, while a Jack Cullen one-hitter won the nightcap 2–1 for the home team. Greensboro ended the 1960 season with an attendance mark of just under 100,000.

Yet these kinds of promotions were controversial. In those days, most team owners felt that fans attracted by free tickets wouldn't be likely to return at full price, and that the promotions weren't worth the effort. Ferraris's aggressive approach didn't catch on until a later generation.

The Glamour of the Minor Leagues

Because of movies like *Bull Durham*, minor league baseball has taken on a certain cachet. Young, healthy, skilled athletes chase their dreams in an atmosphere of male bonding before adoring fans.

The reality is quite different. Carolina League baseball is fiercely Darwinian. Perhaps one in six Class A players eventually makes the major leagues, and fewer than that become regulars. The operative rule is move up or go home. Most Carolina League players are no older than their mid-twenties. Players older than that have either moved on to a higher classification or been released out of professional baseball altogether.

Off the field, the minor league lifestyle is decidedly unglamorous. Although a few players receive substantial bonuses when they sign professional contracts, most make do on modest salaries. Those salaries rarely topped $1,000 per month during the 1980s, for example. Meal money buys hamburger, not sirloin, while road trips are by bus, not airplane. Lou Pinella, who played for Peninsula in 1963, described these trips: "We rode smelly buses without bathrooms, drinking water, or leg room for eight or ten hours at a time without a rest stop. . . . We had drivers, but

Jack McKeon
Greensboro News & Record

they would switch off with a veteran player once in a while to get a snooze. It was a little hairy going around on some of those curving roads when the veteran outfielders were driving. We'd get to a park, haul our own stuff to the field, and start batting practice with a lot of well-used old bats." Pinella was probably exaggerating about the 10-hour rides, but the point is clear.

Living accommodations in the minors are equally spartan. It was common practice for many years for three, four, or five players to share an apartment.

Of course, some players have families.

In addition to winning the title, Greensboro drew over 97,000 fans, the best single-season attendance mark in the league since 1951. Nonetheless, attendance for the league increased by only 2,000 from the previous season. Raleigh and Durham were particular trouble spots, each drawing barely 30,000.

1960 First-Half Final Standings

* Greensboro	48–22	playoff winner
Raleigh	42–27	
Wilson	36–34	
Winston-Salem	30–39	
Durham	26–42	
Burlington	26–44	

Second-Half Final Standings

Burlington	41–29
Wilson	37–31
Greensboro	36–33
Durham	31–36
Winston-Salem	31–37
Raleigh	28–38

✦

In 1973, Kinston pitcher Ron Guidry and his wife considered themselves lucky to be able to rent a decrepit house trailer, complete with a family of mice. As Guidry put it, "Every time the wind blew I had visions of *The Wizard of Oz*. I figured the trailer would be lifted away to Kansas." In midseason, Guidry went away for two weeks of National Guard duty. When he returned, the landlord had removed the trailer, and the Guidrys spent the rest of the season sharing a trailer with another family. Ron Guidry—young, talented, with a bright future ahead of him—spent his Carolina League season having nightmares. In the worst of them, he became lost in the woods and was captured by hillbillies and used as bait to capture wild animals.

Living conditions in the minors have improved considerably since Pinella and Guidry played in the Carolina League. Still, few players get rich or live comfortably. Players endure such hardships for a chance at fulfilling a dream—making "the Show," the major leagues. Most know they will never achieve that dream.

The tension of playing in the minor leagues can be released in a number of sophomoric ways. Jim Bouton told writer Bob Cairns of a wager he made one day in the Greensboro bullpen. A teammate bet him that the crowd that night would be between "two and four thousand."

Bouton looked around at the slowly filling stands and took the bet. When the attendance was announced at 955, Bouton confidently asked for the payoff. He was then informed that 955 was indeed between two and four thousand—that is, between two and 4,000.

Managers are not immune from this kind of by-play. In 1960, Wilson manager Jack McKeon was having problems with his shortstop, Juan Visteur, who continually ignored his signals to stop at a certain base. Jokingly, McKeon told Visteur that he would shoot him the next time he did this. McKeon then purchased a starter's pistol at a sporting-goods store and waited for his opportunity. It came quickly enough. The irrepressible shortstop ran through a McKeon stop sign at third and headed for home. When Visteur was about halfway there, McKeon "shot" him with the starter's pistol. The terrified Visteur never even made it to home, but he did begin paying attention to his coaches.

Usually, however, recreation for the minor league player is quite modest. As Winston-Salem player Wayne Harer put it in the mid-1970s, "Three things to do. You can sleep, or read, or play cards. The choice is yours, such as it is." Many managers even limit pool time in order to guard against sunburn. Such is the glamorous life of a minor leaguer.

Lee Stange
Greensboro News
& Record

Nineteen sixty-one was a memorable year for major league baseball. The American League added two expansion teams, shattering a stable system that had been in existence since 1901. This was also the year that Roger Maris broke Babe Ruth's single-season home-run record.

The Carolina League did not share in this history-making. The league had no franchise changes for the 1961 season. It did have some changes in major league affiliations, however. Winston-Salem became a farm team of the Boston Red Sox, beginning what eventually grew into the longest such relationship in league history. Less auspicious was Raleigh's agreement with the expansion New York Mets, who started their minor league system a year before their inaugural season in the National League. The Mets were the laughingstock of major league baseball for much of the 1960s, and their minor league system wasn't much better, at least at the beginning. Raleigh general manager Herb Brett attempted to compensate for his team's lack of talent by hiring Enos Slaughter as manager. Slaughter, a native of Roxboro, North Carolina, had only recently completed his Hall of Fame playing career. His punchless Caps got off to slow start, put together a seven-game winning streak in mid-May, and then faded out of first-half contention.

While the Caps were slipping into the cellar, the Wilson Tobs were blowing the league race wide open. Twenty-five-year-old Wilson catcher-outfielder Chuck Weatherspoon had one of the most extraordinary months in league history in May. He hit two grand slams on May 2 against Greensboro in a 9–6 win. During an eight-game period in the early part of the month, he hit six home runs and drove in 23 runs. For the month, Weatherspoon hit 12 home runs, four of which came with the bases full, and drove in 49 runs. He ended the season with a .271 batting average, 31 home runs, and 123 runs batted in. The real strength of the Wilson club was its pitching staff, which included Willie Jones, 18-year-old Gary Dotter, and 20-year-old Joel Kiger; the trio combined for 41 victories.

Wilson took over first place on May 17 and gradually pulled away, beating second-place Durham by 5½ games. The Alamance Indians fell from second at the end of May to fifth at the conclusion of the first half.

The split-season format practiced by the Carolina League during the early 1960s had one serious flaw. Since only the first-half and second-half champs made the playoffs, it was always possible that the same club would win both halves, thereby eliminating the need for a playoff.

This wasn't a concern in the early part of the second half. Raleigh got off to a hot start, busting loose for an uncharacteristic 21–12 victory over Greensboro on July 2. On July 12, the first-place Caps were 10–6, while Wilson was only 5–11. The Tobs began their comeback on July 15 against Greensboro when they overcame a 7–0 deficit to edge the Yankees 8–7. They were aided by the midseason acquisition of bonus-baby pitcher Jim Roland, a Raleigh teenager.

Chuck Weatherspoon
Greensboro
News & Record

For much of July, the pennant race was extremely close. At the end of the month, only 1½ games separated first-place Raleigh from last-place Alamance.

Chuck Weatherspoon got hot again for Wilson during the August stretch run. He hit his sixth grand slam on August 5 against Alamance in a 6–1 win. The following day, Greensboro third baseman Gene Domzalski drove in seven runs to pace the Yankees to a 10–7 win over Winston-Salem. The Alamance Indians won eight times in nine starts in early August to move into first place, while Wilson and Winston-Salem stayed close and the other three teams dropped back. Raleigh dropped all the way back to the cellar, finishing the second half in last place again, a disappointing collapse after a promising start.

The Caps did participate in a memorable August 14 doubleheader. In the opener, 22-year-old Raleigh pitcher Tracy Rivers threw a no-hitter against Greensboro, winning 2–0. In the nightcap, Greensboro's Chuck Loyd pitched a one-hitter in a 9–0 win.

That same day, Wilson moved into first with a pair of one-run victories over Alamance. On the 15th, the Tobs beat the Indians again to go ahead by 2½ games. On the 16th, Weatherspoon hit his seventh grand slam of the season in a win over Winston-Salem. Despite his heroics, Wilson was unable to pull away from Greensboro. The Yankees won seven straight in mid-August. On the 22nd, Ed Merritt beat Wilson 3–0 with a two-hitter to move Greensboro percentage points ahead of Wilson. The Tobs beat the Yanks 5–3 the next day to go back in front.

Fortunately for Wilson, the hapless Caps came to town during the season's crucial final days. On August 24, the Caps hit rock bottom in a 13–2 loss to Wilson. Eleven of Wilson's runs were unearned, as the losers committed eight errors. The Tobs scored eight runs in the eighth inning on only two hits. The next day, Raleigh committed five errors in a 7–3 loss. The two-day, 13-error gift helped Wilson pull away from Alamance and Greensboro to win the second half. For the first time in its history, the Carolina League did not have a postseason playoff to determine its champion.

Alamance ended the season with the league's second-best overall record. Catcher Duke Sims (.304, 21, 88), outfielder Fred Krase (.307), and Al Eisele (15–11) sparked their team's late run.

Durham had a solid batting attack but poor pitching. Danny Briner (.286) had a 28-game hitting streak, while fellow outfielder and future Detroit Tiger Gates Brown (.324, 15, 72, 33 stolen bases, 33 doubles) led the league in hitting. Future big leaguer Chico Salmon batted .292. Dick Klunder and Joel McDaniel keyed the pitching staff, which also included a struggling Pat Dobson. Mickey Lolich finally overcame his control problems and was promoted to a higher league.

Greensboro was led by second baseman Ike Futch (.305), power-hitting first baseman Chuck Reidell (28 homers), and Ed Merritt (15 wins). Shortstop Ronnie Retton stole 35 bases, showing some of the agility inherited by his daughter Mary Lou, who later won Olympic gold as a gymnast.

Winston-Salem's lineup included several players who had suited up the previous season with Raleigh, including catcher Russ Gibson, Ben Tench, and Wilbur Wood, who went on to become one of the majors' best pitchers. Bill MacLeod (15–8, 2.31) prospered despite (or perhaps because of) the fact that he hit a league-record-tying 30 batters.

League attendance dropped to 261,000, a loss of 63,000 from the 1960 figure. Only Winston-Salem and Greensboro had decent attendance counts, while the last-place Caps drew only 26,000, an average of less than 400 per game.

1961 First-Half Final Standings

Wilson	41–28
Durham	35–33
Greensboro	34–35
Winston-Salem	33–37
Burlington	32–36
Raleigh	31–37

Second-Half Final Standings

Wilson	*42–28*
Burlington	*39–30*
Greensboro	*36–33*
Winston-Salem	*35–35*
Durham	*30–40*
Raleigh	*27–43*

—◆—

Despite the poor 1961 attendance, the Carolina League added two new teams for 1962. Jessup, who was always looking to expand, felt that the six-team format was less attractive to fans than an eight-team format.

The league gave Kinston another chance after its 1957 debacle. Making its first appearance in the league was Rocky Mount, a city with sporadic experience in such minor leagues as the Virginia League and the Coastal Plain League. It was in Rocky Mount in 1909 that Jim Thorpe had made his ill-advised professional baseball debut. Kinston signed a working agreement with the Pittsburgh Pirates, while Rocky Mount became affiliated with the Cincinnati Reds. Durham became a farm team of the expansion Houston Colt 45s (later the Astros), while Raleigh switched from the expansion Mets to the equally hapless expansion Washington Senators. Chastened by the Wilson experience, the league dropped the split season and went back to a four-team playoff format.

Some league officials were also convinced that the broadcast of major league games into Carolina League territory hurt league games. At that time, no major league game could be broadcast within 50 miles of a minor league game without permission. Prior to the 1962 season, Jessup, who was prepared to live with major league broadcasts, reached an agreement with local television stations designed to increase promotional considerations in exchange for this permission. League directors overruled Jessup and embarked on an unsuccessful attempt to get more money from local television stations in exchange for broadcast rights. This angered major league fans, who blamed the league for restricting broadcasts. The entire episode gave the league unneeded negative publicity.

The league did increase its attendance to 479,000, an average of about 60,000 for each of the eight clubs. The revamped Kinston franchise did exceptionally well at 141,000.

Fans were attracted by an unusually bright galaxy of future major league stars. Houston gave Durham a number of bonus babies, including Wally Wolf, a pitcher from the University of Southern California, and shortstop Glenn Vaughan. The most promising Bull, however, was a highly touted 18-year-old first baseman from New Orleans named Daniel "Rusty" Staub. Cincinnati sent top prospects

Rain, Anyone?

Most baseball fans know that once five innings have been completed, a game is official. A rainout prior to that point means that the game never happened, at least officially. The approach of rain prior to the completion of five innings presents an interesting opportunity for the team trailing in the contest. Delay the game long enough and maybe mother nature will wash it away. Stalling in such situations is a baseball tradition.

Few teams have taken stalling farther than the Kinston Eagles did one day in 1962. Their July 21 game at Rocky Mount started under drizzling skies which threatened to turn into a downpour. After the Eagles fell behind, they began stalling shamelessly in an attempt to delay the game long enough to force the umpires to call a rainout. Eagles manager Pete Peterson made no fewer than six defensive changes in the bottom of the fourth inning. In the top of the fifth, Kinston batters made such a show of going back to the dugout to change bats that the umpires ordered Rocky Mount's Joe Carboni to pitch to a batterless plate. Carboni actually got a strikeout that way.

Adding to Kinston's humiliation, the rain stopped, and the game went the full nine innings. In the bottom of the eighth, Kinston shortstop Gene Michael took the mound and gave up a grand slam. Rocky Mount won the charade 12–2.

Tony Perez (third base) and Cesar Tovar (second base) to Rocky Mount. Winston-Salem shortstop Rico Petrocelli and outfielder Jim Gosger, Alamance outfielder Tommie Agee, Kinston pitchers Steve Blass and Frank Bork, Greensboro pitcher Mel Stottlemyre, and Wilson pitcher Jimmy Roland were all rated "can't miss" prospects. Thirty-five-year-old major league veteran Clint "Scrap Iron" Courtney came down from AAA to shepherd Houston's young pitchers.

Winston-Salem got off to a great start, winning 14 of its first 16 contests. Two outstanding pitching performances brightened the early part of the season. Wilson's Pete Cimino struck out 20 Alamance batters on April 30, equaling Charlie Timm's 1945 league record. Cimino struck out the side in the second, third, sixth, and eighth innings in the 7–3 victory. He also walked six batters and sent Alamance catcher Buddy Booker to the hospital with a fastball to the side of the head. Even more impressive was Joe Carboni's May 4 performance. The Rocky Mount hurler dominated Wilson in perhaps the most overpowering pitching performances in league history. Carboni allowed no hits, walked six, and struck out 19. At one point, 11 consecutive outs were by strikeout. Rocky Mount won 10–0.

Durham won nine straight in early May, while Kinston won 10 straight. After the games of May 14, Winston-Salem led at 21–7, Durham was 17–9, and the other six clubs had losing marks. On May 16, a crowd of 2,889 filled Kinston's Grainger Stadium to see Pittsburgh Pirates left-hander Joe Gibbon, in the minors while recuperating from a sore elbow, pitch three scoreless innings against Wilson in a 10–0 romp.

Rico Petrocelli and Jim Gosger

Gary Waslewski, Steve Blass, and Frank Bork

Bill Jessup, Carolina League President
Greensboro News & Record

The streaking Bulls caught slumping Winston-Salem in late May. They were paced by the hitting of Staub and the pitching of Wolf. The latter won his first eight decisions before losing to Alamance 3–2 on May 29. Two days later, the Bulls beat the Red Sox 8–0, Winston-Salem's 12th loss in 14 starts. The Bulls finished May with a 3½-game lead after winning 20 times in 28 games that month. Kinston moved into second place.

Durham, Kinston, and Winston-Salem fought it out through June. Kinston beat Durham at home on June 10 and 11 to move percentage points ahead of the Bulls; an appreciative crowd of 4,537 saw the game of the 11th. Durham won seven straight to regain the lead later in June. Included in that streak were consecutive wins over Alamance on June 18 and 19 by scores of 17–13 and 16–15.

Even that offensive explosion paled beside Raleigh's 25–11 win over Greensboro on June 17. The same two teams squared off in another wild game June 30. Greensboro jumped to a 9–0 lead, but Raleigh sent 16 men to the plate and scored 10 runs in the top of the fourth before Greensboro recovered for a 16–11 win. At the end of June, Durham was 45–28, Kinston 43–27, and Winston-Salem 41–32.

Wilson's Pete Cimino no-hit Winston-Salem 1–0 in early July, retiring the first 22 batters he faced before walking Moose Imbriani on a 3–2 pitch; Imbriani was the only baserunner. Cimino's occasional brilliance was surpassed by the consistency of Durham's Wolf, who ran his record to 13–1 before losing his second decision, and Kinston's Blass, who was virtually unhittable down the stretch.

Rocky Mount changed managers in mid-July and immediately won eight straight under new skipper Jack Cassini. Perez hit five homers in a five-game period. Rocky Mount's pitching was too weak for a serious pennant run, however, and the Leafs slipped back into the second division.

Around that time, Durham began to pull away from Kinston. The Bulls opened their lead to 3½ games by July 14, five games by July 21, and seven games by July 23, when Wolf beat Kinston 6–4 to run his record to 16–2.

There were some memorable second-half games. On July 28, Raleigh defeated Greensboro 16–0, as Juan Gomez threw a no-hitter in his first league appearance after being promoted from Pensacola of the Alabama-Florida League. Gomez struck out 11 and walked three, while John Kennedy went four for four with five runs batted in. Durham ended July with a 66–38 record and a five-game lead over Kinston.

The Eagles closed to within four games on August 1 but could get no closer. The Bulls led comfortably through August and finished the season with a 6½-game lead over Kinston. Durham led the league with 132 home runs and 779 runs scored. Staub (.293, 23, 93, 115 runs, 116 walks) hit three grand slams and won the league's Player of the Year award. Glenn Vaughan, outfielder Ron Davis, and third baseman Tommy Murray (26 homers) supported Staub on offense, while Wolf (16–3), Marvin Dutt, and Don Bradey supplied the pitching. Winston-Salem finished a solid third.

Most of the drama down the stretch occurred during a closely contested but poorly played race for fourth place among Alamance, Greensboro, and Wilson. Alamance lost its last five regular-season contests but still backed into the final playoff spot when Wilson and Greensboro each lost its final two games to finish one game behind the Indians.

Shortly before the playoffs began, the league shortened the first round to three games. The regular-season-champion Bulls quickly won a pair of one-run decisions over Alamance.

The other semifinal series went the distance. In the opener, Winston-Salem pulled a 15–3 shocker, knocking out Kinston ace Blass and ending his 10-game winning streak. The resilient Eagles recovered and won the last two games 12–1 and 2–0.

Durham and Kinston squared off in an exciting seven-game championship series. Blass was hit hard again in the opener, but the Bulls left 11 men on base and lost 4–3. Kinston center fielder Ed Napoleon had three hits and two runs batted in. Durham won the next two games, but Kinston evened the series with an 8–2 win in the fourth game. In the fifth game, Blass was ineffective for his third consecutive appearance, giving up seven runs and 15 hits in 7 ²/₃ innings in a 7–1 loss. Bork beat Dutt 4-3 to win game six for Kinston and even the series again. Kinston won the deciding seventh game in a 3–2 thriller. The Eagles broke a 2–2 tie in the top of the seventh when Rudy Welch doubled and advanced to third on an error. Welch attempted to score on a fly ball to center fielder Aaron Pointer, who made a perfect throw to home plate. Unfortunately, Bulls catcher Doug Holmquist dropped the ball. Kinston's Nobby Lewandowski closed out the win and Kinston's first Carolina League title.

Despite being hit hard in the playoffs, there was little doubt that Blass was the league's best pitcher. He ended the season with a 17–3 record, a 1.97 earned-run average, and 209 strikeouts. Teammate Frank Bork (19–7, 2.00) led the league in wins. Outfielders Ed Napoleon and Rudy Welch supplied much of the Kinston power. Future big-league shortstop, manager, and general manager Gene Michael batted .215.

Third-place Winston-Salem was led by Jim Gosger (.283, 19, 83), 19-year-old rookie Rico Petrocelli (.277, 17, 80), first baseman Jim Russin (24 home runs), and Jerry Stephenson (11–5).

Alamance had Gil Garrido, Tommie Agee, and first baseman Bob Chance, all of whom eventually made the big leagues.

Greensboro had two future big-league standouts, Curt Blefary and Mel Stottlemyre (17–9, 2.50).

A superb Wilson pitching staff which included Cimino (12–13, 3.36), Jim Roland (10–8, 1.98), Gerry Fosnow, and George Miller was undermined by a punchless offense.

Rudy Welch (left) and Gene Michael (right)   Greensboro News & Record

Its neighbor in Rocky Mount had the opposite problem. Despite the presence of such sluggers as Cesar Tovar (.329, 10, 78, 35 doubles, 56 stolen bases, 115 runs), Tony Perez (.292, 18, 74), Ron Flender (.324), Bill Whitley (.306), and Bert Barth (.286, 33, 136), the Leafs' 4.73 team ERA kept them out of the playoffs.

Raleigh's best player, shortstop Ed Brinkman (.324), was promoted to Washington in midseason. Second baseman John Kennedy (a name that generated some attention in 1962) batted .302.

The Carolina League class of 1962 produced an unusually large number of big-league stars. Perez, Staub, Petrocelli, Tovar, Agee, Stottlemyre, Brinkman, and Blass were all among the best players of the 1960s and 1970s. And they were not the only baseball stars associated with the league that year. The vice president of the Rocky Mount club was Walter "Buck" Leonard, a Rocky Mount native and former star of the Homestead (Pa.) Grays of the Negro National League. Leonard worked with the club as an unofficial batting instructor but later lamented that few of the players knew who he was, or cared. Yet the Hall of Famer remained a part of the Rocky Mount club into the mid-1970s.

1962 Final Standings

Durham	90–51	
* Kinston	83–57	playoff winner
Winston-Salem	76–64	
Burlington	66–74	
Greensboro	65–75	
Wilson	65–75	
Rocky Mount	60–80	
Raleigh	56–84	

✦ ✦ ✦

Joe Morgan, 1963 Durham Bulls
Courtesy of Miles Wolff

CHAPTER FOUR
1963 — 69

♦ ♦ ♦

The Carolina League moved back into Virginia in 1963 after an absence of four seasons. The territory was entirely new, however. For the first time, league teams were located in the rapidly growing Virginia Tidewater. The Newport News–Hampton area was represented by the Peninsula Senators, while the Tidewater Tides operated out of Portsmouth. Peninsula acquired a player-development agreement with Washington, but Tidewater was forced to operate as an independent in its maiden season.

The expanded 10-team circuit split into two five-team divisions. The Virginia clubs were joined by Kinston, Wilson, and Rocky Mount in the Eastern Division, while Raleigh, Durham, Greensboro, Winston-Salem, and Burlington comprised the Western Division. The postseason playoffs would involve the top two teams from each division and an east-west championship final.

These changes took place in the context of larger changes in the world of minor league baseball. A new major league–minor league agreement came into force in 1963 which compressed the minor leagues into AAA, AA, A, and rookie classifications. The Carolina League became an A circuit. The new agreement also required all major league teams to field a certain number of minor league teams. If the agreement guaranteed a certain level of major league support for the minors, it also solidified major league control of the minors. Of course, this continued a trend that had been in evidence since the early 1950s. From 1963 onward, virtually every minor league team would have a formal Player Development Contract, or PDC, with a major league team.

The Raleigh Mets started the season with two former big leaguers, pitchers Sherman "Roadblock" Jones (12–6) and Bob Morehead (13–5), both of whom were trying to recover from sore arms. However, the parent club didn't give the team much else to work with, and it ended up in the cellar. Not surprisingly, attendance in Raleigh was poor.

The early leader in the Western Division was Burlington, paced by exciting Cuban-born pitcher Luis Tiant. On May 7, the right-hander threw a 4–0 no-hitter at Winston-Salem. The nine-strikeout performance ran his scoreless-inning streak to 35⅓. It reached 38 before ending ⅓ inning shy of Ben Rossman's league record. Later in the season, Kinston's Bruce Kunkle equaled Tiant's mark.

Tiant wasn't the only exciting newcomer. In early June, Houston promoted rookie second baseman Joe Morgan from Modesto in the California League to Durham. The future Hall of Famer hit a pinch-hit two-run homer on June 8 in his first at-bat as a Bull. Morgan's blast was part of a dramatic comeback that saw Durham erase an 8–0 Winston-Salem lead to claim a 13–9 victory. The win was secured when Bulls manager Billy Goodman, the 1950 American League batting champ, hit a pinch-hit home run with the bases loaded and two outs in the bottom of the ninth.

Burlington ended May 4½ games ahead of second-place Durham and Greensboro. Both closed the gap late in June. By the end of the month, Burlington's margin over the Bulls had been cut to half a game, with the Yankees only a game back. Raleigh won 18 of 24 in late June and early July to climb temporarily into the race. Jones paced this surge by winning 11 of his first 12 decisions. The Mets couldn't maintain this pace, however, and soon dropped back.

Tiant and Raleigh's Grover Powell squared off in the best pitching duel of the season on July 6. The game was scoreless after eight, with Powell working on a one-hitter. Burlington scored a pair of unearned runs in the top of the ninth for a 2–0 win; both pitchers ended up with three-hitters, Tiant striking out eight and Powell a dozen.

Burlington surged again in early July, opening a 5½-game lead by the middle of the month. In addition to Tiant (14–9, 2.56, 207 strikeouts), Burlington's solid pitching staff featured Chuck Kovach (17–11) and George Pressley (16–7). Outfielders Lee Green (.304) and Jerome Kelly (85 RBIs) paced the attack. Burlington's lead over Durham reached 6½ games on August 1 before the Bulls took a twin bill over the leaders. Burlington still maintained a lead into mid-August.

Just when Burlington fans began making plans for the postseason, the wheels fell off. Tiant missed three weeks with an ankle injury, the bats went silent, and Greensboro and Durham began closing in. Greensboro was paced by second baseman Roy White (.309, 117 runs) and outfielder Curt Blefary (.289, 25, 67), both of whom had long and productive major league careers in their future. Ted Dillard (11–5, 2.21) and Jim Horsford (12–4, 1.41) keyed the pitching staff. Durham countered with Morgan (.332, 13, 43), league home-run champ Walt Matthews (.283, 30, 89), and third baseman Tommy Murray (.256, 25, 102), while Darrell Brandon and Jim Holbrook won 14 games apiece. Manager Goodman batted .354 in limited action.

On August 22, Greensboro pounded Kinston 20–3, hitting four home runs. Three days later, the Yankees beat Rocky Mount to move percentage points ahead of slumping Burlington, 2–0 losers to Peninsula on a one-hitter by Don

Curt Blefary
Greensboro
News & Record

Loun. The following day, Phil Swimley hit a two-run homer to give Greensboro a 4–2 win over Rocky Mount in 14 innings. On August 29, Greensboro beat Tidewater twice to run its winning streak to 11 games. The streak ended the next day, but on August 31, Greensboro beat Burlington twice by identical 3–2 scores to drop the Indians 3½ games back.

As the season entered its last week, Burlington found itself in a race for second place and the playoffs. Tiant came back from his ankle injury on September 1 to beat Greensboro 5–2. The next day, Burlington scored five runs in the bottom of the first against Wilson but ended up losing 6–5. On September 4, Durham hit six home runs to take a pair from Kinston. Two days later, the Bulls beat Burlington to move into a tie for second; Morgan went three for four with two home runs and five runs batted in. On the last day of the season, Durham beat Burlington again to finish in second place. Greensboro ran away to a 6½-game margin.

The eastern race ended as a two-team affair between Kinston and Wilson. Peninsula and Rocky Mount had their moments early, however. The fledgling Senators started off 7–3 before fading. Rocky Mount had a nine-game winning streak in early May to keep pace with Kinston.

Led by star catcher and league Player of the Year Jim Price (.311, 19, 109), Kinston started off 19–6. Outfielders Don Bosch (.332, 108 runs, 32 stolen bases) and Rudy Welch (.316), shortstop Gene Michael (.304), and pitchers

Courtesy of Miles Wolff

1963 Durham Bulls

Front row left to right:
Walt Williams, Clint Courtney, Joe Morgan, Guinn Murray, Leon Hartless, Jim Marrujo, Jim Goss
and Johnny Garrett (Bat Boys).

Middle row left to right:
Jack Caffery, Jim Todhunter, Walt Matthews, Tom Burgmeier, Jim Holbrook, Larry Huebner, Ken Pate, Joe
Clement.

Standing left to right:
Bill Goodman (manager), Bobby Black, Bob Rikard, John Marms, Don Arlich, Darrell Brandon, Fred White, Tom
Willwerth, Tommy Murray, Fred McNeill (Trainer)

Rafael Sosa (13–7) and Bruce Kunkle (8–5, 2.58) supported Price. Kinston even
hosted a brief appearance by sore-armed former Pirates star Vern Law, who won
two games on his way back to the majors.

Wilson refused to cave in to Kinston's great start. First baseman Luke Vasser,
third baseman Ron Clark, and outfielder Dan Hagan—all of whom surpassed
the .300 mark—and pitcher Gerry Fosnow (13–9, 2.71) gave the Tobs the weap-
ons to stay in the race. At midseason, Kinston was 39–31 and Wilson 39–32.

The race stayed close to the end. On July 17, Kinston and Wilson were tied for
the east lead at 50–41. On August 7, Kinston's Gene Michael drove in six runs,
four of them with a grand slam, in a 7–5 win over Tidewater. Kinston maintained
a narrow lead into the final days. It took a half-game lead into the last game,
which it won 7–6 over Raleigh.

Having outlasted Wilson over the course of an entire season, Kinston dropped
out of the playoffs to the same team in a matter of days. Wilson won the first
encounter of the east playoffs by a 3–2 score when right fielder Dan Hagan
singled home the winner in the bottom of the ninth. Larry Bohannon won game
two for the Tobs, and a Chuck Holle four-hitter gave the Tobs the series sweep
in game three.

The Western Division final went the distance. Greensboro won the opener 4–0, with Jack Spurgin and Ted Dillard combining for a no-hitter; Spurgin, who had pitched a no-hitter in the regular season, developed a blister during the game, which allowed Dillard to pitch the ninth. Roy White had a two-run homer and made three excellent defensive plays. The Bulls recovered to win game two 5–4 in 10 innings, as Tommy Murray singled in the winning run. Greensboro committed four errors in game three, allowing the Bulls to cruise to an easy victory. The Yankees evened the series in game four, but Greensboro won the championship in game five

Roy White
Greensboro
News & Record

13–9 on a cool, damp night in front of a crowd of only 568. Four Greensboro singles, three walks, and an error led to seven Yankee runs in the fourth.

A pair of rainouts had preceded the Western Division fifth game. Worried that no one would show up for the Greensboro-Wilson final, league officials changed the format to the best two of three games. All three, as it turned out, were decided by a single run. Greensboro won the opener 9–8 in 12 innings, with Butch Cretara singling in the winner. Wilson won game two 7–6 in 13 innings. In the final game, Wilson jumped out to a 6–0 lead after 1½ innings and held on for a 7–6 win. Three of the first six Wilson runs were unearned.

Despite missing the playoffs, Rocky Mount had a solid season. First baseman Lee May (.263, 18, 80) led the league with 27 errors but more than compensated with his hitting. Outfielder Joe Wilson (.299, 26, 106) hit even better than May in the Carolina League, but his career never reached the heights achieved by his Rocky Mount counterpart, who went on to hit 354 home runs in the majors. Gerry Merz and Don Flynn won 17 and 15 games, respectively, for Rocky Mount.

The two Virginia clubs finished well below .500. Tidewater outfielder Chuck Buheller and catcher Adolfo Suarez combined for 39 home runs. Last-place Peninsula featured league Rookie of the Year and future major league player and manager Lou Pinella (.310, 16, 77, league-leading 23 assists). Future major leaguer Brant Alyea (.254, 16, 71) produced some runs for the Grays despite fanning 170 times.

In the west, Winston-Salem and Raleigh had dismal seasons. Two future Boston starters, Mike Andrews and Joe Foy, made brief stops at Winston-Salem. Raleigh's cellar finish might have been averted had future New York Mets star Cleon Jones (.305) been with the club for more than 49 games.

1963 Eastern Division Final Standings

Kinston	77–66	
* Wilson	77–67	playoff winner
Rocky Mount	72–72	
Tidewater	65–79	
Peninsula	58–86	

Western Division Final Standings

Greensboro	85–59
Durham	78–65
Burlington	77–66
Winston-Salem	67–76
Raleigh	62–82

—◆—

The league stood pat in 1964, with no franchise changes. It did, however, reduce all of its playoff series to three games. The directors also turned down an offer from the Western Carolina League to match champions in a postseason playoff.

The Western Division race was a three-team affair among Winston-Salem, Greensboro, and Raleigh. All three clubs had talent to spare.

Winston-Salem lost star pitcher Jim Lonborg (6–2, 3.20) to promotion early in the season, and third baseman George Scott (.288, 10, 30) missed much of the season with injuries. Nonetheless, outfielders Mike Page (.344) and Chris Coletta (.326), first baseman Tony Torchia (.300), and Mario Pagano (14–7) kept the Red Sox in contention, while the midseason acquisition of second baseman Carmen Fanzone gave them added punch down the stretch.

Greensboro, with 127 homers, was the only league team to reach triple figures in home runs. Considering his 44 errors and .885 fielding percentage, third baseman John Miller (.276, 24, 74) probably needed to hit that many himself to be much of an asset. Outfielder Steve Whitaker (.303, 27, 100), shortstop Chet Trail, and Ted Dillard (12–5) made more balanced contributions.

Raleigh, now affiliated with the St. Louis Cardinals, was led by third baseman Jose "Coco" Laboy (.340, 24, 74), outfielder Ed Chasteen (.257, 28, 90), Don Hagen (16–7), and Ron Cayll (15–7).

Although not a season-long contender, Burlington hosted a brief appearance by one big name, six-foot-eight Gene Conley, a former major league pitcher and NBA player. The sore-armed Conley had been released early in the season by the Boston organization. Cleveland picked him up and sent him to Burlington. His rehab effort was unsuccessful, however, and he never made it back to the big leagues.

Winston-Salem jumped to a 13–8 start in the west and a modest lead over Greensboro. On May 14, the Yankees defeated Wilson 2–0 in the first game of a doubleheader, as Gil Downs and Charlie Payne combined for a no-hitter. Downs was recovering from a sore shoulder, and manager Loren Babe wasn't taking any chances; no-hitter or not, he pulled Downs after five innings and let Payne finish up.

What was perhaps the most entertaining game of the season took place on June 27 when Greensboro outslugged Durham 18–13; Steve Whitaker drove in four runs with a home run, a triple, and a single.

Greensboro's 11–5 victory over Raleigh on July 2 featured fireworks of a different sort. In the fourth inning, umpire W. D. McRoy ruled that Raleigh outfielder Ed Chasteen had made a running catch. Greensboro manager Babe thought Chasteen had trapped the ball off the wall and attempted to make his case by taking a poke at McRoy.

The outfield play was even stranger the next day. Raleigh's Wayne Pietri hit a fly ball to left-center. Greensboro center fielder Steve Dichter, hoping for a ground-rule-double ruling, indicated to umpire John Harris that the ball had disappeared. Harris disagreed. While Dichter argued his case, Pietri circled the bases for an inside-the-park home run.

At the end of June, Winston-Salem led the west at 42–31. Burlington, Greensboro, and Raleigh were close behind. Burlington faded out of contention during July, while Raleigh made a run that put it in the lead. Laboy keyed the run, batting .452 for the month. On July 17, he drove in six runs in an 11–6 win over Durham. Laboy was batting .386 as late as July 26. At the end of July, Raleigh was atop the race, with Winston-Salem and Greensboro staying close.

The Cards suffered two setbacks that undermined their title hopes, however. Ron Willis (9–1) went out with a back injury, while shortstop Eddie Pacheco, who had started the season at Rock Hill of the Western Carolina League, was promoted to Tulsa of the Texas League; Pacheco had batted .392 in his brief stay in Raleigh.

Winston-Salem regained the lead on August 4. Raleigh dropped back with a four-game losing streak, which Don Hagen ended with a 15-strikeout, 2–0 six-hitter over Burlington. The Cards continued to drop behind Winston-Salem, however. Their frustrations boiled over in an ugly August 20 melee against Rocky Mount.

As Winston-Salem pulled away in the west, it became embroiled in a controversial race with east leader Kinston for the league's best overall record and the potential home-field advantage in the playoffs. By this time, Kinston was in the process of pulling away from Tidewater, its only rival for eastern supremacy down the stretch.

The Wilson Tobs had looked tough early in the east. They won 10 of their first 14 before falling apart. By the end of June, they had dropped to 25–49 and were in last place, a position they held at the end of the season.

Tidewater presented a more formidable challenge. The Tides were led by dynamic left-handed pitcher Rudy May. On June 2, May struck out 18 Rocky Mount batters in a three-hit 5–1 victory; nine of these strikeouts were consecutive, a league record. At the end of June, Tidewater was 38–36 and trailed Kinston by eight games. When May (13–6, 2.55) was promoted, the Tides' hopes of staying close were reduced dramatically. Tidewater was left with a weak-hitting but speedy club that stole 219 bases. The biggest thieves were outfielders Ed Stroud (.323, 72 stolen bases) and Buddy Bradford (.285, 48 stolen bases).

Kinston suffered an equally costly call-up when Gary Waslewski (12–1, 1.64)) was promoted to Asheville. Yet the balanced Eagles continued to maintain their lead, paced by Carolina League veterans Rudy Welch and Bruce Kunkle. Kinston led Tidewater by three games going into August and doubled that margin by the end of the season.

Late in the season, the league directors overturned a Bill Jessup ruling and upheld a Winston-Salem protest in a disputed loss to Kinston, giving Winston-Salem home-field advantage over Kinston in the event that the two clubs should meet in the playoff finals. As it turned out, the ruling didn't matter. Perhaps distracted by the controversy, Kinston lost a pair of 7–3 decisions to Tidewater in the opening series of the playoffs.

Bill Jessup and the Torn Sweatshirt

League presidents rarely make headlines, preferring to do most of their work behind closed doors. One exception took place in the Carolina League on August 11, 1964. On that day, ace Kinston pitcher Bruce Kunkle defeated Winston-Salem 9–0 with a one-hitter. Early in the game, Winston-Salem batters had begun complaining that Kunkle's torn sweatshirt was distracting them. Umpire Claude King ruled that the shirt met specifications. Winston-Salem appealed, but the appeal was denied by league president Bill Jessup.

Usually, this kind of thing would have ended right there. However, Winston-Salem and Kinston were fighting for the best regular-season record and home-field advantage for the playoffs. Winston-Salem decided to appeal to the league directors. In early September, the directors voted 5–3 to overrule Jessup and accept the appeal. Kinston president Jack Rider accused Winston-Salem of attempting to steal the pennant and blasted the decision as an attempt to bring Jessup down to size, saying, "Kinston was the innocent bystander that got hit by a street car aimed for Bill." Jessup defended his original decision, saying the game should have been decided on the field, not in a smoke-filled room.

Winston-Salem ended with the best regular-season record in the league but didn't need it against Kinston. The Eagles, perhaps distracted by the uproar, dropped their opening playoff series, while the Red Sox went on to capture the league title.

For Jessup, the incident was just another day on the job, albeit one with more public exposure than usual.

In the west, Winston-Salem beat Greensboro 5–4 and 10–8. Mike Page drove in three runs in game one, while a six-run seventh inning decided the second contest.

Winston-Salem disposed of Tidewater with relative ease in the finals. The Red Sox won game one 6–5. The big hit was a two-run triple in the fifth inning by center fielder Chris Coletta, breaking a 1–1 tie. Fred Hatter scattered seven hits in a 5–2 Winston-Salem triumph in the second game to clinch the title.

After a good start, Burlington had faded to a losing record. Shortstop Orlando Centellas and first baseman Ron Durham (20 homers apiece) and outfielder Sam Parilla (.315, 16, 77, 29 stolen bases) could not compensate for a weak pitching staff.

The Durham Bulls had the league's worst record by a wide margin. Further marring their dismal season was the accidental drowning death of pitcher Sammy Ray Fountain on May 25.

Peninsula, Rocky Mount, and Wilson also finished well below .500, although Rocky Mount pitcher Casey Cox (9–10, 3.16) and Wilson first baseman Rich Reese (.301) eventually advanced to the majors.

1964 Eastern Division Final Standings

Kinston	79–59
Tidewater	75–63
Peninsula	61–76
Rocky Mount	61–77
Wilson	57–82

Western Division Final Standings

* Winston-Salem	82–57	playoff winner
Greensboro	76–61	
Raleigh	76–62	
Burlington	68–70	
Durham	54–82	

———◆———

The league again stood pat for 1965, with the same 10 teams that completed the 1964 season. Burlington became a Washington farm team, while Rocky Mount switched its PDC to Detroit.

The most highly publicized player in the league that year was 19-year-old Greensboro shortstop Bobby Murcer (.322, 16, 90), a hard-hitting native of Oklahoma who evoked predictable, if fanciful, comparisons to another Oklahoma native, Mickey Mantle. Murcer, second baseman Chet Trail (.274, 22,

Bobby Murcer
Greensboro
News & Record

89), catcher Ellie Rodriguez, and pitcher Fritz Peterson (11–1, 1.50) led Greensboro to an 11–3 start and the early lead in the west.

Tidewater jumped on top in the east in more ways than one. On May 8, it was involved in an ugly game at Hampton against Peninsula. In the fifth inning, Tides pitcher Ed Smith brushed back Peninsula's Tom Perdue. Perdue charged the mound, both benches emptied, and a brawl ensued. Things got worse. In the seventh, Peninsula pitcher Wally Wolf hit consecutive batters. The second of these, Don Welsh, took offense, charged the mound, and began swinging his bat. The benches emptied again. Grays pitcher John Keller tackled Welsh, who hit him with the bat and sent him to the hospital. Eventually, 10 Hampton police cars and two police wagons ended up at the site. Tidewater won the game 15–4; Welsh was suspended and fined by Jessup. Incredibly, *Greensboro Daily News* writer Moses Crutchfield applauded this show of spunk: "It is refreshing to know there are baseball players left who will take so much, then forget their inhibitions."

Bobby Murcer sat out early May with a spike wound, and Durham caught Greensboro in the middle of the month. The Bulls had a solid pitching staff, led by Marvin Dutt (15–5), Mike Daniel (10–3), and Jim Holbrook (13–9). Veteran Walt Matthews (.306, 18, 93) led the team's batting attack, which received little help from future major league player and manager Doug Rader, who struggled through a .209 season.

With Murcer ailing, Greensboro dropped to last place by May 22. Late in the month, New York sent outfielder–first baseman Rich Barry to Greensboro from Columbus of the Southern League; Barry hit eight home runs in his first eight games to help Greensboro reverse its slide. By the beginning of June, Greensboro had climbed back to second. On June 5, Trail hit a grand slam to lead Greensboro to a 19–5 win over Kinston. A healthy Murcer sparked the Yanks with a 13-for-20 week in mid-June, with 11 runs batted in. On June 30, Greensboro beat Wilson 2–1, as Peterson threw a three-hitter and stole home.

Despite these highlights, Greensboro was unable to catch Durham. Greensboro's pennant hopes were jolted when Peterson was promoted in mid-July. Still, the Yanks stayed close to the Bulls in what had become a two-team race. Durham got a boost from Venezuelan pitcher Juan Quintana, who pitched a no-hitter against Raleigh on July 16 in his first start after being sent from Amarillo.

At the end of July, Durham led Winston-Salem by two. The Yanks surged again behind Murcer and took a half-game lead on August 6. They then were held scoreless three straight games. On August 9 and 10, the Bulls took two from Greensboro to extend their lead to 3½ games. In the latter contest, Bulls catcher Tom Kowalowski hit a dramatic two-run homer in the bottom of the 14th to win the game 4–3. On August 14, slumping Greensboro scored five runs in the bottom of the first and then proceeded to lose to Raleigh 17–9. Greensboro's last hurrah took place on August 28, when Murcer went five for eight with three RBIs to spark his team to an 8–2, 6–3 sweep of Raleigh; this brought the Yanks to within 1½ games of Durham. The Bulls held together and won by 4½.

The Eastern Division race also had its ups and downs. Tidewater appeared to be in control early. Despite his fine 1964 season, Chicago elected to leave Ed Stroud at Tidewater. Tides general manager Dave Rosenfield offered a glimpse why: "Ed suddenly has learned that base stealing isn't the only thing in this game and to get to the majors you've got to do other things well." Stroud (.341, 31 stolen bases) learned his lesson well enough to make the majors. An even bigger name had less success. Al Lopez, Jr., son of a successful major league player and manager, was demoted to Sarasota. Dennis Lundgren (22 homers) and double-figure winners Ed Nottle and Norbert Rogers helped Tidewater take a six-game lead over Wilson in early June.

Peninsula made a move for the top that same month. On June 9, it mauled Burlington 16–1; Sam Thompson, Stan Swanson, Clyde Mashore, and Ken Peters all homered in the fourth inning. Around the same time, Tidewater unraveled, losing 12 of 13 in the middle of the month to fall behind Peninsula. It recovered enough to pull back ahead by two games at the end of June.

The reprieve was short-lived for Tidewater. Peninsula went 25–8 in July, while Tidewater struggled to a 15–16 month. The combination broke the race wide open. Outfielder Teolindo Acosta (.336), Al Cosgrove, Mashore, Thompson (64 stolen bases), Jim Morio (16–7), and Bernie Kazakavich (12–5, 1.97) gave Peninsula a blend of speed, power, and pitching. A Pony Night crowd of 7,168 at Hampton saw Peninsula take a twin bill from Greensboro by 4–1 and 5–4 scores. Kazakavich struck out 16 in the seven-inning opener. Peninsula coasted to a nine-game margin over Tidewater. The Tides held off a late run by Kinston to hold onto second place and the last playoff spot.

The Tides carried this momentum to a first-round playoff upset over Peninsula. Peninsula won game one 2–0 behind a Kazakavich four-hitter. The Tidewater bats exploded for seven runs in the seventh inning of game two for a 12–1 victory. Tidewater then won the decisive third game 10–7 on a three-run 10th-inning homer by Dennis Lundgren.

The Tides were matched against Durham in the finals. The Bulls had beaten Greensboro in three games but were swept by the Tides for the title, 10–7 and 2–0. In the final game, Roger Nelson threw a three-hitter and struck out 13.

Kinston narrowly missed the playoffs despite the best efforts of home-run king Mike Derrick (.289, 28, 103), outspoken right-hander Dock Ellis (14–8, 1.98), and Silvano Quezada (9–2, 1.71).

Rocky Mount's best player was pitcher Pete DiLauro (12–7).

Wilson's playoff hopes ended when .338 hitter Nestor Velasquez was promoted to Charlotte in midseason. Former league Player of the Year Chuck Weatherspoon batted only .229 in an unsuccessful attempt to put his faltering career back on track. From August 15 through August 19, the Wilson pitching staff threw 38 consecutive scoreless innings; 32 of these were against Rocky Mount.

Like Wilson, Winston-Salem faded after a promising start. First baseman Tony Torchia (.324) was the most effective of the Red Sox. Future major league relief star Albert "Sparky" Lyle struggled through a 5–5, 4.24 season. Lyle's memories of his summer in Winston-Salem were not positive. In *The Bronx Zoo*, he wrote, "The lowest I'd ever been in my entire life was at Winston-Salem. We weren't playing real well, and I wasn't pitching good." Lyle also wrote that he and manager Bill Slack had constant disagreements.

Raleigh had a good season from outfielder Felix DeLeon (.303), but Mike Torrez (4–8, 4.79), who later played with and against Lyle for years in the American League, had a forgettable year.

Last-place Burlington sent catcher Paul Casanova (.287, 8, 76) to a long big-league career.

1965 Eastern Division Final Standings

Peninsula	86–58	
*Tidewater	76–68	playoff winner
Kinston	72–71	
Rocky Mount	70–70	
Wilson	68–75	

Western Division Final Standings

Durham	83–60
Greensboro	79–65
Winston-Salem	65–79
Raleigh	64–79
Burlington	63–81

—✦—

Nineteen sixty-six stands out as both a memorable and an unusual year in Carolina League history. Lynchburg was added to the Western Division, putting the league back in western Virginia and culminating a long effort by Lynchburg president Calvin Falwell. However, no 12th team was available, leaving the league with an awkward 11 clubs. A novel solution called the "mixed doubleheader" was used in an attempt to overcome the scheduling problems caused by the odd number of teams. In a mixed doubleheader, the home team played the first game against one team and the second game against another club. This left the other eight teams to play a more conventional four games.

League fans voted against the unusual format by staying away in droves. Despite the addition of an extra team, attendance dropped precipitously from 560,000 to 480,000. Early in the season, Durham Athletic Park hosted a crowd of 82 on a chilly night to see Rocky Mount's Dick Drago beat the Bulls 8–1.

On a brighter note, those fans who did come out saw a stellar assortment of future major league stars, including two eventual Hall of Famers.

Raleigh was affiliated with the Pittsburgh Pirates for the first time. Pittsburgh sent the renamed Raleigh Pirates two future major league stars, catcher Manny Sanguillen (.328) and first baseman Al Oliver (.299, 10, 57). Gene Garber joined the Pirates later in the season. Paced by Oliver and Sanguillen, Raleigh won 15 of its first 20 games to jump to an early lead in the west; Winston-Salem stayed close. Wilson started off 15–11 to take the early lead in the east.

The league had several exceptional pitching performances in the early going. On April 19, Durham's Juan Quintana beat Peninsula 8–0 with his second Carolina League no-hitter; he became the first pitcher to accomplish this feat. Nine days later, Wilson's Curt Sauer no-hit Greensboro 2–0. Only an error by promising Panamanian second baseman Rod Carew kept Sauer from a perfect game. Sauer went 6–0 before being promoted. On May 11, Winston-Salem's Dave Gray struck out 16 Burlington batters in seven innings in a 4–0 triumph.

These performances paled beside what happened in Greensboro on May 15. In the first game of a doubleheader, Rocky Mount's Dick Drago beat Greensboro 5–0 with a no-hitter; he struck out four and walked two. In the second game, his teammate Darrell Clark threw another no-hitter, winning 2–0, although he walked five. Both no-hitters were in seven-inning games, of course. Nonetheless, this is believed to be the only time in organized baseball history that a team has pitched no-hitters in both ends of a doubleheader.

Raleigh was unable to maintain its fast early pace in the Western Division. It stopped hitting in May and lost nine straight, 18 of 21. By the end of the month, Winston-Salem had taken over first place for good. The Red Sox were led by first baseman Jose Calero (.330, 26, 94), outfielder Jerry Dorsch (.297, 22, 79), second baseman Syd O'Brien (.302), and Bill Farmer (14–6). Their most indispensable player, however, was pitcher Robbie Snow (20–2, 1.75), the last Carolina League pitcher to win 20 games, as of this writing.

At the end of May, Winston-Salem led Lynchburg by two and Burlington by three. Lynchburg stayed close through June before falling out of contention. Winston-Salem opened a working margin in July and led by eight games on the 23rd. The Red Sox needed every bit of that lead during August, when both Raleigh and Burlington made runs for the top. A rejuvenated Raleigh club won eight straight in the middle of the month to close within two games. Winston-

Satchel Paige in the Carolina League

Satchel Paige was one of baseball's great treasures. Forced by segregation to spend most of his career in the Negro Leagues, the hard-throwing right-hander dominated his regular circuit and excelled in unofficial but highly competitive off-season contests against major leaguers. When he finally got a chance to pitch in the majors in 1948, Paige helped Cleveland to a World Series despite being in his 40s. His rules for living included the oft-quoted, "Don't look back, something might be gaining on you."

Paige was blessed with a rubber arm. Even after his big-league career ostensibly ended in 1953, he continued to pitch for barnstorming teams such as the Kansas City Monarchs.

In 1955, Greensboro general manager Rufus Blanchard signed Paige to take the mound August 17 against Reidsville. League president Ted Mann approved Paige's temporary contract. However, National Association president George Trautman responded to a Phillies protest by ruling the contract invalid and criticizing the proposed game as "a cheap pub-licity stunt." Trautman did leave the door open for an exhibition game involving Paige, however. Before Greensboro could decide, Hurricane Diane hit North Carolina and made the point moot by raining out the August 17 schedule.

Paige continued to pitch, even taking his turn on the mound for the Kansas City Athletics in 1965. The Carolina League tried to arrange an appearance again the following season, this time with more success. Paige pitched two innings for Peninsula against Greensboro on June 21, 1966. His appearance attracted 3,118 fans to Peninsula's home ballpark in Hampton. Paige gave up two runs on four straight hits in the first inning before pitching a one-hit, no-run second. Greensboro won the game 4–2, but Paige was not involved in the decision.

Although it was obviously a publicity ploy, Paige did have a league contract and did pitch in an official league game. League president Bill Jessup approved, and the National Association did not stand in the league's way. This was Paige's last appearance in organized baseball. He was elected to the Hall of Fame in 1971.

Salem skipper Bill Slack was ejected three times in five days and was fined $225 by Bill Jessup. Just when it appeared Raleigh might pull the race out, Sanguillen was promoted to AAA. The Pirates lost seven straight and dropped out of contention.

Burlington had a 10-game winning streak that came too late to catch Winston-Salem but did enable it to overtake Raleigh for second place and the last playoff spot. The Senators had a talented outfielder in Dick Billings (.312, 14, 70), along with hurlers Bill Haywood (17–9), Bill Gogolewski, and Ruperto Toppin (13–4).

Winston-Salem clinched the west title on September 1 with a 4–0 win over Durham; six-foot-five 19-year-old Bill Farmer struck out 16 Bulls.

Wilson maintained its lead in the east well past midseason. The Tobs had a hot prospect, second baseman Rod Carew (.292, 28 stolen bases). The future Hall of Famer was so advanced that he not only jumped to the majors the following season but also won the American League Rookie of the Year award. Catcher George Mitterwald, outfielder Dan DiPace (.329), veteran Chuck Weatherspoon

Two No-Hitters Are Better Than One

Many baseball fans go their entire lives without seeing a no-hitter in a professional game. Imagine the delight of the 617 fans who attended the Rocky Mount–Greensboro doubleheader at Greensboro's Memorial Stadium on the evening of May 15, 1966. Those lucky patrons got to see a pair of seven-inning no-hitters, both, unfortunately, thrown against the home team. Rocky Mount hurler Dick Drago threw a no-hitter against the G-Yanks in the first half of the twin bill. His teammate Darrell Clark followed with another in the nightcap.

Drago's gem was the more likely of the two. A highly regarded prospect, he went into the game with a 4–1 record. Several G-Yanks hit the ball hard, but always at a fielder. Only a pair of walks marred Drago's performance. He struck out four in a 5–0 victory.

Greensboro played most of the second game without its manager, Gary Blaylock, who was ejected in the second inning. Clark went into the game with a 1–2 record. Fittingly, his no-hitter was more

difficult than Drago's. Clark's control was shaky, leading to five walks. His Greensboro counterpart, Bill Burbach, was almost as effective as he was. The two teams were scoreless through six innings. Rocky Mount finally punched across a couple of runs in the top of the seventh, aided by an errant pick-off attempt by Burbach. Clark finished off Greensboro in the bottom of the inning for a 2–0 no-hit victory.

Rocky Mount skipper Al Federoff summed up the reaction of his team: "We were all too excited at the end to really realize what had happened. It's one of those once in a lifetime experiences, something I never expect to see or hear about again." Federoff's prediction was accurate. The double no-hitter has never been duplicated.

Federoff also correctly predicted that Drago would advance to the majors in a short period. Drago made the major leagues in 1969 and won 108 games in a 13-year big-league career. Darrell Clark never made the majors. However, for one night, he was part of baseball history.

Bill Slack and Bob Meyer

1966 Wilson Tobs with Rod Carew on the left

Greensboro News & Record

(.252, 23, 69), and Dick Sommer (16–8) were other top Tobs.

As good as Carew was, he was probably not the league's top prospect. Peninsula catcher Johnny Bench wowed observers with his hitting power, throwing arm, and savvy. Greensboro manager Gary Blaylock, a former major league pitcher, summed up the consensus on Bench: "For a youngster just one year out of the rookie league he's the most polished player I've ever seen." Blaylock further observed, with considerable understatement, that Bench "also hits with authority." Unfortunately for Peninsula, Bench (.294, 22, 68) hit Carolina League pitching with enough authority that Cincinnati promoted him to AAA Buffalo shortly after the All-Star break. Even with second baseman Hal McRae (.287, 11, 56), third baseman Bernie Carbo (.269, 15, 57), Clyde Mashore, and Steve Mingori (2.50 ERA), Peninsula dropped into the second division without Bench.

Mashore hit what is probably the shortest home run in league history on July 22 in a 9–3 win over Durham. Durham right fielder Charlie Murray thought Mashore's shallow pop fly was foul and let it drop. The umpires, neither of whom was in position, called it fair. While Murray argued with the umpires, Mashore kept running. He ended up with a 200-foot home run, while Murray ended up with an ejection.

Kinston took over the east lead from Wilson in late July and pulled away from the troubled Tobs. Wilson's George Mitterwald and Dan DiPace spent much of August in the Army Reserves, while key pitchers Curt Sauer and Ron Keller were promoted to AA Charlotte and Carew had a series of injuries that dropped his batting average below .300. Kinston was led by .300 hitters Juan Guzman and

1966 Peninsula Pilots manager Pinky May with Peninsula catcher Johnny Bench   Courtesy Carolina League

Al Cambero, outfielder Barry Morgan (.281, 28, 104), and hurlers Conrad Noessel (12–4), and Ron Reed (5–2, 1.76).

Rocky Mount made a late run which nudged Wilson out of second place and gave it the final playoff spot. Rocky Mount's standout pitching staff included Drago (15–9, 1.79), Jim Rooker (12–5, 2.05), and Clark. Light-hitting catcher Jim Leyland (.243, 0, 16) never made it to the majors as a player but managed the Pittsburgh Pirates to three National League Eastern Division titles in the early 1990s.

With the race decided, Winston-Salem and Greensboro gave the fans a treat on the last day of the season when managers Bill Slack and Gary Blaylock opposed each other on the mound. The younger Blaylock prevailed 6–3. Slack had other problems as the playoffs approached. Jerry Dorsch and shortstop Don Fazio both left the team to go back to school.

Having snuck into the playoffs at the end of the season, Rocky Mount dominated the postseason with its pitching. In its first game against regular-season champ Kinston, Rocky Mount jumped to a 13–0 lead after 3½ innings and cruised to a 15–5 win. Dick Drago won the second game 2–1 to put Rocky Mount into the finals.

Winston-Salem's pitching staff matched Rocky Mount's in the first round. Bill Farmer threw a one-hitter in the first game as the Red Sox beat Burlington 6–1, while Jim Thornton followed with a three-hitter for a 2–0 win in the second game.

Underdog Rocky Mount continued its winning ways in the finals. Bill Butler won the opener 4–1. In the second game, Rocky Mount scored a run in the bottom of the ninth to tie the game, then won 6–4 on a two-run 10th-inning home run by outfielder Larry Haggitt.

As usual, the also-rans had some talented players.

Tidewater's best players were outfielder Jim Perkins (.312, 34 stolen bases) and 17-game-winner Frank Pollard.

Lynchburg's first Carolina League campaign was memorable especially for two games. On July 7, Lynchburg lost to Tidewater 4–3 in 18 innings. One month and one day later, it defeated Kinston by the same score in 19 innings. At the time, this was the longest game in league history. It was also the second game of a doubleheader, meaning that the two clubs played 26 innings in one day.

Durham finished in the cellar.

Greensboro had one of the more unusual aggregations of talent in league history. The Yanks led the league with a superb 2.61 team earned-run average, yet countered that with a minuscule .208 batting average. The lack of offense neutralized outstanding pitching by Bill Burbach (3–14, 2.19), Gary Girouard (9–7, 2.13), Jim Fink (12–11, 2.21), and Alan Closter (11–7, 2.25).

Hard-Luck Burbach

One of the universal baseball characters is the "hard-luck" pitcher, a hurler who can't seem to win no matter how well he pitches. The model for the Carolina League was Greensboro Yankees pitcher Bill Burbach, who could have sued his 1966 team-mates for nonsupport and won in any court. In fact, the entire pitching staff could have done so. Despite squaring off against such formidable hitters as Rod Carew, Johnny Bench, Al Oliver, and Manny Sanguillen, the Yanks led the league with a superb 2.61 team earned-run average. Yet they lost a dozen more games than they won. The reason was not hard to find. They had a pathetic team batting average of .208 and scored only 444 runs in 140 games.

No Yankee pitcher suffered from the lack of run production as much as Burbach. Consider his outing on July 8. That night, Burbach pitched a no-hitter for 10 innings against Lynchburg. When Greensboro loaded the bases with no outs in the bottom of the 10th in the scoreless game, Burbach's gem appeared safe. Manager Gary Blaylock sensibly elected to remove him for a pinch hitter. Unfortunately, the Yankees proceeded to botch a squeeze play and failed to score. Lynchburg won the game 3–1 in 16 innings. After this no-decision, Burbach had a 1.78 ERA and a 1–7 record.

His luck never improved. Burbach ended the season with an excellent 2.19 ERA and a miserable 3–14 record. Three years later, the resilient right-hander made the big leagues. However, he won only six games for the New York Yankees in three years. He still holds the title as the Carolina League's all-time hard-luck pitcher.

1966 Eastern Division Final Standings

Kinston	76–63	
* Rocky Mount	72–63	playoff winner
Wilson	72–65	
Peninsula	63–75	
Tidewater	58–81	

Western Division Final Standings

Winston-Salem	82–58
Burlington	76–62
Raleigh	71–66
Lynchburg	64–75
Greensboro	64–76
Durham	62–76

—♦—

The league balanced its divisions again in 1967 with the addition of the Asheville Tourists, longtime members of the Southern League. Although new to the Carolina League, Asheville did have one familiar name, general manager Jim Mills.

Since Asheville was placed in the Western Division, Raleigh switched over to the Eastern Division.

Asheville attracted almost 3,000 to its home opener. Paced by outfielder Danny Walton (.302, 25, 78), first baseman Keith Graffagnini (.261, 24, 87), catcher Hal King (.288, 30, 87), and Mike Daniel (15–5, 2.63), the Houston farm team went 11–3 during April. The Tourists couldn't maintain the pace of their first month; in fact, they eventually finished in last place.

Greensboro was next to take over the lead. The Yankees had winning streaks of 10 and six games during May, led by left-handed pitcher Gary Jones (15–9, 2.42), who won his first 10 decisions. On June 3, he pitched a one-hitter against Kinston, giving up a single to Al Cambero with two outs in the ninth inning. Jones finally lost 4–1 to Asheville on June 16.

Durham stayed close to Greensboro. However, the Bulls suffered a major loss in mid-June when ace pitcher Danny Frisella (9–3, 1.49, 121 strikeouts in 109 innings) was promoted to AAA. Greensboro suffered promotion loses, too, including that of five-foot-four spark-plug second baseman Matt Galante (.314).

Late in July, Lynchburg put together an 11-game winning streak to climb into the race. At the end of the month, Greensboro led the west, followed closely by Asheville, Durham, Lynchburg, and Burlington, all of which were within five games of the top.

Greensboro lost five straight in early August to drop behind Durham. The Yankees suffered a gut-wrenching defeat on August 14, blowing an 11–1 lead over Winston-Salem and losing 13–12 in a 19-inning marathon that lasted five hours and 47 minutes. Winston-Salem got a spectacular relief performance by Jim Thomas, who came in during the ninth and proceeded to strike out 19 Yankees in 10 scoreless innings. This loss seemingly took the fight out of Greensboro, which dropped all the way to fifth place.

Burlington and Lynchburg also kept treading water, allowing Winston-Salem to sneak into second. Only Durham played well down the stretch. The Bulls ended up beating Winston-Salem by 4½ games.

Wilson led the east for the first five weeks of the season. The campaign was enlivened by a brief appearance by former Cincinnati Reds standout Joey Jay, who came to Tidewater in an attempt to rehab a sore arm. Although Jay finished 3–1, his arm continued to bother him, and his comeback failed.

The Raleigh Pirates got hot in mid-June and climbed into first place. The Pittsburgh farm club, managed by future Boston Red Sox skipper Joe Morgan, was led by future major leaguers Don Money (.310, 16, 86), Gene Garber (8–6, 1.89), Richie Hebner (.336), Al Oliver (.297), Angel Mangual, and Gene Clines. The Pirates also got excellent pitching from Harold Clem (15–3, 1.64), whose efforts included a one-hitter and a two-hitter.

Tidewater, led by Ron Allen (.288, 24, 100), second baseman Denny Doyle,

Jack Nutter (12–6), and future major league standout Larry Hisle (.302, 23, 78, 31 stolen bases), was also playing well. At the end of June, it trailed Raleigh by only 1½ games. On the last day of that month, Tidewater's Lowell Palmer, a 19-year-old from Sacramento, threw a no-hitter at Kinston. He walked only two batters in the 7–0 win and faced the minimum 27 batters, as both baserunners were retired on double plays.

Tidewater took over first from Raleigh in mid-July, and the two clubs traded the top spot throughout the rest of the month. Raleigh was hampered by some serious injuries, most notably a broken wrist that ended Hebner's season. In addition, Clines had bursitis, while valuable utility man Duncan Campbell (.331, 10, 64) broke a finger.

Raleigh regained the lead when Tidewater lost six in a row during early August. It pulled away later in the month with a 17–6 streak. On August 9, Raleigh took a pair from Burlington by scores of 6–0 and 6–3. In the first game, Garber's sinking fastball helped the Raleigh infield turn a league-record seven double plays, a mark achieved in only seven innings. On August 20, a fully recovered Campbell hit three homers to lead Raleigh over Wilson 11–6. Peninsula made a late run for the top and finished only one game behind Raleigh.

The 1967 postseason consisted of a curious and inflated eight-team format. The first round was only a single game, matching the first-place and third-place teams in each division in one game and the second-place and fourth-place teams in the other. In the best game of the first round, Raleigh's Clem outdueled Rocky Mount's Jim Brown (14–11, 2.82) by a 1–0 score. In the other eastern matchup, Tidewater, a club whose late slump had dropped it eight games below .500, upset Peninsula. In the west, Durham defeated Burlington, while Lynchburg pounded Winston-Salem.

The two second-round series were a more conventional three games. Durham cruised to a pair of comfortable victories over Lynchburg, while Tidewater won twice from Raleigh. The Tides won their second game largely because of four unearned runs they scored in the fifth inning.

Durham put an end to Tidewater's unlikely title run in the championship series. The Bulls won the opener 1–0, as Rich Folker and Gerry Wild combined for a shutout. Barry Lersch's three-hit, 12-strikeout 2–0 win evened the series. Durham then rode a three-run seventh to a 6–3 win and the league championship in game three.

The champion Bulls were led by pitchers Malcolm "Bunky" Warren (12–6, 2.25), Jim Bethke (10–8, 2.58), and Gerry Wild (14–13, 2.70).

Other top players in the Western Division were outfielders Joe Lahoud (.287) and Bob Speer (.313) of Winston-Salem; Burlington's Luis Penalver (12–9, 2.37); and Lynchburg first baseman Gail Hopkins (.312, 20, 79).

Their Eastern Division counterparts included Jim Holt (.312), Frederico Velazquez (.312), Nicky Curtis (11–5), and Jackie Earls (12–6) of Peninsula;

Jim Covington (.276, 21, 67) and Jon Warden (15–11) of Rocky Mount; and Van Kelly (.323) and Hal Breeden (.305) of Kinston.

1967 Eastern Division Final Standings

Raleigh	77–65
Peninsula	74–64
Rocky Mount	74–68
Tidewater	70–68
Wilson	61–72
Kinston	60–75

Western Division Final Standings

*Durham	74–64	playoff winner
Winston-Salem	69–68	
Burlington	70–69	
Lynchburg	68–68	
Greensboro	66–72	
Asheville	64–74	

———◆———

The league underwent an eventful few months following the 1967 season. Asheville rejoined the Southern League, the Pirates dropped their PDC with Raleigh, and Salem, Virginia, moved into the league as a Pittsburgh affiliate. Raleigh merged with Durham to form the Raleigh-Durham Mets, splitting their home games between the two cities. Atlanta dropped Kinston, which signed a PDC with the New York Yankees. High Point-Thomasville came back on board as the 12th team but was forced to operate as a co-op.

Even though the league managed to come up with 12 teams for 1968, there was still much concern among league officials over PDCs. The league constitution was amended so that member clubs could not cancel PDCs unless they gave 15 days' written notice. Given the dominance of the major league clubs in such matters, this was about the best the league could do. The directors also turned down a suggestion to change the league's name to the Carolina-Virginia League.

The Salem Rebels made their Carolina League debut season a memorable one. Aided by weak Western Division competition, they won their division easily after a slow start. Lynchburg took an early lead at 11–5. The sensation of the Western Division, however, was Hi-Toms first baseman Tolia "Tony" Solaita, a native of exotic American Samoa. Solaita hit five homers in his first 12 games, the beginning of an ultimately unsuccessful season-long assault on Muscle Shoals's league home-run record.

Lynchburg maintained its hold on first place into June. On May 18, it was 23–9 and held a 3½-game lead over Salem. The lead was reduced to 1½ games at the end of the month, however, and it disappeared entirely in early June.

Salem stretched its lead in the second half of the season. Fiery manager Don Hoak, a former Pittsburgh standout, had a stellar aggregation which included second baseman Dave Cash, outfielders Wilbert Hammond (.307, 39 stolen bases), John Jeter (.296, 18, 79, 38 stolen bases), and Dave Arrington (league-record 17 triples), infielder Charlie Howard (.281, 27, 94), and pitchers Robert Settle and Calvin Bailey. Lynchburg slumped badly, and no one else in the division made a run. Salem finished the season with an 85–55 record, the only team in the division to win more than it lost.

High Point-Thomasville passed Lynchburg for second but still trailed Salem by 16 games. Solaita (.302, 49, 122) finished with the third-best home-run season in league history. Joe Dodder and Ed Moxey hit 24 and 21 home runs, respectively, as the Hi-Toms accumulated an impressive 152 round-trippers. However, a league-worst 4.21 earned-run average kept the high-scoring team mired in mediocrity.

The Eastern Division race was much more competitive, with Wilson and Tidewater taking turns in the lead in the first part of the season. Raleigh-Durham began to close ground on Tidewater during June. On June 4, Jon Matlack

Tolia "Tony" Solaita
Greensboro News & Record

(13–6, 2.55), a highly regarded 18-year-old left-hander, struck out 17 Tidewater batters in a 9–1 win. At midseason, Raleigh-Durham made three key moves, acquiring first baseman Mike Jorgensen (.315), third baseman Joe Moock (.318), and shortstop Ted Martinez (.330) to go along with Matlack, outfielder Lee Stanton, Gerry Bark (14–7, 2.49), Charles Hudson (16–7, 2.22), Bill Seals (10–4, 1.83), and Jim Bibby. Raleigh-Durham did lose future Baltimore Orioles star Ken Singleton to promotion early in the season, however.

Also gaining ground was Peninsula, which put together a 12-game winning streak to get into the race.

The season's best individual performance came on July 17, when Winston-Salem's Ed Phillips pitched a perfect game against Rocky Mount. In addition to striking out 10 in the 3–0 win, Phillips hit a two-run homer.

Raleigh-Durham took over the Eastern Division lead on July 20 with a 2–0, 3–2 sweep over Salem. A seven-game Raleigh-Durham winning streak helped push the margin over Tidewater to three games at the end of July. The two teams maintained this gap during August. Raleigh-Durham ended up 3½ games ahead of Tidewater.

Again, the Carolina League had a bloated eight-team playoff format, which enabled Greensboro to advance to the postseason with a 61–79 regular-season mark. Again, the playoffs opened with a single game in the first round. The risks of this system were obvious: even the best team could come up short in a single game. That was exactly what happened to Salem, owner of the league's best regular-season record since Durham's 1962 team. The Rebels lost 5–4 to Lynchburg on a 10th-inning RBI single by Lynchburg star Carlos May (.330, 13, 74). In the other Western Division first-round matchup, the Hi-Toms beat Greensboro. In the east, Raleigh-Durham beat Peninsula and Wilson beat Tidewater.

The Hi-Toms advanced to the finals by beating Lynchburg twice. In their first victory, they scored four unearned runs in the top of the ninth for a 9–5 win.

Their opponent in the final was Raleigh-Durham, the winner of a three-game series against Wilson. Raleigh-Durham's Jim Bibby won the opener against Wilson and also hit a solo homer. The Tobs evened the series on a Charlie Murray one-hitter, but Raleigh-Durham won the deciding game 4-0 behind Jerry Bark's four-hit effort.

Solaita led High Point-Thomasville to an upset win in the finals. The league Player of the Year hit a three-run homer in the top of the fourth off Matlack to key a 6-5 Hi-Toms victory in the first game. The Mets made things easier for the visitors by committing four errors. In the second game, Solaita again hit a three-run homer, this time in the second inning, and the Hi-Toms cruised to an 11–1 win. John Miller scattered eight hits for the win. Future major league skipper

Jack McKeon managed this unlikely title run, the first time in league history that the postseason championship was won by a team with a losing record in the regular season.

In addition to Carlos May, Lynchburg had solid seasons from James Jedelsky (.300), Ed Smith (16–7), and Marcelino Dominguez (10–7, 2.35). Future Kansas City Royals standout Al Fitzmorris could do no better than 11–11.

Greensboro was led by slugging outfielders Olivero Sparks (.319, 22, 76) and Glenn Adams.

Tidewater finished with the league's third-best regular-season record, thanks to the efforts of outfielders Joe Lis (.293, 32, 94) and Bob Kelly (.304) and double-digit winners Bill Champion (15–5, 2.03), Dave Bennett, Ken Reynolds, and Dick Seminoff.

Peninsula was also competitive, with catcher Gene Tenace (.283, 21, 71), first baseman Gonzalo Marquez (.311), outfielder Bob Brooks (26 homers), Greg Conger (13–6, 1.76), and Larry Abbott (10–4, 2.53).

Proving again that minor league success is not always an accurate predictor of major league success, several future major league regulars struggled through forgettable Carolina League seasons. These included Kinston outfielder Ron Blomberg (.251, 7, 43), Burlington shortstop Toby Harrah (.239, 6, 39), Raleigh-Durham outfielder Jerry Morales (.225), and Raleigh-Durham pitcher Ed Figueroa (0–2, 6.23), who missed much of the season with a sore arm. Blomberg achieved fame in 1973 when he became the American League's first regular-season designated hitter.

Ron Blomberg   Greensboro News & Record

1968 Eastern Division Final Standings

Raleigh-Durham	*83–56*
Tidewater	*80–60*
Peninsula	*75–65*
Wilson	*71–68*
Rocky Mount	*70–70*
Kinston	*62–75*

Western Division Final Standings

Salem	*85–55*	
*High Point-Thomasville	*69–71*	*playoff winner*
Lynchburg	*68–72*	
Greensboro	*61–79*	
Winston-Salem	*56–81*	
Burlington	*56–84*	

—♦—

After the 1968 season, the Carolina League began a period of decline that saw it drop from 12 teams to four in less than a decade.

Tidewater dropped out of the league when the New York Mets decided to move their AAA franchise from Jacksonville, Florida, to the Virginia Tidewater. The Mets paid the league $25,000 for the rights to the territory. Raleigh-Durham picked up Tidewater's PDC with the Philadelphia Phillies. Charter member Greensboro dropped out, citing problems with aging Memorial Stadium. Peninsula dropped its PDC with Oakland and picked up Greensboro's contract with Houston. High Point-Thomasville became a Kansas City farm team and dropped its distinctive nickname, becoming known, like its parent club, as the Royals. The most dramatic change was the transfer of the Wilson team—and its PDC with Minnesota—to Red Springs, a small town in the southern part of North Carolina.

The league retained its Eastern Division–Western Division format. Surprisingly, it also retained the eight-team playoff structure, meaning that only two teams would miss the postseason. The league did expand the first-round playoffs to three games. It also adopted the designated hitter.

Raleigh-Durham had the league's most spectacular player, Greg Luzinski (.289, 31, 92), a powerful slugger whose tape-measure home runs elicited gasps of admiration across the league. Outfielder Roy Foster, Gordy Knutson (10–6, 1.90), and John Penn (15–9, 2.45) were also highly regarded by the Philadelphia brain trust.

Kinston led the east for much of May, jumping out to a 22–11 record on May 17 before hitting a bad patch and dropping to 27–20 at the end of the month. It was supplanted at the top by Rocky Mount, which rode a 10-game winning streak to a 31–16 record at the end of May.

The west was not as strong as the east. At the end of May, Salem was 25–21, Winston-Salem 23–22, and everybody else below .500. High Point-Thomasville won 10 straight in early July to move into first place but was unable to hold onto the top spot for long.

Kinston and Rocky Mount traded first place in the east through June. Raleigh-Durham was bolstered in midseason by the addition of sixth-round draft pick Bob Boone (.300) of Stanford and hard-hitting outfielder Sammy Parilla (.383, 28, 85 in only 321 at-bats). Parilla was a six-year minor league veteran who had been released by the Cleveland organization. Ironically, Boone, who later became one of the best defensive catchers in major league history, played third base for Raleigh-Durham.

Kinston gradually slumped out of contention in the east, leaving Rocky Mount and Raleigh-Durham to fight it out at the top. Sparked by outfielder Elliott Maddox (.301), Ronnie Chambers (.301), Tim Hosley (27 homers), Dave Cook (8–1, 2.12), and Jerome Donahue (10–0, 1.89), Rocky Mount opened up a five-game lead by the end of July. Raleigh-Durham's Luzinski was beaned in early August and was slow in recovering his previous form. However, the veteran Parilla kept the Phillies in contention with a spectacular 26-game hitting streak down the stretch. On August 26, the Phillies scored seven runs in the bottom of the ninth to beat Burlington 9–8, the last three runs scoring on a Parilla homer. Two days later, Parilla hit a three-run homer in the top of the ninth to give Raleigh-Durham a 10–8 win over Salem. The following day, he hit two more home runs (giving him six in five days) in a 9–8 win over first-place Rocky Mount. This cut Rocky Mount's lead to 2½ games with three left. But when Rocky Mount beat Raleigh-Durham 4–3 on August 30, it clinched the east title.

In the west, Winston-Salem and Salem remained the only two teams over .500 for most of the season. The two closely matched clubs entered the last day of the season tied for the lead. Salem's Dennis Malseed beat Lynchburg 3–0 with a four-hitter, while Winston-Salem fell to Burlington. Salem was led by third baseman Luther Quinn (.314, 20, 74), the league's Player of the Year. Jerry Branch, Mel Civil, and outfielder Richie Zisk joined Quinn in the .300 circle. Bob Cluck (10–4, 2.25), John Lamb (11–4, 1.95), and Malseed were the key pitchers in Salem's title run.

Rocky Mount, Raleigh-Durham, Salem, Winston-Salem, Kinston, Peninsula, Burlington, and High Point-Thomasville all advanced to the inflated playoffs. In

The Red Springs Experiment

In the 1930s, 1940s, and 1950s, numerous small towns in North Carolina and Virginia hosted minor league baseball. But after the demise of such leagues as the Virginia League, the Tobacco State League, and the Tar Heel League in the 1950s, minor league ball increasingly became the province of large metropolitan areas. In 1969, the Carolina League briefly attempted to reverse the trend. That season, the league's Wilson team, fighting years of low attendance, moved to the small southeastern North Carolina community of Red Springs.

Red Springs had a population of about 4,000, making it the smallest community represented in minor league baseball. The town had previously fielded a club in the Tobacco State League, a Class D circuit that went under in 1950, and skeptics openly wondered what business professional ball had in a town of that size. Yet the community's enthusiasm convinced the Minnesota Twins to transfer their PDC from Wilson to Red Springs. The town sold over 350 season tickets and several thousand dollars' worth of fence and program advertising. It also used a federal grant to bring aging Robbins Field up to Class A standards.

The experiment eventually drew national attention, including an article in *Sports Illustrated*. The article observed that Red Springs "was on its way to the best time the town has had since the night in 1913 when most everybody went to jail following a raucous celebration of the semipro team's state championship."

Despite hosting a last-place team, the community of Red Springs turned out to the tune of 40,000, double the figure drawn in preceding years in Wilson. Owner–general manager Matt Boykin optimistically predicted that small towns were the salvation of the minor leagues: "Here, baseball is the only thing to do, and there are a bunch of little places like this with ball parks that can be fixed over. We should forget the big towns and go to the small ones."

Boykin's optimistic assessment proved premature. In the end, the town's small size was more of a handicap than its proponents realized. A lack of housing and leisure activities for players proved a particular hardship. The league did not return to Red Springs the following season, and it appears likely that 1969 was the town's swan song in organized baseball.

the best tradition of Carolina League playoffs, the also-rans made their share of trouble.

In the west, Winston-Salem was handicapped by the loss of two players who left for teaching jobs and another who went back to college. Not surprisingly, the Red Sox lost to Burlington two games to one, scoring only five runs in the process. Salem beat High Point-Thomasville 2–1 and 14–0 in the other west semifinal.

In the east, Raleigh-Durham won two squeakers from Kinston, 3–2 and 6–4, the latter in 10 innings. In the other matchup, Peninsula upset the regular-season champs from Rocky Mount in two close contests.

Burlington continued its upset run with a surprisingly easy two-game sweep of Winston-Salem.

The east final was an exciting series. Peninsula won the opener 10–8 on the strength of a seven-run sixth inning, but Raleigh-Durham captured the second contest. In the final game, Cliff Davis hit a grand slam in the top of the seventh to give Peninsula a 7–6 lead, which it extended to 8–6 in the eighth. With its back to the wall, Raleigh-Durham stormed back with five runs in the bottom of the eighth for an 11–8 win.

The Phillies continued their hot play in the final series. Parilla homered, doubled twice, and drove in three runs in an opening-game victory. Burlington drew even with a 10-inning 4–3 victory in game two, scoring the winning run on a wild pitch. In the decisive third game, Luzinski's three-run homer in the fourth propelled the Phillies to an 8–2 win.

Burlington might have won the title had it been able to hold onto its talented shortstop, Toby Harrah (.306), who was promoted in midseason to the Southern League. Harrah ended the season with Washington, beginning a 17-year big-league career. The Burlington pitching staff, led by Frank Bolick (10–3, 2.00), Dickie Nold (13–8), and Mike Thompson (9–5, 2.09), carried the team to within one victory of a championship.

Pitching was also Winston-Salem's long suit. Don Newhauser turned in an exceptional year, finishing 11–3 with a 1.11 earned-run average.

Shortstop Mario Guerrero, Tim O'Connell (.304), outfielder Rusty Torres, and Bruce Olson (13–6, 2.83) led Kinston to a winning mark.

Peninsula fell short of that level despite the presence of Cesar Cedeno (.274, 24 stolen bases), a Dominican who went on to play 17 seasons in the majors. Ed Armbrister, Ken Forsch, and Walt Harris (12–4, 1.84) were also highly regarded.

The springtime hopes of the Red Springs team faded amidst the losses of summer. Outfielder Steve Brye overcame his .234 season to make the majors.

Lynchburg brought up the rear in the west. Outfielders Ron Lolich (.309, 26, 90) and Howard Wood had good seasons at the plate, but poor pitching doomed the White Sox to the cellar.

To his surprise, Bill Jessup's contract was not renewed after the season. Gradually, a rift had opened between Jessup and the Virginia clubs. Jessup owned a beer distributorship in Wilson, and some of the clubs felt that his business obligations kept him from devoting his full attention to the league, and especially to the more distant Virginia cities. Jessup felt that the Virginia teams had ganged up on him. Over two decades after his dismissal, Jessup called the infusion of Virginia teams into the league "a big mistake . . . because eventually they banded together and took control of the league."

1969 Eastern Division Final Standings

Rocky Mount   82–62
* Raleigh-Durham   79–62   playoff winner
Kinston   74–68
Peninsula   67–76
Red Springs   57–84

Western Division Final Standings

Salem   78–66
Winston-Salem   77–67
Burlington   71–71
High Point-Thomasville   69–74
Lynchburg   60–84

♦   ♦   ♦

Salem Municipal Field

Courtesy of Miles Wolff

CHAPTER FIVE
1970 — 76

♦ ♦ ♦

Bill Jessup was replaced as league president by 51-year-old Wallace McKenna, a Lynchburg businessman and former Lynchburg general manager, and a man described by *Newport News Daily Press* sportswriter Bob Moskowitz as "virtually dedicated to seeing the brighter side of life, no matter how dark the clouds above." The clouds got dark indeed for McKenna, who proved unable to halt the decline of the Carolina League.

Both Red Springs and High Point-Thomasville went under after the 1969 season. Minnesota moved its PDC to Lynchburg, while Philadelphia transferred its contract to Peninsula. Raleigh-Durham was unable to pick up a contract for the 1970 season and operated as a co-op. With only eight teams, the league went back to a single-division split-season format. Only the two half-season winners would make the postseason playoffs, a dramatic contrast to the eight-team play-offs of recent seasons.

McKenna and other league and team officials tried numerous promotional gambits in an attempt to attract more fans to the ballparks. McKenna pushed a "Guess the Attendance" contest for opening night, in which the person coming closest to the total attendance was the winner. Raleigh-Durham general manager Walter Brock tried a "Guaranteed Victory Night"; if the home team lost, all in attendance got free admission the next night. Traditional attractions like baseball clown Max Patkin still turned up at regular intervals.

Increasingly, however, Carolina League fans ignored the traditions and found something else to do. Attendance dropped throughout McKenna's tenure.

Despite the decline in fan interest, the Carolina League continued to enhance its stature as a fast Class A league. Many baseball people agreed that it was a league that separated the men from the boys. On occasion, this reputation even hurt the league. In the words of longtime Lynchburg executive Calvin Falwell, "Many farm directors found it hard for their clubs to compete in this league if sufficient experienced players were not available." When talented prospects were available, some major league teams felt that if they were good enough for the Carolina League, they might as well bypass that league and go straight to AA.

Making matters even more ominous for the league was the fact that many major league teams cut their number of minor league affiliates during the 1970s, making it increasingly difficult to procure PDCs. This difficulty, combined with poor attendance, made the 1970s a decade of survival.

The Carolina League continued to receive some bright prospects during the 1970s, however. One of the brightest was Cliff Johnson, a six-foot-four, 225-pound catcher-outfielder who dominated the 1970 season for the Raleigh-Durham Triangles. Johnson had played the previous year with Peninsula without distinction, batting only .221. The added maturity of an extra season made a dramatic difference for the burly slugger, however.

The Raleigh-Durham team that year was a ragtag conglomeration of players from 11 separate franchises; Johnson was in the Houston organization. Cliff Davis, a 31-year-old veteran of assorted Houston minor league clubs, accepted the difficult assignment of bringing this disparate group together. Johnson made Davis's job substantially easier. On May 5, he hit two home runs and drove in six runs in a single inning in a 14–2 win over Salem. Four days later, he went four for four with a home run and four RBIs in an 11–1 win over Burlington. The following day, Johnson was overshadowed by Burlington first baseman Jim Kuehner, who went six for six with a home run, three doubles, six runs scored, and 10 runs batted in during a 19–11 win over Raleigh-Durham. At the end of May, Raleigh-Durham was 2½ games ahead of Winston-Salem; Johnson was batting .447 with 14 home runs and 47 runs batted in.

Johnson obviously couldn't maintain that pace, and when his batting average dropped from the stratosphere, the Triangles dropped with him. The slide began June 12 when they dropped a pair of one-run decisions at home to Winston-Salem, beginning a five-game losing streak. The Kinston Eagles took over first place on June 14 with a doubleheader sweep of Lynchburg; Bob Elliott pitched a no-hitter in the nightcap. By that point, Winston-Salem and Peninsula had joined Kinston and Raleigh-Durham in a tense pennant race. A crowd of 5,832 packed Devereaux Meadow on June 15 to watch Raleigh-Durham regain first place temporarily with a 2–1 win over Peninsula; Johnson hit a two-run homer in the first, his 19th round-tripper of the year.

Peninsula, Raleigh-Durham, Winston-Salem, and Kinston were all within two games on June 19. The next day, Red Sox ace Lynn McGlothen beat Rocky Mount 5–0 on a three-hitter to bring Winston-Salem to within half a game of Peninsula. After the games of June 21, Peninsula led with a 39–29 record, while the other three contenders were all 38–29. On June 22, Triangles center fielder Alonzo Harris (.302, 28 stolen bases) went six for six to lead his team to a 13–2 win over Salem.

The Triangles, Peninsula, and Winston-Salem were tied for first with two games to play. All three won their games on June 23, leaving them tied at 40–29 with one game to play; Kinston had dropped to 38–31. The next day, McGlothen's four-hitter beat Burlington 4–0, while Peninsula nipped Rocky Mount 2–1. The Triangles, however, dropped a 5–4 heartbreaker to Kinston.

The Carolina League had never had a split-season tie before. Wallace McKenna decided to have a one-game playoff to decide the title. Rained out on the 25th, the game was played the next day in Winston-Salem. Red Sox center fielder Roger Nelson hit Gary Schlieve's third pitch of the game for a home run. When the dust settled, Winston-Salem had a crushing 9–1 victory and the first-half title.

Both clubs had a carry-over from this short playoff. Winston-Salem won eight of its first 10 games to jump on top in the second half, while Peninsula dropped seven of its first nine and was never a factor. At the end of July, Winston-Salem was 22–13, trailed by Raleigh-Durham at 18–14 and Burlington at 17–14.

On August 5, Cliff Johnson was promoted to AAA Oklahoma City of the American Association, ending the Triangles' pennant hopes. The promotion also ended Johnson's triple-crown drive. Although he led the league in batting average (.332), home runs (27), and runs batted in (91), he fell 12 at-bats short of the minimum number necessary to qualify for the batting title.

Outfielders David Moates (.311, 44 stolen bases), Jasper Dixon, and Willie Brown sparked Burlington to a late run that caught Winston-Salem at the end of August. The Red Sox lost their last two games to Raleigh-Durham and finished two games behind Burlington.

After two close half-season pennant races, the two-team, three-game playoff was something of an anticlimax. Winston-Salem won the opener when Rod Austin's two-run homer in the sixth broke a 1–1 tie and propelled his team to a 4–1 win. McGlothen won the second and final game 1–0 with a four-hitter. Frank Mannerino drove in the only run with a second-inning double.

McGlothen finished the season as the league's dominant pitcher, compiling a 15–7 record and a 2.24 earned-run average. Robert Snyder (13–5, 2.77), John Clifton, and James Thornton helped the club compile a 2.90 team ERA. Speedy Juan Beniquez and Roger Nelson combined for 75 stolen bases to spark the offense.

In addition to Johnson, Raleigh-Durham featured the slugging of first baseman Ed Powell (.270, 24, 86). The Triangles finished with the second-best overall record in the league, but mediocre pitching kept them out of the playoffs.

A solid Kinston club was led by outfielder Johnnie Fenderson (.293), Frederic Frazier (33 stolen bases), and pitchers Bill Olsen (13–5, 2.26), Walter Walters (11–7, 2.39), and Roger Hambright (15 saves). Future big leaguer Wayne Nordhagen hit a mediocre .230.

Rocky Mount stayed around .500 for most of the season. Leafs hurler Dan Bootcheck (13–8, 1.92) led the league in earned-run average.

After almost winning the first-half race, Peninsula stopped hitting and dropped to the cellar in the second half. First baseman Mike Anderson (.312, 22, 67), outfielder Richard Giallella, and future major league standout Andre Thornton (.249 in 70 games) led the batting attack, while Gary Schlieve (8–10, 2.35) and Craig Saramuzzo (8–16, 2.76) pitched much better than their records indicated.

Salem and Lynchburg brought up the rear. Nonetheless, each had a pair of players who advanced to the big leagues. Salem second baseman Rennie Stennett led the league in batting at .326, while Marietta College graduate Kent Tekulve (4–6, 1.94, 7 saves) began his illustrious career as a professional reliever. Lynchburg had future major league regulars in third baseman Steve Braun and second baseman Jerry Terrell, both of whom batted .279.

1970 First-Half Final Standings

* Winston-Salem	41–29	playoff winner
Peninsula	41–29	
Raleigh-Durham	40–30	
Kinston	39–31	
Rocky Mount	34–36	
Burlington	32–38	
Salem	29–41	
Lynchburg	24–46	

Second-Half Final Standings

Burlington	40–27
Winston-Salem	38–29
Rocky Mount	36–32
Raleigh-Durham	37–33
Kinston	33–34
Lynchburg	33–37
Salem	31–39
Peninsula	26–43

—◆—

Despite poor 1970 attendance, league officials talked optimistically of expansion prior to the 1971 season. Danville was interested in returning to the Carolina League but was still handicapped by the lack of an adequate ballpark.

Raleigh-Durham was unable to come up with a PDC and again operated as a co-op. Because of the nationwide energy crisis, many league games were started earlier in the evening.

The Salem Rebels won 11 of their first 15 games to take an early lead. Salem third baseman Art Howe batted .500 through April. Kinston third baseman Otto Velez (.310, 16, 73) and a much-improved Wayne Nordhagen (.294, 14, 76) led a surge that put their club in first place. When Velez hit two home runs in an 8–0 win over Salem on May 8, Kinston had a 2½-game lead. Salem regained first place briefly in mid-May but fell victim to a nine-game Peninsula winning streak. At the end of May, Peninsula led Salem by 2½, Kinston by 3, and Lynchburg by 5.

Winston-Salem was an also-ran but did feature the league's best player, hardhitting first baseman Cecil Cooper, who was batting .400 as late as May 23. Art Howe wasn't far behind. On May 31, he hit for the cycle in a 7–6 victory over Kinston. Second-division Raleigh-Durham had pitcher Jerry Bell, who beat Lynchburg 9–1 on June 4 to run his record to 8–1. He was then promoted to AAA Evansville of the American Association. About the same time, Boston moved Cooper to AAA Pawtucket. He ended his Carolina League season with a .379 batting average. Cooper hit .343 in Pawtucket and completed the season in Boston. He was eventually traded to Milwaukee, where he became a Brewers mainstay.

Kinston took over first place in early June. Peninsula hung tough until a 15–1 loss to Winston-Salem on June 18 and a doubleheader loss to Burlington the following day. Kinston swept Raleigh-Durham on June 20 to clinch the first-half title; Charlie Spikes (.270, 22, 79) homered in each of those games for the Eagles. Spikes, Velez, Nordhagen, first baseman Jack Pierce (.292, 20, 81), and Jim

Golden helped Kinston to the title. Future big-league standout George "Doc" Medich (7–4, 2.43) joined the team in midseason from medical school.

Even without Cooper, Winston-Salem jumped to a 7–1 start and an early lead in the second half. Winston-Salem's top players included shortstop Rick Burleson (.274) and outfielder Dwight Evans (.286, 12, 63), both of whom went on to star for Boston well into the 1980s, along with outfielder Mike Cummings (.291, 43 stolen bases), Ken Watkins (12–6, 2.84), and Charles Pfeiffer (15 saves).

The Red Sox ran their record to 18–5 on July 18 but couldn't shake Peninsula. The Phillies won seven straight, keyed by center fielder Nelson Garcia (27 stolen bases), who had a 20-game hitting streak during July. Late in the season, Peninsula got a boost when spark-plug outfielder Richard Giallella (.299) returned from a six-week absence caused by a broken arm. First baseman Bob Beall (.314), catcher Jim Essian, and Garcia led the sluggers. However, Peninsula's real strength was its pitchers, who compiled a superb, league-leading 2.65 ERA. Richard Fusari (19–6, 2.19) and Mike Coble (12–8, 2.72) led the staff.

Kinston moved past Winston-Salem into second place but was unable to catch Peninsula.

Peninsula continued its hot streak in the brief playoffs, sweeping first-half champion Kinston in two games. In the first game, Peninsula scored a run in the top of the first on a groundout by Giallella, and Mike Coble made it stand up for a 1–0 win. Richard Fusari continued Peninsula's pitching dominance when he won the second game 3–1.

A League of Her Own

The possibility of a woman playing professional baseball has long intrigued baseball observers and writers. So far, this possibility has stayed in the realm of fiction. But in 1971, at least for a few days, fiction almost became reality in the Carolina League.

In the final days of that season, Walter Brock, general manager of the Raleigh-Durham team, announced that his club was prepared to sign 23-year-old Jackie Jackson, a first baseman-outfielder (normally a cost analyst) from Burtonsville, Maryland. Jackson had tried out the previous week with Pittsfield of the AA Eastern League.

It's not clear whether Jackson's playing in the Carolina League was a real possibility. Raleigh-Durham was doing badly at the gate, and Brock, a man whose tightness with the dollar was legendary in minor league circles, certainly recognized that a little free publicity might help his struggling franchise.

The publicity didn't last long. The league office discouraged Brock's adventurism, and he quickly reversed himself and withdrew the offer amidst reports that Jackson was "weak with the bat." Whatever publicity Brock generated for his club was too little, too late. The Raleigh-Durham team went under following the 1971 season.

Over the course of the season, Lynchburg won one more game than it lost, led by slugging outfielder Craig Kusick (.267, 20, 91) and pitchers Arnold Johannes (16–11) and Mike Wagner (14–6).

Four clubs had losing marks, among them Rocky Mount, whose better players included outfielder Marvin Lane, third baseman Jeffrey Hogan, and first baseman Joe Staton, all of whom were .300 hitters.

Salem's Howe ended the season with a league-leading .348 batting average and added a dozen home runs and 79 runs batted in. Jose Gonzalez (.308, 13 triples) supported Howe. Kent Tekulve (11–5, 10 saves) pitched the entire season for the Rebels. He eventually became one the game's best relievers and broke Hoyt Wilhelm's record for major league games pitched.

1971 First-Half Final Standings

Kinston 43–26
Peninsula 41–29
Lynchburg 37–30
Salem 36–31
Raleigh-Durham 31–36
Rocky Mount 30–38
Winston-Salem 27–40
Burlington 27–42

Second-Half Final Standings

*Peninsula 44–24   playoff winner
Kinston 40–26
Winston-Salem 40–27
Rocky Mount 35–31
Lynchburg 31–37
Salem 29–40
Burlington 27–42
Raleigh-Durham 25–44

—◆—

The league endured a painful 1971–72 off-season. Attendance for 1971 had been less than 40,000 per team, the lowest average yet. Rocky Mount and Burlington were in particular trouble.

Wrestling promoter Pat Apostolou of Roanoke, Virginia, announced that he wanted to bring a Carolina League team, probably Burlington, to that city. However, Apostolou couldn't do anything without permission from nearby Salem; when that town refused to grant a waiver to the National Association's 10-mile rule, he was stymied.

When the Montreal Expos announced that they were moving their AAA franchise from Winnipeg to Newport News, the league lost its Peninsula territory. On December 10, 1971, Wallace McKenna announced that the Carolina League would operate with only six clubs in 1972. All of the clubs had PDCs, including Raleigh-Durham, which was scheduled to be a Texas farm team. Burlington was apparently gone.

In mid-January, however, Raleigh-Durham president Mike May dropped a bombshell. Despite the fact that his team had earned the league's third-best attendance figure in 1971, he announced that the club had lost too much money to continue. McKenna and May began a last-ditch attempt to uncover local investors to save the franchise but came up empty. Burlington was hastily drafted as the sixth team.

The Carolina League had suddenly disappeared from both the populous Virginia Tidewater and the equally important North Carolina Triangle.

The league opened its 1972 season with its first black umpire, 30-year-old Wayne Beasley, an employee of a food catering service. Beasley, who had umpired in the California League the previous season, was the first black umpire in the South and one of only four in organized baseball. However, Beasley didn't last long. Although he reported relatively few racial incidents, he left the umpiring ranks on June 22, citing, of all things, boredom: "I am despondent. I can't find enough to do during the days. I have read about all the books I can and I still can't find enough to keep me busy." Beasley was replaced by another black umpire, Joe Myers, who moved from the New York–Penn League.

Burlington dominated the first half. Led by second baseman Mike Cubbage (.281), infielder Dane Iorg (.321), and pitcher Erskine Thomason (11–6), the Rangers started off 14–4 and finished May with a 31–14 record.

Only hard-hitting Lynchburg maintained contact with Burlington. The slugging of league home-run leader Bob Gorinski, Jack Maloof (.308), and Robert Koeppel helped the Twins stay close. Lynchburg was as close as three games on June 15 but finished 4½ back. The other four teams ended the first half with losing records.

The second half bore scant resemblance to the first. Iorg was promoted out of the league, and Burlington was never in contention. The second-half race was between Kinston and Salem, each of which had an exceptional half-season. At the end of July, Kinston was 26–10 and Salem 24–11. Kinston was led by Dave Pagan (14–9, 2.53), Mike Krizmanich (.309), and Tom O'Connor (.283, 19, 89). Salem featured pitcher Jim Minshall, catcher Ed Ott, and, most notably, league Player of the Year and future major league star Dave Parker.

On August 9, Minshall beat Kinston 10–1 to run his record to 12–1 and cut the Eagles' lead to a tenuous half-game. The next day, Salem took over first with a nail-biting 10–9 win over Kinston. The Pirates scored two runs in the bottom

Kill the Ump!

Occasionally, some major league executive will argue for the total elimination of the minor leagues. Why not just keep the prospects in Florida or Arizona all year, play games against other teams, and give young players the kind of intensive tutoring not possible during a regular season?

This has never come to pass, of course. A minor league season more closely replicates the strain of a major league season than could any extended spring training. The lengthy season, the endless procession of game after game, and the travel all test the young minor leaguer. How will a player perform in the face of a hostile crowd in the middle of a road trip, sometimes after a bus ride of four, five, or six hours? The minors are the place to find out.

Yet even the most tired minor leaguer returns home eventually to play before friendly crowds and sleep in his own bed. Some even get a day off once in a while.

But consider the plight of Carolina League umpires. They never play before a friendly crowd; every game is a road game; days off are rarer than an uncooked steak; and their friends can be counted on one hand. Wayne Beasley, the league's first black umpire, resigned because the constant travel and between-game boredom became more than he could handle.

Two or sometimes three umpires work Carolina League games. This means that the demanding assignment of calling balls and strikes comes up more frequently than in the four-man umpiring teams in the majors. It also means that the umpire calling the bases spends much of the game scrambling from base to base.

In an umpire's world, well-called games are routinely ignored, while close calls always carry the potential for argument. Verbally abusing umpires has been a part of baseball since its inception. A close call that goes against the home team may result in "Three Blind Mice" being played over the sound system or a heckler yelling, "You must be blind, I've seen your wife!"

Carolina League fans have occasionally gone farther than verbal abuse. In 1948, umpire Bull Davis needed a police escort to escape angry Raleigh fans after he called a forfeit for the visiting team. Later that season, he was punched by a fan in Winston-Salem after a hotly contested game. Perhaps the worst incident occurred in June 1973, when Rocky Mount fans broke down a dressing-room door going after umpire Keith Stover.

Umpires usually have more problems with players than fans, of course. Language can be vicious. Umpires easily offended by four-letter words tend to have very short tenures. Some protests are more physical. Over the years, players have attacked Carolina League umpires with bats, balls, and fists. On June 2, 1951, Danville's Mike Romello slugged umpire Emil Davidzuk after a call went against him. Romello was arrested by a Durham judge who happened to be in the stands. Romello's modern counterpart was Lynchburg infielder Frank Moscat, who punched out umpire Jim Trusiani in 1985 after being called out on a check swing. Moscat was suspended for 15 days and fined.

Managers can be just as difficult. Some skippers, such as Raleigh's Joe "Ducky" Medwick and Durham's "Dirty" Al Gallagher, have transformed umpire baiting into an art form. At one time or another, virtually every manager has covered home plate by kicking dirt. After being ejected from a game, Durham manager Willie Duke once left the ballpark and returned with a bucket of water, which he poured over the plate. In 1970, Lynchburg manager Tom Umphlett delayed a game 15 minutes arguing a call by umpire Gene Tompkins.

Some of these disputes have given the fans their money's worth. A 1980 performance by Winston-Salem manager Buddy Hunter has become legendary in Carolina League circles. Hunter and umpire Bob Serino had been at odds for several days over a disputed home-run call. In the sixth inning of a May 13 game in Durham, Serino ejected Hunter after a game's worth of bickering. Following the ejection, Hunter walked to the dugout but returned to the field with a baseball. He then sprinted down the right-field line, where he threw the ball against the wall. Hunter next pantomimed flipping a coin, catching it on his arm, and making a home-run call, an obvious reference to the earlier disputed call. He then slid into first base, called himself safe, took off both shoes, and chewed on them for a brief period before throwing them at Serino. He then left the field to what one newspaper referred to as "a thunderous ovation by fans and players alike." Durham's manager acknowledged that Hunter's display "was one of the all-time greats. You've got to give the man credit. That was an outstanding act."

Almost as entertaining was Durham's Bobby Dews in 1982. Dews and umpire Mark Stalker had been feuding for several days. On May 28, the manager lost his composure when Stalker called two Durham baserunners out on steal attempts. He first removed second base and hurled it into the stands. Dews then left his jacket and jersey on the mound, powdered under his arms with a rosin bag—a trick he borrowed from baseball clown Max Patkin—punted the rosin bag in the air, and threw a bag of balls onto the field.

Umpires have the most difficulty keeping control when teams exchange beanballs. One 1964 exchange between Raleigh and Rocky Mount led to the arrest of Raleigh's Jose "Coco" Laboy after he cracked an opposing player's head with a bat. In 1992, Durham and Salem had a series of bench-clearing brawls that resulted in fines for virtually the entire teams.

During the early years of the Carolina League, its umpires were mostly veterans, many of them former league players such as Jim and Joe Mills. Lou Bello, well known as an Atlantic Coast Conference basketball referee, umpired in the Carolina League during the early 1950s. Certainly, some eyebrows were raised when former major league pitcher Johnny Allen, a native of Lenoir, North Carolina, joined the Carolina League umpiring staff in 1950. The hot-tempered Allen had abused more than his share of arbiters during his long professional career, but he made a realistic reassessment once he put on the umpire's suit: "Like all umpires, I've had my share of arguments with managers and players, but honestly my disputes have been mostly minor ones.... On the ball field there are always a lot of things that an umpire need not see, need not hear." Indeed, the cardinal rule that most successful umpires follow is that a good ump is rarely noticed.

One umpire who broke that rule in a big way was Spook Jacobs. Early in the 1982 season, Jacobs announced that the strike zone was too small and began calling games accordingly. League president Jim Mills blasted Jacobs in the press: "He better cut that crap out. If he's going to do that, he shouldn't tell people." By the middle of the season, throwing objects at Jacobs had become a fan ritual.

Today, the career minor league umpire has gone the way of the career minor league player. Under the Umpire Development Program, umpires are assigned to the Carolina League and other leagues. Like players, they either move up the ladder or find another job. Evaluating umpires takes up a large percentage of league presidents' time.

Quite a few Carolina League umps have learned their lessons better than the hapless Spook Jacobs. Among the league alumni who have made the jump all the way to the big leagues are Jerry Crawford, Ken Kaiser, Dale Ford, Fred Brocklander, Craig Emerson, Philip Durkee, Greg Henley, Steve Palermo, Dave Pallone, Vito Voltaggio, Darryl Cousins, David Slickenberg, Steve Storie, Joe West, and Bob Willman. These successful umpires all learned how to deal with the pressure and the abuse in their own way.

Umpire Harry "Ike" Reeder came up with perhaps the most distinctive manner of coping. In July 1954, after a near-riot in Durham, *Durham Morning Herald* sports editor Jack Horner blasted Reeder in a column entitled "Incompetent Umpires Always Wind Up in Rhubarbs." The column questioned Reeder's ability and invited league president Ted Mann to dismiss the beleaguered arbiter: "It's up to President Mann to rid his staff of any incompetents to prevent disturbances of this type." Mann did not renew Reeder's contract the following season, but the ump got his revenge. He sued Horner and the newspaper in 1955 and received a hefty out-of-court settlement.

Few umpires get that kind of satisfaction. Most work long and hard in an unglamorous profession, chasing the same dream that inspires the players. Umpires strive for the big leagues every bit as fiercely as players, knowing equally well that there are few vacancies at the top and that their quest will most likely prove fruitless.

of the ninth, the winner on a squeeze play by Mario Mendoza. Ron Mitchell went three for five for Salem, with four runs batted in. The resilient Eagles regained the lead the following day by nipping Salem 12–11. Kinston pounded usually reliable Salem pitcher Doug Bair for nine runs in $3^{2}/_{3}$ innings as they jumped to a 12–7 lead, then held on.

The two clubs continued to seesaw. Salem held a half-game lead when it traveled to Kinston on August 14 for a crucial four-game series. Salem won a big doubleheader that day by scores of 3–0 and 5–4. Dave Parker drove in four runs in the two games. Kinston's Bill Olsen beat Salem 3–1 the following day to cut the lead back to 1½ games; Parker was ejected in the third inning for slamming down his helmet after being called out on a third strike. In the series finale, Bair pushed the margin back to 2½ when he beat Kinston 5–0, allowing only a seventh-inning single by M. L. Prince; 32-year-old Felix Santana drove in three runs in that game.

On August 18, Kinston lost two games to last-place Rocky Mount. It never got back into the race, finishing 2½ games behind Salem. Winston-Salem finished third despite not having a single top-caliber player. It was followed by first-half champ Burlington and Lynchburg. Despite the presence of talented infielder Ron Cash (.301), Rocky Mount suffered through a 12-game losing streak and finished in the cellar, a distant 27 games behind Salem.

Managed by Tim Murtaugh, Salem ended the season leading the league in batting average, home runs, and runs scored. Two players in particular dominated the league. Minshall (16–1, 3.38) ended the regular season with a record-equaling 16 consecutive wins, while the extraordinarily talented Parker (.310, 22, 101, 30 doubles, 38 stolen bases) missed the triple crown by a single home run. Ott (.304), Mitchell (.306, 21, 89), smooth-fielding shortstop Mario Mendoza, and Doug Bair (15–7, 2.85) helped make Salem a formidable team.

Burlington won the first game of the playoffs 2–1 in 11 innings. Bair evened the series for Salem in an 11-inning 2-1 thriller. Salem took the title in the third game, overcoming a 4–1 deficit behind a Dave Parker home run and a three-run seventh to win 6–4.

Attendance for 1972 plummeted to 202,000, an average of fewer than 35,000 per team. Burlington drew an anemic 18,000, the lowest single-season total in league history. The poor condition of that city's ballpark—especially the inadequate lighting—was another cause for concern.

Dave Parker

1972 First-Half Final Standings

Burlington	*43–25*
Lynchburg	*39–30*
Salem	*33–34*
Rocky Mount	*30–37*
Kinston	*30–38*
Winston-Salem	*29–40*

Second-Half Final Standings

*Salem	*46–24*	playoff winner
Kinston	*43–26*	
Winston-Salem	*36–34*	
Burlington	*34–36*	
Lynchburg	*31–38*	
Rocky Mount	*19–51*	

—◆—

After the 1972 season, the troubled Burlington franchise moved to Wilson. The city of Wilson promised $20,000 for improvements to venerable Fleming Stadium. Wilson had suffered poor attendance prior to its disappearance from the league following the 1968 campaign, but new owner Marshall Fox, a 23-year veteran of pro ball as a player, executive, and owner, was willing to try again. Fox had served as general manager in Peninsula during the middle and late 1960s, so he had some familiarity with the league. In one break with tradition, the Wilson team was called the Pennants, not the traditional Tobs. The new nickname proved to be wishful thinking of the highest order.

Wilson was unable to procure a PDC and was forced to operate as a co-op. Also that year, Kinston operated as a Montreal farm team, while Rocky Mount became a Phillies affiliate.

The league had an exciting pennant race in each of its half-seasons.

Lynchburg and Rocky Mount were the primary contenders during the first half. Rocky Mount led most of the way, finishing May with a small lead over Lynchburg. The two clubs fought it out through June, exchanging the lead several times. Lynchburg won on the last day to clinch the title, finishing only percentage points ahead of Rocky Mount; Lynchburg was unable to make up two early rainouts, creating an unbalanced schedule. Winston-Salem made a late run to finish 2½ back.

The Lynchburg Twins had no stars but put a balanced attack on the field that included first baseman Jim O'Bradovich (.304, 18, 71), outfielder Willie Norwood, and second baseman Rob Wilfong. Bill Stiegemeier (15–6, 2.56), Dave Allen (12–5, 2.86), and relief ace Bill Clauss led the pitching staff.

Rocky Mount jumped to an early lead again in the second half. On June 30 and July 1, Rocky Mount's Greg Pryor (.293) had eight straight hits against Kinston. Virtually every club was in contention until Winston-Salem and Lynchburg separated themselves from the pack in late August. The Red Sox swept Rocky Mount in the last series of the season, while Lynchburg lost a crucial doubleheader to Salem on August 27 to finish one game behind Winston-Salem.

Like first-half champ Lynchburg, the Red Sox featured a balanced attack. Infielder Steve Dillard and catcher Ernie Whitt both had big-league careers ahead of them. Veteran manager Bill Slack could also call on first baseman Chuck Erickson (.296, 16, 101), second baseman Al Ryan, and pitchers Steve Foran (13–10) and Bill Moran (12–7).

The playoffs were expanded back to five games for 1973. The result was one of the better championship series in league history. The Red Sox won the first two games from Lynchburg. Game two was especially exciting. Winston-Salem came back from a 5–1 deficit to pull out a 10–9 win, keyed by an eighth-inning grand slam by Erickson. Facing elimination in game three, Lynchburg found itself trailing 6–4 after eight innings. However, it stayed alive with a dramatic four-run outburst in the top of the ninth for an 8–6 win; three of the runs were unearned, following an error by second baseman Ryan. Lynchburg won the fourth game 5–3, as Frank Schuster hurled a four-hitter.

The deciding fifth game went down to the wire. Lynchburg led 4–2 going into the bottom of the eighth and was only six outs from an improbable come-from-behind championship. However, Winston-Salem scored single runs in the eighth and ninth to send the game to extra innings. The tying run came home in an unusual manner. Whitt was on second base when Dillard hit a liner to left field. The ball was trapped by left fielder John Klitsner, but Whitt hesitated and was caught in a rundown. With the championship staring Lynchburg in the face, Jim O'Bradovich threw the ball away, allowing Whitt to score. In the bottom of the 10th, Winston-Salem third baseman Lanny Phillips reached first on an error by third baseman Mike Poepping. Pitcher Jim Wright was then hit by Bill Clauss while attempting to bunt. Tony McLin followed by beating out a sacrifice. With the bases loaded and no outs, Al Ryan walked to force in the deciding run. Winston-Salem wrapped up the 5–4 win and the title without getting the ball out of the infield in the 10th inning.

Winston-Salem and Lynchburg did not have a monopoly on good prospects, of course. In addition to Greg Pryor, Rocky Mount featured catcher Bill Nahorodny (.262, 14, 76) and pitchers Quency Hill (14–4, 2.93, 13 consecutive wins) and Roy Thomas (15–8, 2.24, 193 strikeouts).

Salem outfielder Omar Moreno (.284, 112 runs) stole a league-record 77 bases, while shortstop Craig Reynolds (.287, 13, 86) impressed league observers. Both went on to become regulars at the big-league level.

Kinston had the league Player of the Year, 20-year-old outfielder Terry Whitfield (.335, 18, 91, 19 stolen bases), along with outfielder Jimmie Collins (.325), Jody Norris (14–8), and future big-league relief standout Felix "Tippy" Martinez (13–8, 2.66, 15 saves). The Eagle with the brightest future, however, was left-handed pitcher Ron Guidry (7–6, 3.21). The third-year pro from Louisiana spent part of the season with the Army Reserves and suffered from control problems, as evidenced by 70 walks in only 101 innings. Once Guidry straightened out his fastball, he became one of the best pitchers in baseball, compiling a 25–3 record for the New York Yankees in 1978.

Wilson brought up the rear in both half-seasons.

Attendance improved slightly during 1973.

Terry Whitfield   Ron Guidry

1973 First-Half Final Standings

Lynchburg	40–28
Rocky Mount	41–29
Winston-Salem	38–31
Kinston	34–34
Salem	31–28
Wilson	23–47

Second-Half Final Standings

*Winston-Salem	39–31	playoff winner
Lynchburg	38–32	
Salem	35–34	
Kinston	34–35	
Rocky Mount	34–36	
Wilson	29–41	

—◆—

After the 1973 season, Wallace McKenna was reelected for a three-year term. The league president admitted that expansion back to eight teams was unlikely in the near future and claimed that the big leagues were penalizing the Carolina League for being too good, preferring to send prospects directly from lesser-quality A leagues to AA.

Despite good support from the town's fans, Wilson dropped back out of the league, apparently for good this time. The franchise relocated to Peninsula and continued to operate as a co-op.

The 1974 pennant race was virtually devoid of drama. The Pittsburgh Pirates gave their Salem affiliate a powerhouse that eventually produced as many solid major league players as any team in Carolina League history. League Player of the Year Miguel Dilone (.331, league-record 84 stolen bases), catcher Steve Nicosia (.305, 15, 92), outfielder Mitchell Page (.296, 17, 75), and pitchers John Candeleria (11–8) and Rick Langford (11–7) all found a measure of fame and fortune in the big time. The Pirates also had a host of other successful Carolina League players, including Alfredo Edmead (.314, 7, 59), second baseman Pablo Cruz (.330), and Paul Djakonow (98 RBIs). Pitchers Doug Nelson, David Nelson, Mike Gonzalez, and Dick Standart all won 10 or more games.

The Pirates got off to a sluggish start, splitting their first 18 games, and finished April in fourth place. A 23–8 May ended the first-half suspense, however. The Pirates finished seven games ahead of runner-up Lynchburg.

Lynchburg jumped to an early lead in the second half before fading badly. Winston-Salem stayed close to Salem until the final week but finished 3½ games behind the Pirates.

Kinston was Salem's polar opposite. The Montreal farm club had a serious shortage of talent, fans, and luck. An early nine-game losing streak turned off the fans. The team finished in the cellar by a wide margin in both half-seasons. Road trips were particularly harrowing. On the team's first trip to Salem, it traveled around for hours looking for a nonexistent inn. On a later trip, the team bus blew two tires on a mountainous Virginia road; fortunately, no one was injured seriously. On August 19, the power went out in Kinston during a game against Lynchburg, resulting in a long delay. More than one wag suggested that the troubled franchise had failed to pay its light bill.

Salem's romp to the league title was marred by the late-season death of Alfredo Edmead, who was killed as a result of a collision with teammate Pablo Cruz.

The Pirates' victory in both halves of the season meant that the league would not have a playoff series.

Salem's dominance obscured the fact that both Lynchburg and Winston-Salem had fine clubs. Lynchburg boasted powerful first baseman Randy Bass (.256, 30, 112), third baseman Frank Grundler (.335), outfielder Willie Norwood (.309, 10, 91), Mike Gerakos (.304), Russell Noah (.301, 15, 86), and John Maier (10–2). Winston-Salem had the league's best pitcher, big right-hander Don Aase (17–8, 2.43, 176 strikeouts). Manager Bill Slack favorably compared Aase to

The Death of Alfredo Edmead

Baseball can be a dangerous game. However, it is rarely a fatal one. Only one major league player has died of injuries received during a game, the ill-fated Ray Chapman, who died after being hit in the head by a pitch in 1920.

Tragically, the Carolina League has also had one on-field fatality. The death took place in Salem, Virginia, on August 23, 1974, in a relatively meaningless late-season contest. The accident occurred when Rocky Mount's Murray Gage-Cole hit a pop fly into shallow right field. Salem outfielder Alfredo Edmead came in on the ball, while second baseman Pablo Cruz went out. As the two men concentrated on the ball, Edmead's head collided with Cruz's knee, which was protected by a heavy brace.

The 18-year-old outfielder collapsed unconscious, bleeding heavily from the head. Edmead was rushed to a local hospital, where he was pronounced dead on arrival. The game continued. "Nobody wanted to play," one player later told sportswriter Frank Dolson, "but they kept going with the game. I think the reason we kept playing, nobody wanted to admit he might die."

Edmead was considered a good bet to become a major league player. A native of the Dominican Republic, he had been signed to a professional contract largely through the efforts of his close friend and countryman Pablo Cruz, the same man with whom he collided that sad day.

---

former Winston-Salem ace Jim Lonborg. Most of the team's offense came courtesy of Mike Bennett (.300) and Joe Krsnich (.293).

Rocky Mount's top player was pitcher Dan Greenhalgh (14–9, 2.68).

Peninsula and Kinston had miserable seasons. Kinston did have two future major leaguers, 17-year-old Tony Bernazard, who hit .200 in 54 games before being demoted to the Gulf Coast League, and Joe Kerrigan (4–10, 4.64). Neither player was ready for the fast Carolina League.

1974 First-Half Final Standings

Salem	47–23
Lynchburg	40–30
Winston-Salem	39–30
Rocky Mount	37–32
Peninsula	25–43
Kinston	19–49

Second-Half Final Standings

Salem	40–27
Winston-Salem	37–31
Lynchburg	38–32
Rocky Mount	35–35
Peninsula	33–33
Kinston	19–44

—⬥—

The Carolina League hit rock bottom in 1975, when only Salem, Rocky Mount, Winston-Salem, and Lynchburg got out of the gate. McKenna was unable to procure PDCs for Peninsula and Kinston, both of which dropped out. Lynchburg signed a PDC with Texas, while Salem, Rocky Mount, and Winston-Salem kept their agreements with Pittsburgh, Philadelphia, and Boston, respectively.

Four-team leagues are hardly models of stability. Each team in the Carolina League had to play almost 50 games against each of the other three clubs, a degree of familiarity and repetition guaranteed to turn off all but the most ardent fans.

McKenna hastily put together an agreement with the nearby Western Carolina League, a Class A league with teams in the South Carolina cities of Spartanburg, Columbia, Greenwood, and Charleston. According to the agreement, teams would play two home series and two away series with each of the clubs from the opposing league. However, McKenna declined to match the Carolina League champ against the WCL champ after the season, arguing that the superior Carolina League had nothing to gain from such a match.

The unusual interlocking schedule gave Carolina League fans a chance to see such WCL prospects as Greenwood catcher Dale Murphy, Spartanburg out-

The Carolina League's Disappearing Act

On May 7, 1975, only 109 fans attended a Carolina League game at Ernie Shore Field between Winston-Salem and visiting Salem. The Winston-Salem newspaper sardonically noted that "there was considerably more noise emanating from nearby Hanes Hosiery field where a softball game was going on."

This wasn't unusual at the time. The Carolina League just about disappeared during the 1970s. The league declined to a paltry four teams in 1975 and drew only 130,000 paying customers for the entire season. Attention from local newspapers was equally minuscule.

Since this decline took place during the tenure of league president Wallace McKenna, it's tempting to see some kind of relationship. Yet close observers agree that McKenna was not to blame for the league's ailments. Other sports were drawing fans away from baseball, and the minor leagues were imperiled throughout the country. Looking to save money, major league clubs increasingly saw the minor leagues as a drain on their finances; shortsighted major league executives attempting to cut corners by reducing their minor league systems were more to blame for the league's troubles than anything else. Attempts to expand the league by McKenna and his successor, Jim Mills, were frequently derailed because of the absence of major league support.

Both McKenna and Mills resisted suggestions to merge the Carolina League with the Western Carolina League, another four-team circuit. Instead, they held the Carolina League together until it could rebound. Longtime Lynchburg official Calvin Falwell credited McKenna for his toughness: "In my opinion, Wallace was one of the Carolina League's finest presidents and we credit him with holding the league together during some troubling years."

fielder Lonnie Smith, and Charleston pitcher Ed Whitson. It also enabled Winston-Salem fans to enjoy the antics of hotheaded Spartanburg manager Lee Elia, who pulled his team from the field during the eighth inning of a game against the Red Sox, resulting in a forfeit. The rhubarb began when umpire Delvis "Mac" McCadden ejected Spartanburg catcher Bob DeMeo for questioning a strike call.

The four-team pennant races weren't much more compelling than the six-team races of the previous year. In the first half, Rocky Mount jumped to a 17–5 start and held off a late Winston-Salem run to win easily. In the second half, Rocky Mount dropped behind Salem early but came from behind to nip the Pirates. Rocky Mount's star was manager Cal Emery, who held his club together despite an unusually high number of call-ups.

Spectators responded to all of this with something approaching total apathy. Attendance was appallingly low. For the season, the league drew a mere 130,000 paying customers, an average of just over 30,000 per club. League champ Rocky Mount brought up the rear with 24,000. Many potential spectators were no doubt deterred by the poor condition of the stadium in that town. The lighting was so inadequate that playing in Rocky Mount was compared to playing on the dark side of the moon.

Rocky Mount was led by third baseman Jim Morrison (.288, 20, 88), first baseman John Poff, and outfielder John Hughes. Warren Brusstar, Oliver Bell, and Roger Quiroga combined for 38 victories.

Winston-Salem third baseman Ted Cox (.305, 10, 80) won the batting title, albeit with the lowest mark to ever lead the league. His teammate Rick Jones was 13–3 when he was promoted to AA Bristol at the end of June. Allen Ripley (14–7, 2.76) and Breen Newcomer (9–3, 2.57) were other reliable hurlers. Future major league catcher Bo Diaz batted .263 in 59 games.

Salem boasted the league Player of the Year, 21-year-old outfielder Luke Wrenn (.293, 12, 57), along with outfielder Alberto Louis (.302) and Larry Angell (13–1, 2.46).

Last-place Lynchburg had a solid double-play combination in second baseman Brian Doyle and shortstop Rick Albert.

1975 First-Half Final Standings

Rocky Mount	*48–24*
Winston-Salem	*44–27*
Salem	*33–36*
Lynchburg	*30–36*

Second-Half Final Standings

Rocky Mount	43–27
Salem	41–30
Winston-Salem	37–35
Lynchburg	30–42

—◆—

During the off-season, McKenna made an unsuccessful bid for the vacant position of National Association president. The job went to Bobby Bragan, although McKenna was named to the three-man executive committee.

He had no more success getting the Carolina League back up to a more desirable number of teams. Despite its 1975 title, Rocky Mount dropped out, and Peninsula came back in again. Peninsula took over Rocky Mount's working agreement with Philadelphia and added manager Cal Emery to boot. Rocky Mount's departure left Winston-Salem as the only North Carolina team in the Carolina League. The league elected to continue its interlocking schedule with the Western Carolina League, although teams would play only one home and one away series with each club from the opposing league.

For the third straight season, one team won both half-season pennants. This time, it was the Winston-Salem Red Sox.

In the first half, the Red Sox started off 9–3 before dropping eight in a row (seven of them at home) to fall to third place behind Peninsula and Salem. They then reversed themselves, winning 20 of 24 in late May and early June to put the competition away.

The second half was much closer. Winston-Salem lost six of its first seven to fall five games behind Lynchburg. The Red Sox won their next seven but then lost ace pitcher Breen Newcomer (14–6) to the Eastern League. Left-hander John Tudor took up the slack with five straight wins down the stretch. Winston-Salem and Lynchburg traded the lead throughout the first half of August.

The close race was decided in a pair of head-to-head series.

The first took place in Lynchburg beginning on August 16. Winston-Salem won the opener 8–1, keyed by Ken Huizenga's seventh home run in eight games. Lynchburg won the next two games, with shutouts by Juan Berenguer and John Pacella, to cut Winston-Salem's lead to half a game. Lynchburg was poised to take over the lead in the last game of the series when it took a 4–2 lead into the top of the ninth. But the Red Sox erupted for five runs to win the game 7–4 and push their lead back to 1½ games.

Winston-Salem led by one game when it hosted Lynchburg in a series beginning August 23. The Red Sox put on an offensive explosion to take the first two games by scores of 9–3 and 9–2, opening the margin to three games. Lynchburg's frustrations boiled over in the third game of the series. An exchange of beanballs resulted in a 20-minute brawl in the sixth inning and injuries to four Lynchburg players. Winston-Salem went on to win the tense game by an 8–7 score. The brawl was the result of bad blood that had existed between the two clubs for much of the season. Winston-Salem manager Tony Torchia later criticized his Lynchburg counterpart, Jack Aker: "He tried to provoke an inept club. . . . It just showed his own ineptness."

Lynchburg captured the series finale 6–5, as Berenguer outdueled Tudor. Three batters were hit during the game. Tempers flared, but there was no repeat of the previous game's fisticuffs. The moral victory was too little, too late for Lynchburg, as Winston-Salem ended up winning by 1½ games. For the third straight year, the Carolina League would not have a playoff.

Winston-Salem's title was largely the result of the pitching of Newcomer, Tudor (5–2, 2.74, 5 saves), Walt Bigos, Al Faust (11–5, 2.50), Bruce Poole, and Rich Waller (13–0, 3.04). Waller's undefeated season included a no-hitter against Charleston. Third baseman Ron Evans, outfielders Luis Delgado (.294) and Ken Huizenga, and Otis Foster (.282, 12, 83) supplied the runs. Mike O'Berry was named the All-League catcher despite batting only .200, a telling commentary on the circuit's decline.

Lynchburg had the league Player of the Year, first baseman Marshall Brant (.258, 23, 93), a six-foot-four, 215-pound slugger who batted .331 with 18 homers after the All-Star break. Pitchers Berenguer and Pacella both advanced to the majors.

Peninsula outfielder Bobby Brown, signed by the Phillies organization after being released by Asheville, ended up leading the league with a .349 batting average. Peter Manos (9–4, 1.16) set a still-standing league record for lowest earned-run average. Future Philadelphia standout Keith Moreland batted .282 before being promoted to Reading.

Salem had little to brag about other than standout pitcher Ed Whitson (15–9, 2.53, 186 strikeouts).

Wallace McKenna became ill after the season and died on December 3. He was 57. *Lynchburg News* columnist Calvin Porter eulogized him as "a gentleman and the kind of person every reporter dreams of working with."

1976 First-Half Final Standings

Winston-Salem	42–26
Peninsula	36–31
Salem	35–32
Lynchburg	27–42

Second-Half Final Standings

Winston-Salem	38–31
Lynchburg	37–33
Peninsula	35–34
Salem	33–37

◆ ◆ ◆

1981 Kinston Eagles with Tony Fernandez on first row, far right

CHAPTER SIX
1977 — 83

♦ ♦ ♦

Wallace McKenna was replaced as league president by Jim Mills, a familiar name to league officials and a man with more than three decades of experience in minor league ball. The new president resisted renewed pressure to merge the league with the Western Carolina League and vowed to carry on with the four-team alignment until more teams could be brought on board.

The four-team circuit gave fans a close second half after a one-sided first half. The Lynchburg Mets were never challenged seriously in the first half. Manager Jack Aker's club won 15 of its first 20 contests and cruised to a five-game victory over Winston-Salem. The pitching-rich Mets featured two future big-league standouts in Neil Allen and Jeff Reardon, the latter of whom joined the team after completing his college career at the University of Massachusetts.

The second-half race was much closer. Allen went on the disabled list with an illness in late July and didn't come back until September. Peninsula jumped to an early lead with 18 wins in its first 25 starts but was soon challenged by both Lynchburg and Salem. As the season entered its final weekend, Salem and Peninsula were tied for first, only a game ahead of Lynchburg. Winston-Salem was a distant fourth. Peninsula's Dickie Noles beat Winston-Salem 8–1 on August 31, while Salem lost to Lynchburg and dropped out of first. The following day, Peninsula's Derek Botelho beat Winston-Salem 3–2 to wrap up the second-half title. Lynchburg beat Salem to secure second place.

Lynchburg and Peninsula squared off in a hotly contested championship characterized by bad blood. Lynchburg scored 10 runs in the first two innings of the opener and cruised to a 12–5 win. Glenn Brummer and Dave Cover each had four hits for the winners. Jeff Reardon benefited from Lynchburg's 19-hit explosion. The next game was a distinct contrast. Peninsula's Larry Hertz shut the Mets out 6–0, allowing only five hits. John Hughes went three for five and drove

Jim Mills

Perhaps no one has served minor league baseball in the North Carolina–Virginia area longer and in more different capacities than Apex, North Carolina, native Jim Mills. At various times and in various places, Mills has worn the hats of player, manager, umpire, general manager, field manager, roving expert, and league president.

James Bowie Mills was born in 1919. He and his twin brother, Joe, attended North Carolina State College in 1940. After a single baseball season, the Mills brothers (no, they didn't sing) left to begin their professional baseball careers. Jim batted .331 for the Owensboro, Kentucky, club of the Kentucky-Ohio-Missouri League. He was set to report to Louisville for the 1942 season when the war intervened. He spent four years in the United States Army Air Corps, assigned mostly to the mainland.

Mills never got as close to the major leagues after the war as he did before it. He starred for the Raleigh Caps in 1946 and 1947, reuniting with brother Joe; Jim was an acknowledged team leader as the Caps beat Durham for the postseason championship both years. He left Raleigh in 1948 for a chance to be a player-manager for a club in Concord. Mills continued as a player-manager through the 1953 season for Concord, Mooresville, and Rocky Mount in, respectively, the North Carolina State League, the Coastal Plain League, and the Tar Heel League. He compiled a 308–255 record as a manager and finished his career with a .310 batting average, including a .386 mark for Mooresville in 1949.

Mills returned to the Carolina League in 1954 as an umpire. For financial reasons, he left umpiring the next season for a job as a sporting goods salesman. His basketball and football officiating careers lasted longer. In fact, Mills spent 18 years as a top-notch Atlantic Coast Conference basketball referee.

Football and basketball officiating left his summers open, and Mills got back into baseball in short order. In 1956, he became general manager of Fayetteville's North Carolina State League team. He remained a minor league general manager through the 1971 season, including Carolina League stops at Wilson and Asheville.

in a pair of runs for the Grays. Following the game, Lynchburg's Juan Monasterio and Peninsula's Luis Reyes squared off in a spirited fistfight. The series moved to Peninsula for the duration. The first two games there were as one-sided as the two in Lynchburg. Peninsula won game three 8–1, and Lynchburg evened the series in game four with a 7–0 win. The clubs finally played a close contest in the fifth and deciding game. Peninsula scored two runs in the bottom of the first, aided by sloppy Lynchburg fielding. Trailing 3–0, Lynchburg came up with single runs in the seventh and eighth innings but could come no closer off reliever Jeff Schneider. Peninsula won its first Carolina League title by a 3–2 score.

Peninsula featured several future major leaguers, including Noles, second baseman Luis Aguayo, and designated hitter John Hughes (.264, 22, 99, 33 doubles). Pitchers Jeff Schneider (15–7) and Botelho (13–5) also were key performers. Future American League Rookie of the Year Joe Charbonneau played briefly and badly for the Pilots, batting only .172.

Despite losing in the playoffs, Lynchburg boasted the league's best overall

His 1959 Wilson club won the league title, upsetting Raleigh and Carl Yastrzemski in the playoffs. In 1972, Mills became a field representative for the National Association of Professional Baseball Leagues.

He came back to the Carolina League in 1977 under unusual circumstances. Following the untimely death of Wallace McKenna late in 1976, the league set about electing a new president, a task that proved unusually difficult. On January 16, the four clubs split their votes between two candidates. Lynchburg and Salem cast their votes for Rex Angel, a Lynchburg accountant who had handled the league's books since 1970. Winston-Salem and Peninsula voted for John Moss, president of the Western Carolina League. Lynchburg president Calvin Falwell moved that Salem general manager Morris Cregar, who had been serving as acting president, break the tie. Ten days later, Cregar cast his tie-breaking vote for Angel. Winston-Salem and Peninsula protested the legality of this vote; the embattled Angel resigned as league president. Meanwhile, National Association president Bobby Bragan was pushing Mills. Mills was finally elected and

began an eventful seven-year term.

He took over an ailing four-team circuit that had draw an anemic 167,000 paying customers in 1976. Before long, the Carolina League had individual clubs drawing more fans than that.

From the beginning of his tenure as league president, Mills was expansion-oriented. The league went from four to six clubs prior to the 1978 season and added two more teams for the 1980 season. It has had eight clubs ever since. The addition of Rocky Mount in 1980 was a disaster, and Alexandria didn't work out much better. On the other hand, the addition of Durham in 1980, a goal for which Mills worked long and hard, was a resounding success. Equally successful was the league's expansion into Maryland in 1981.

After a number of controversies, Mills's contract was not renewed following the 1983 season, a year in which the eight-team Carolina League drew over 600,000 paying customers. He has spent the decade since in the Durham front office.

The Carolina League awards the Mills Cup annually to the winner of its postseason championship.

record. Injury-hampered Neil Allen was 10–2 in the 20 games he was able to pitch. Future major league relief standout Reardon was 8–3 in his tenure at Lynchburg. Outfielder Bob Bryant (.360 in 225 at-bats), catcher Butch Benton (.343 in 233 at-bats), David Covert (.316), and Francisco Perez (.284, 17, 86) combined to give Lynchburg a solid batting attack.

Salem had the league's most formidable offensive attack. Outfielder Oswaldo "Ozzie" Olivares was named the league Player of the Year on the strength of his league-leading .370 batting average, 14 triples, and 46 stolen bases. Olivares ended up with a still-standing league-record 208 base hits. Fellow outfielder Eugenio Cotes hit .341, with 16 home runs and 102 runs batted in. Infielders Luis Salazar and Pablo Cruz (.341) had solid seasons at the plate. Future big-league standout catcher Tony Pena joined the team at midseason from the Western Carolina League. Poor pitching doomed Salem's pennant hopes.

Despite finishing with the league's worst record, Winston-Salem had what turned out to be the circuit's best prospect, although he was not so highly regarded at the time. Third baseman Wade Boggs batted .332 for the Red Sox on his way to a distinguished career in Boston and New York; as of this writing, he has won five American League batting titles. Pitcher Kevin Stephenson went 12–5 and threw a seven-inning no-hitter against Salem.

League attendance dropped slightly to 165,000, an average of about 600 per game.

1977 First-Half Final Standings

Lynchburg	39–27
Winston-Salem	34–32
Peninsula	31–35
Salem	28–38

Second-Half Final Standings

*Peninsula	40–32	playoff winner
Lynchburg	39–33	
Salem	38–34	
Winston-Salem	27–45	

—◆—

At the league's 1977 postseason meeting, Jim Mills was reelected for one year and praised for doing a good job under difficult circumstances. Alexandria and Kinston were voted into the league as the fifth and sixth teams for 1978 after an attempt to bring Greensboro back proved fruitless. National Association president Bobby Bragan encouraged the expansion and assured the league that he would work to find working agreements for league teams, a process helped by the addition of Toronto and Seattle to the American League for the 1977 season.

The addition of Alexandria was a bold attempt to tap into the Washington, D.C., market. Unfortunately, the market was a good deal less glamorous than hoped. The Alexandria team was forced to play its first season at a small field at Cora Kelly Elementary School, and only after the club survived a lawsuit by disgruntled local citizens upset over spending $120,000 in tax money to bring the ballpark up to professional standards. Not surprisingly, D.C. baseball fans stayed away from Alexandria in droves.

Further complicating matters was the fact that both of the new teams in the league operated as independents, fielding lineups with free agents and an assortment of players from various organizations. Neither club fielded a competitive team.

The first half was a race between two clubs loaded with top prospects. On one side were the Lynchburg Mets, led by shortstop Wally Backman (.302), catcher Jody Davis (.262, 16, 94), second baseman Ronald MacDonald (.325), and a solid pitching staff. Their competition came from the Peninsula Pilots, led by catcher and league Player of the Year Ozzie Virgil, Jr. (.303, 29, 98), third baseman Nick Popovich (81 RBIs), outfielder George Vukovich (.311), and a deep and talented pitching staff. Lynchburg led by three games in the middle of May, but Peninsula caught up late in the month. The Mets surged in the middle of June, opened the margin back to 3½ games, and held on for a one-game margin.

Salem won seven of its first nine to take the early lead in the second half. The Pirates faltered, however, and Peninsula took over. The Pilots won 10 of 11 in early July and were never challenged after that. Lynchburg was not a factor in the second half; relief ace Russell Clark was promoted to AA Jackson of the Texas League at midseason, after which the Mets' bullpen was ineffective.

Peninsula had one of the best pitching staffs in league history. Bob Walk (13–8, 2.12), Marty Bystrom (15–7, 2.83), Henry Mack (15–4, 2.79), Fred Martinez (13–2, 2.07), and Sam Welborn (13–5, 2.42) dominated opposing hitters. Mack pitched a no-hitter on July 1 but lost 3–2 to Lynchburg. Eleven days later, he beat Kinston 3–0, giving up only a broken-bat single to Clay Elliott in the second inning. On August 12, Bystrom hurled a perfect game against Winston-Salem. Jerry Reed started the season at Spartanburg but finished at Peninsula, collecting seven saves down the stretch.

Lynchburg met Peninsula in the championship series for the second consecutive season. Lynchburg jumped all over the Pilots in the opener. Jody Davis hit a grand slam in the third inning and a solo homer later as the Mets pounded Peninsula ace Henry Mack 7–0; Jim Burton threw a two-hitter for Lynchburg. Game two was tied 6–6 in the seventh when Bob Rossen's bases-loaded single gave Lynchburg an 8–6 victory; Wally Backman had three hits, including a solo home run. The Mets captured the title in a dramatic third game. The Pilots took a 2–1 lead into the top of the ninth behind Bystrom's one-hitter. Ronald MacDonald and Sergio Beltre led off the ninth with singles, at which point Peninsula manager Jim Synder relieved Bystrom with Jerry Reed, whose brief appearance was a disaster. Reed walked all three batters he faced, forcing in the tying and go-ahead runs. Peninsula then botched a suicide squeeze, allowing two more runs to score. After Backman's sacrifice fly, Lynchburg had put five runs on the board. Peninsula loaded the bases in the bottom of the ninth, but Pete Hamner secured the 6–2 Lynchburg win and the series sweep by retiring Ozzie Virgil and Nick Popovich on fly balls.

Lynchburg was surprisingly matter-of-fact about its upset title. Manager Jack Aker claimed that "there's nobody in the league we'd rather have faced in the playoffs than Peninsula. . . . We knew we could beat them anytime we needed."

Although they missed the playoffs, the Salem Pirates had a better combined regular-season record than did Lynchburg. Shortstop Vance Law (.319), infielder Luis Salazar (.292), and pitcher Pascal Perez (11–7, 2.61) all became good major league players, although the latter's promising career was cut short by drug use. First baseman Chuck Valley (19 home runs), second baseman Jerry McDonald (.324), and veteran shortstop Pablo Cruz (.302) augmented the Salem batting attack.

The Alexandria Dukes, Winston-Salem Red Sox, and Kinston Eagles brought up the rear. Alexandria's Calvin King had the league's best batting average, .339, but batted only 180 times in the league. Kinston featured pitcher Tim "the Butcher" Costello (9–6, 2.50). The disappointing Red Sox had the league's worst mark for the second straight year despite some solid prospects, including catcher Roger LaFrancois (.311) and pitcher Steve Crawford.

None of the 1978 Carolina League players became major league stars, although Virgil and Davis were two of the National League's better catchers in the mid-1980s. Walk, Bystrom, Backman, and Crawford were all respectable major league players.

Attendance was 267,000 for the six-team league, an average of about 44,000 per team, the highest since 1970.

1978 First-Half Final Standings

*Lynchburg	43–27	playoff winner
Peninsula	42–28	
Salem	34–35	
Alexandria	29–37	
Winston-Salem	28–38	
Kinston	29–40	

Second-Half Final Standings

Peninsula	48–21
Salem	38–28
Lynchburg	30–37
Alexandria	29–38
Kinston	28–37
Winston-Salem	27–39

—◆—

With attendance on the upswing for the first time in almost a decade, there was much talk of expansion during the off-season. Former league members Greensboro, Rocky Mount, Wilson, and High Point were possibilities bandied about. Nothing was done for the moment, however, because of an absence of PDCs, and the Carolina League remained a six-team circuit for 1979.

After several lean years, the Red Sox stocked Winston-Salem with a superb pitching staff and a formidable everyday lineup. Manager Bill Slack's charges dominated the 1979 season from the outset. The Red Sox started off 16–5 to open up an early working margin. A mid-May slump allowed Peninsula, then Alexandria to get into the race. Winston-Salem regrouped in late May and pulled away during June. When the dust settled on the first half, Winston-Salem had won by 4½ games over Alexandria.

Winston-Salem didn't look like a repeat winner in the early part of the second half. The erratic Red Sox lost seven of their first 10, then won seven straight, then lost four in a row. Salem led much of July after finishing in the first-half cellar. Peninsula and Alexandria were in pursuit. On July 30, Winston-Salem was in fifth place.

Salem and Winston-Salem both had dramatic turnarounds in August and September. The Pirates lost 24 of their final 37 to finish the season in fifth place. During that period, the Red Sox surged into first. A 10–4 run put them on top for good on August 13.

Keying the Winston-Salem run was an extraordinary hot streak by outfielder Reid Nichols, a speedy native of Ocala, Florida. In fact, Nichols came close to getting a hit in every August game. He put together a hitting streak that began attracting attention as it passed 20 games, then took aim at Pat Cooper's league record of 31. On August 24, Nichols ran his streak to 26 with an eighth-inning double against Salem. The following night, he increased it to 27 with a 10th-inning bunt single in a 13-inning 2–1 win over Salem. On August 28, Nichols hit safely in his 30th consecutive game in Winston-Salem's final home contest, a 5–4 win over Salem before an enthusiastic crowd of almost 3,000. With a chance to equal Cooper's record on August 29, Nichols squared off at Alexandria against Dukes ace Bryan Clark, arguably the league's best pitcher. Clark stopped Nichols and ended the streak at 30. Nichols flied out to deep right field in his final at-bat.

Considering the high level of competition faced by Nichols and the dramatic turnaround of Winston-Salem—going from fifth place to first—Nichols's August 1979 ranks as perhaps the finest individual month in Carolina League history. He ended the season with a .293 average, 12 home runs, and 59 RBIs and led the league with 107 runs scored and 156 hits. Surprisingly, Nichols was not named Player of the Year.

Augmenting the Red Sox attack were designated hitter Craig Brooks, second baseman Erwin Bryant, and outfielder Jack Sauer. Steve Crawford, Mark Baum, Mike Howard (12–3, 2.30), Marty Rivas, Steve Shields, and relief ace Dave Tyler (9–4, 1.43) paced an unusually deep pitching staff.

The Alexandria Dukes finished both half-seasons in second place. Had promising catcher Dave Valle (.213, 6, 25) not missed most of the second half with injuries, they might have held off the Red Sox. Infielder Gary Pellant and pitchers Clark (14–5, 2.64), Jeff Cary, and Bob Simond couldn't quite carry them to first place. The switch-hitting Pellant homered from both sides of the plate in the same inning on April 30 in a 20–7 rout of Salem.

Kinston was led by second baseman Ed Dennis (.307, 20-game hitting streak in mid-June) and catcher Pat Kelly (.309). First baseman Greg "Boomer" Wells batted .356 before being promoted to AAA Syracuse on May 24. Future American League home-run champ Jesse Barfield hit only eight homers for the Eagles.

Peninsula had several of the league's best prospects. Player of the Year Bob Dernier (.291) led the league with 77 stolen bases, while first baseman Greg Walker and designated hitter Tom Lombarski (.306) helped score runs for a pitching staff led by Tom Hart (14–6, 2.22) and Ed Gause (11–8).

Lynchburg had the league's RBI champ, catcher Mike Fitzgerald, while second baseman Brian Giles batted .299 but missed five weeks with an injury.

Second baseman Mike Barnes (.300) led Salem.

Winston-Salem's second-half title meant that the Carolina League would not have a postseason playoff for the fourth time in six years. A new format for 1980 was to guarantee a postseason in future years.

The 1979 season was dominated by pitchers to an unusual extent. Kelly's .309 batting average, Fitzgerald's 75 RBIs, and Pellant's 18 home runs are among the lowest figures to ever lead the league in those categories.

Nichols, Dernier, Barfield, and Walker were among the league players who went on to the majors.

Attendance for the league jumped to 282,000.

1979 First-Half Final Standings

Winston-Salem	44–26
Alexandria	38–29
Peninsula	35–32
Kinston	33–36
Lynchburg	31–36
Salem	22–44

Second-Half Final Standings

Winston-Salem	41–29
Alexandria	36–33
Kinston	34–33
Peninsula	33–36
Salem	32–38
Lynchburg	30–37

—◆—

Encouraged by the rise in attendance and the availability of PDCs, the Carolina League decided to expand to eight teams for 1980. Durham and Rocky Mount were readmitted to the league. However, Alexandria lost its PDC with Seattle and was forced to operate as a co-op. With eight teams, the Carolina League divided into a North Carolina Division and a Virginia Division. The split-season format was kept.

It would be an understatement to claim that this expansion was a mixed success. A starker contrast than that between the 1980 Durham Bulls and Rocky Mount Pines could scarcely be imagined. The Bulls were operated by 34-year-old Miles Wolff, a native of Greensboro and an experienced minor league baseball executive, despite his age. Durham Athletic Park was brought back to professional standards, and Durham signed a PDC with the Atlanta Braves, that franchise's first venture into the Carolina League since 1967. The independent Rocky Mount team was owned by Lou Haneles and managed by Mal Fichman. Haneles owned a baseball school in Florida and attempted to stock his Carolina League team mostly with players from that school, along with players released by other organizations. Haneles quickly found out that he had badly overrated the quality of his talent.

Durham and Rocky Mount immediately went in opposite directions. The Bulls drew 4,418 in their home opener, a 12–8 win over Salem in which they stole nine bases. The Bulls won 12 of their first 14 and jumped off to a big lead. By the

The Hapless Rocky Mount Pines

In recent years, virtually every minor league team has obtained its players by way of a working agreement with a major league team. In 1980, the Rocky Mount Pines tried a different approach. The result was one of the most spectacular failures in minor league baseball history.

The Carolina League expanded from six teams to eight in 1980 with the addition of the Durham Bulls and Rocky Mount. The Pines were owned by Lou Haneles and managed by Mal Fichman. The two had operated, with some success, an independent team called the Co-Pilots in the New York–Pennsylvania League in 1979. They were enthusiastic when Carolina League president Jim Mills offered them a chance to take their act to a higher league.

Rocky Mount's method of player procurement set it apart from its minor league brethren. Fichman and Haneles operated a baseball school in Miami, comprised of players ignored by professional teams. They had stocked the Co-Pilots with players from this school in 1979 and saw no reason why the same system wouldn't work in the Carolina League in 1980, especially since they could augment their roster with players released from other organizations. In other words, they expected to profit from the evaluation mistakes of other teams.

Mills and other league officials recognized the risks of this plan. Rocky Mount was voted into the league with the proviso that its roster be stocked with at least a dozen players with league experience. Fichman bravely told Mills that he hoped the other league teams would be able to keep up with his club.

As it turned out, the other league teams did just fine against Rocky Mount. Haneles consistently fell well short of the league mandate of 12 professional players. The hapless Pines finished April with a 4–13 mark. They then went 4–29 during May. By that time, it was apparent that a first-class debacle was under way. *Sports Illustrated* came to call. The magazine found that "the coaching is questionable, the fan support scarce, and the owner has never seen the team play—which under the circumstances may be forgivable. Still his frugality should qualify the entire team for welfare." The hapless Mal Fichman quickly became known as "Mal Function" around the league. Rocky Mount finished the first half of the season with a 14–55 mark.

Things got worse. Rocky Mount had its devoted baseball fans, but even they stopped coming to games. Attendance for the season was only 26,000. The Pines were able to continue down the stretch only with the financial assistance of other league clubs, especially the other new team, the Durham Bulls, who were enjoying a banner year. Late in the season, Durham captured the second-half title when Rick Behenna threw a no-hitter against the Pines.

Rocky Mount finished the campaign with a 24 –114 mark, easily the worst in league history. Its season included separate losing streaks of 18, 14, 13, and 11 games. The Pines didn't go gracefully. The season ended in a rash of recriminations. The manager blamed the owner. The owner blamed the fans and the city for lack of support and a poor ballpark and the league for not finding better ballplayers. For its part, the league simply wanted Haneles to go away. The franchise was revoked in the off-season in a series of heated meetings. Rocky Mount has not been back in organized baseball since.

end of May, they were 34–15 and held a 6½-game edge over runner-up Kinston. They were also drawing fans in numbers not seen since the early years of the league. Wolff's philosophy was to "sell the sizzle with the steak . . . the steak being the baseball and the sizzle being everything else that goes with it." The baseball included a volatile manager in "Dirty" Al Gallagher and an aggressive team loaded with speed, including outfielders Albert Hall and Milt Thompson (.290) and first baseman Gerald Perry (.249, 15, 92, 37 stolen bases, 102 runs). Joe Cowley (6–0), Ike Pettaway (11–4), Mike Smith (11–3) and Rick Coatney (9–2) anchored the pitching staff. Rocky Mount, on the other hand, went 4–29 in the month of May and became a victim of national derision.

The Bulls extended their North Carolina Division lead to nine games in early June before losing Jeff Mathews to AA Savannah. His loss precipitated a slump in which they lost 11 of 14. Around the same time, Kinston won nine of 13 to close within three games of the lead. Durham led by only two games when it hosted a four-game series against Kinston to close out the first half. Durham won a doubleheader on June 17 to wrap up the title.

Neither the triumphant return of the Bulls nor the misadventures of Rocky Mount could obscure the fact that the Virginia Division featured an exceptional team. The Philadelphia Phillies had given Peninsula a team full of hot prospects, including shortstop Julio Franco (.321, 11, 99, 44 stolen bases), outfielder Will Culmer (.369, 18, 93), outfielder Joe Bruno (.305), and pitchers LeRoy Smith (17–6, 2.60), James Wright (13–1, 1.85), and Don Carman (14–5). The Pilots won six of their first seven and were never headed.

Lynchburg had a solid club, led by first baseman Mike Anicich (.266, 22, 73) and Rick Owenby, who went 8–1 before being promoted to the Texas League. The Mets stayed close for a month before losing eight of their last nine games in May. By that time, Peninsula was 34–14 and had demolished the competition. It finished the first half with a huge 16-game margin over second-place Lynchburg.

Peninsula maintained this lofty standard during the second half. Nonetheless, it faced a stern challenge from a surprisingly strong Salem team. The Redbirds, in the last year of their long-running PDC with Pittsburgh, started off the second half 12–3 and matched Peninsula win for win down the stretch. Jose Rodriguez and Terrell Salazar (.285, 18, 83) provided Salem with some punch, while Johnny Taylor (13–6) and Dale Mohorcic (2.18 ERA, 17 saves) keyed the mound corps. At the end of July, Salem had a small lead over Peninsula, but Peninsula's superior firepower won in the end. Franco and Culmer delivered a series of big hits as the Pilots took over the lead in late August. They held off Salem by three games.

The North Carolina Division second-half race came down to Winston-Salem and Durham. Kinston got off to a good start but fell back. Despite the best efforts of outfielder Mitch Webster (.295 after being demoted from AAA

Tony Fernandez
Courtesy of
Kinston Indians

Syracuse), Paul Hodgson (.352), and Mark Eichorn (14–10), Kinston faded out of the race. Rookie shortstop Tony Fernandez batted .278 in limited action.

Led by slugging veteran Craig Brooks (.327, 24, 83) and Jay Fredlund (15–6), Winston-Salem stayed close to Durham through July and into August. Atlanta subjected the Bulls to an large number of roster moves. Milt Thompson was promoted to Savannah, but his loss was more than compensated for by the midseason acquisition of outfielder Brett Butler (.366, 36 stolen bases) from Anderson. Mathews was also returned to Durham.

Winston-Salem carried a one-game lead over Durham into a crucial three-game series in mid-August. Durham won the opener 6–4 on Gerald Perry's two-run homer in the bottom of the ninth. Winston-Salem won the next two games to move back in front by two; Brooks won one of those contests with a two-run homer with two outs in the top of the ninth. The Red Sox couldn't maintain their momentum, however, and dropped back into a tie on August 26. The schedule called for Durham to finish the season at home against Rocky Mount, an advantage that Winston-Salem couldn't overcome. The Bulls clinched a tie on August 29 when Rick Behenna, who struggled through a disappointing 8–13 season, no-hit Rocky Mount 8–0; Albert Hall stole his 100th base during that game. Durham beat the Pines the next night 5–4 on a 13th-inning single by Butler to wrap up the title.

The Behenna no-hitter was the finishing touch on Rocky Mount's 24–114 record, easily the worst in league history. Special condolences were due Rocky Mount pitcher Scott Gibson, who suffered through an 0–12 season, and reliever Mike Brown, who pitched in a league-record 78 games.

Alexandria was almost as bad. The highlight of the Dukes' season was Tim Lewis's record-equaling 20-strikeout performance against Winston-Salem.

Peninsula blasted Durham in a surprisingly one-sided championship series. The Pilots scored five runs in the top of the 10th to win the opener 7–2. They hit four home runs, including a grand slam by Paul Kless, to win the next game 9–3. The final game was an 8–2 Peninsula rout. The Pilots finished the season with a record of 100–40—achieving the best winning percentage in league history—a three-game playoff sweep over a very good Durham club, and a legitimate claim as the best team in Carolina League history.

Despite the disaster in Rocky Mount and poor attendance in Alexandria, the league drew over 600,000 paying customers, an average of 75,000 per team.

Durham set the pace with 175,000, a total higher than the entire league drew in each year from 1975 through 1977, and the best single-season mark since 1947.

1980 North Carolina Division First-Half Final Standings

Durham	42–28
Kinston	38–32
Winston-Salem	38–32
Rocky Mount	14–55

Virginia Division First-Half Final Standings

*Peninsula	51–19	playoff winner
Lynchburg	35–35	
Salem	33–36	
Alexandria	28–42	

North Carolina Division Second-Half Final Standings

Durham	42–28
Winston-Salem	38–32
Kinston	31–37
Rocky Mount	10–59

Virginia Division Second-Half Final Standings

Peninsula	49–21
Salem	46–24
Lynchburg	36–33
Alexandria	26–44

—✦—

Rocky Mount's membership in the league was terminated during a series of heated off-season meetings. With Rocky Mount gone but not mourned, the Carolina League returned to normalcy in 1981. The hapless Pines were replaced by the Hagerstown Suns, the Carolina League's first venture into the state of Maryland. The Suns were a co-op team but had much better success going that route than had Alexandria the season before, largely because of the support they received from the nearby Baltimore Orioles. In fact, Hagerstown was a resounding success both on the field and at the ticket office.

With the addition of Peninsula, the North Carolina Division became the Southern Division, while the Virginia Division was renamed the Northern Division.

The Pittsburgh Pirates changed their PDC to Alexandria, while Salem became affiliated with the San Diego Padres.

In one important respect, 1981 was not a normal year. The Carolina League, along with the rest of the minor leagues, reaped a publicity bonanza when major league players struck for much of the season, leaving baseball-starved fans no option but the minor leagues. The minors were all too happy to fill the gap in newspapers and magazines and on television and radio.

Much of the league's early attention was focused on three highly touted prospects.

Durham outfielder Brad Komminsk and Winston-Salem pitcher Mike Brown got off to fabulous starts. Brown, a first-round draft pick out of Clemson University, pitched four consecutive shutouts, including a one-hitter and a two-hitter, and set a league record with 42 consecutive scoreless innings, breaking Ben Rossman's 1952 mark of 38⅓. Komminsk, a former Atlanta first-round draft pick, hit eight home runs in April as the Bulls jumped to a 13–6 start. Nicknamed "the Franchise," Komminsk was considered the heir apparent to Atlanta star Dale Murphy. He appeared to be a sure triple-crown winner before a late-season bout of mononucleosis led to a home-run drought. One league manager reportedly offered a six-pack to any of his pitchers who could hold Komminsk hitless.

Darryl Strawberry, the first pick in the 1980 free-agent draft, had more trouble in the Carolina League. A native of Los Angeles, the six-foot-six outfielder suffered from the demands of Mets fans and the New York media, which regularly reported on his failings in the Carolina League. At the All-Star break, Strawberry was batting less than .200, striking out frequently, and fielding poorly.

Durham and Lynchburg were the early leaders in their respective divisions, but neither was able to hold on. Kinston, led by All-Star shortstop Tony Fernandez, overtook the Bulls in early May. The Mets suffered a major loss in mid-May when first baseman Mike Anicich was promoted to Jackson. He was batting .410 at the time, not the kind of loss a team shrugs off. After his departure, Lynchburg lost 16 of its final 20 first-half games to fall from contention.

Hagerstown, which trailed by 5½ games when Anicich left Lynchburg, ended up as the only Northern Division team with a winning record. It won 23 of its last 37 behind the efforts of Matt Tyner, designated hitter David Rivera, and catcher John Stefero.

Durham and Kinston produced their share of fireworks in the Southern Division race. As the Bulls lost eight of 13 to fall behind Kinston, manager Gallagher's considerable temper boiled over. After a closed-door meeting failed to end the slide, Gallagher was ejected from a game when he covered home plate with dirt during a dispute.

Gallagher finally went ballistic during a crucial May 22 doubleheader against

"Can't Miss" Prospects

As useful as the minor leagues are in the development of major league baseball players, projecting major league success on the basis of minor league play is a risky business. Some of the best Class A players are unpolished gems who never improve or run into a higher level of competition that exposes some fundamental flaw. On the other hand, some mediocre Carolina League players develop into top-level major leaguers.

Consider the contrast between two teammates on the 1952 Burlington Pirates. Pitcher Ron Necciai was a "can't miss" prospect who dazzled fans and scouts alike with his blazing fastball. One of his teammates was pitcher Ron Kline, who struggled to a 3–6 record. Yet arm trouble and a chronic stomach problem ended Necciai's career prematurely; he won only a single game in the majors. Kline, on the other hand, went on to post 114 major league victories.

Or consider Mickey Lolich, who posted a losing record in three seasons with the Durham Bulls. Once Lolich figured out how to throw strikes consistently, he went on to become one of the major leagues' top hurlers, winning 217 games, most of them for the Detroit Tigers.

Rarely has the difficulty of predicting stardom been more pronounced than in 1981, the year Durham Bulls outfielder Brad Komminsk tore up the Carolina League. Komminsk seemed to have it all, a rare combination of speed and power that made him as highly regarded a prospect as the Carolina League has had in recent years. Komminsk led the league in batting average and runs batted in, finished second in home runs, fielded well, and ran the bases with surprising agility for his six-foot-two, 205-pound frame. Delighted Atlanta officials saw him as their replacement for Dale Murphy. Komminsk was the ultimate "can't miss" prospect. Yet miss he did. Several observers have blamed Atlanta for tampering with his swing. Whatever the reason, Komminsk never became more than a journeyman outfielder in the major leagues.

Contrast Komminsk with one of his 1981 rivals, Lynchburg outfielder Darryl Strawberry. Although he was as highly regarded as Komminsk, Strawberry struggled throughout the 1981 season, striking out frequently, hitting for a low batting average, and fielding his position with a noticeable lack of interest. Yet he eventually became a prolific slugger for the Mets and Dodgers, albeit a controversial one.

Komminsk and Strawberry are archetypes for numerous Carolina League players whose major league careers could not reasonably be predicted solely on the basis of their ability to play at the Class A level.

Kinston at Durham Athletic Park. The Bulls went into the games trailing by five, so they desperately needed a sweep. In the first game, Gallagher, Durham coach Cito Gaston, and Kinston manager John McLaren were all ejected by umpire Coleman Coffett before the game was half over. In the nightcap, Gallagher caused a 10-minute delay by arguing with the umps. The teams split the two games, leaving the Bulls no closer than when they started. League president Jim Mills, who was in attendance at the games, called Gallagher on the carpet. "In my 40 years of baseball," Mills told the press, "I've never seen anyone try to show up two umpires as bad as that. The whole thing was bush." Mills, who had a reputation for leniency toward managers in these matters, announced that he would crack down on umpire abuse, but he also conceded that the umpiring staff was not up to par and that at least two of his men did not meet Carolina League standards.

A June 2 game between Durham and Lynchburg vividly confirmed Mills's concerns. Mets center fielder Billy Beane robbed his Durham counterpart, Gary Cooper, of extra bases by acting out a catch on a ball that actually bounced past him. The umpires were fooled and called Cooper out. Mills began shuffling umpiring crews in an attempt to get better results.

The Bulls got hot in June, spurred by outfielder Alvin Moore, who took over a starting spot when Ronnie Rudd was traded; ironically, the trade was canceled when Ed Putnam, the player Rudd was traded for, refused to report and retired instead. Moore's 18-game hitting streak (and perhaps Gallagher's antics) inspired the Bulls, who regained first place on June 8 with a 19–1 thrashing of Salem. Komminsk had two of the Bulls' eight homers in that game; he also singled, tripled, scored five runs, and drove in five. Moore had two homers and six runs batted in, while first baseman Keith Hagman also homered twice. The home-run explosion tied a record set by Greensboro in 1958.

The Bulls swept Alexandria 2–1 and 1–0 on June 9 and beat them again the next day 3–2. These three wins ran the Bulls' winning streak to nine games and gave them a two-game lead over Kinston. The losses cut Alexandria's lead over Hagerstown to half a game. Alexandria ended the Bulls' streak with a 4–3 win on June 11.

Durham's comeback was stopped for good by streaking Hagerstown. On June 15, the Suns knocked the Bulls back into second place by winning a doubleheader by identical 5–4 scores, while Kinston beat Lynchburg 7–3. Hagerstown won both games in the bottom of the last inning; in the first game, Kurt Fabrizino hit a two-run homer to win the game, while pinch hitter John Stefero singled in the winner in game two. Kinston clinched the Southern Division first-half pennant two days later when it scored four runs in the top of the seventh to beat Winston-Salem 6–5. The Bulls had overcome a 6½-game deficit to lead by two, only to fall short by two games.

Meanwhile, Hagerstown pulled away from slumping Alexandria to win the Northern Division by 3½ games.

Kinston and Durham both suffered from midseason call-ups. Kinston lost shortstop Tony Fernandez (.318) and pitchers Jim Baker (11–1) and Tom Lukich (10 wins and 11 saves), while Durham lost Scott Patterson, who had won all nine of his decisions.

Decimated Kinston was never a factor in second half, finishing well below .500. Durham jumped off to a 9–3 start before losing seven of eight and fading. On July 17, it dropped out of first with a 4–1 loss to Lynchburg's Jeff Bittiger, who fanned 18 Bulls and hurled a three-hitter.

The second-half Southern Division championship became a race between Peninsula and Winston-Salem, the two first-half also-rans. The Pilots opened up a four-game lead in the middle of August and held off the Red Sox by three.

In the Northern Division, Hagerstown jumped off to a 13–7 start but also faded down the stretch. Salem and a revived Lynchburg team fought it out for the divisional title. Anicich was sent back to Lynchburg, Strawberry came around, and the Mets were much improved in the second half. In fact, Lynchburg took a three-game lead over Salem into August. It held that lead until the final week, when Salem moved into first place. Keyed by outfielder Gerald Davis, Salem held on for a one-game win over the Mets.

The first round of the playoffs consisted of a single game. In the Southern Division, depleted Kinston was no match for Peninsula. Pilots ace Kelly Downs allowed only four hits in a 9–0 win. In the Northern Division, Hagerstown outslugged Salem 11–6.

The championship appeared to be an even match on paper. Hagerstown's hopes were pinned largely on the slugging of Matt Tyner (.301, 31, 77), William Butler, David Rivera, John Stefero (.287, 25, 82), and Paul Croft (.282, 20, 60). Lighter-hitting Peninsula countered with Steve Jeltz (38 stolen bases) and a solid pitching staff led by Kelly Downs (13–7) and Dennis Thomas (8–2). This time, good hitting beat good pitching. The Peninsula pitching staff could not cool off the hot Hagerstown bats. Hagerstown made it a three-game sweep by scores of 11–8, 12–1, and 9–4. The Suns scored an impressive 43 runs in their four-game run to the title.

Durham's Brad Komminsk finished the season with some impressive statistics himself, including a .322 batting average, 33 home runs, 104 runs batted in, 108 runs scored, and 35 stolen bases. Alvin Moore, Miguel Sosa, and Keith Hagman helped Komminsk generate considerable offense. However, only Rick Behenna (13–12) was consistently effective on the mound. Future Atlanta Brave Jeff Dedmon (7–8) struggled through a difficult season.

Salem outfielder Gerald Davis (.306, 34, 103) denied Komminsk the triple crown by one home run. Catcher Mark Parent and infielder Luis Quinones overcame ho-hum Carolina League seasons to make the majors, something Davis never accomplished.

Lynchburg's Darryl Strawberry completed his disappointing season on an upswing that left him with a .255 batting average, 13 home runs, 78 runs batted in, and 31 stolen bases. Other noteworthy Mets included Anicich, shortstop Jose Oquendo (38 stolen bases), Lloyd McClendon, Jeff Bittiger (11–6), and Jay Tibbs, all of whom eventually played in the majors.

The same can be said about Alexandria's exceptional defensive shortstop, Rafael Belliard (.216), and his teammate Tim Burke, along with Winston-Salem's Mike Brown (14–4, 1.49), Steve Lyons, and Marc Sullivan.

A basic minor league conflict—that between winning games and developing talent—was illuminated dramatically in 1981 when the Braves dismissed the tempestuous Gallagher after the conclusion of the season. "Dirty Al" had established himself as a fan favorite but had lost favor with some of his players, one of whom refused to shake his skipper's hand during pregame introductions. Atlanta felt that Gallagher emphasized winning games to the detriment of developing its expensive talent. Gallagher and Atlanta's minor league brain trust argued over player assignments and lineups. For his part, Gallagher argued that the conflict between winning and development was artificial: "I believe that the two are together, absolutely the same. I don't see the difference between the two." Obviously, his bosses disagreed.

1981 Northern Division First-Half Final Standings

*Hagerstown	37–31	playoff winner
Alexandria	33–34	
Lynchburg	32–38	
Salem	26–44	

Southern Division First-Half Final Standings

Kinston	42–28
Durham	40–28
Winston-Salem	34–35
Peninsula	30–36

Northern Division Second-Half Final Standings

Salem	40–30
Lynchburg	39–31
Hagerstown	33–37
Alexandria	29–41

Southern Division Second-Half Final Standings

Peninsula	41–29
Winston-Salem	38–32
Durham	30–40
Kinston	30–40

—◆—

The Carolina League did not have any franchise changes following the 1981 season. Hagerstown signed an agreement with the nearby Baltimore Orioles, a profitable arrangement for both clubs.

Much of the early attention was focused on Durham pitcher Brian Fisher, a hard-throwing 20-year-old from Aurora, Colorado. On April 30, Fisher beat Salem 6–3, striking out 20 Redbirds, including the first nine. Both equaled league records. Fisher entered the ninth with 19 strikeouts and fanned the last batter, Pat Casey, to equal the record. It was Casey's fourth strikeout of the evening. The game was further enlivened by a streaker who ran across the field and disappeared over the left-field wall. Fisher's win gave the Bulls a Southern Division–leading 15–7 mark, two games ahead of Kinston.

A potent Alexandria team finished April with a seven-game lead over Hagerstown in the Northern Division. Both Durham and Alexandria held their leads through the end of the first half, although the former had considerably more difficulty.

The Bulls won 19 of their first 27 and cruised through the early weeks. On May 5, Fisher struck out 17 in a 7–1 win over formidable Alexandria. At that point, he had 27 strikeouts in consecutive starts and a total of 95 in 57 $^{2}/_{3}$ innings. However, in his next start, Fisher injured his arm during pregame warmups at Winston-Salem. He later blamed the injury on a poor bullpen pitching mound. Fisher unwisely continued to pitch and tore a muscle in his right elbow. He missed almost two months. Other Bulls were injured about the same time, including pitcher Mike Payne, outfielders Joe Lorenz and Bryan Neal, and catcher Pat Kelly. The Bulls hit a 9–13 stretch.

While the Bulls were struggling, Peninsula put together a 12-game winning streak. On June 4, it beat Durham to pull within a game of the lead. The next day, Peninsula beat the Bulls 6–4 to move into a tie for first. The game was enlivened by a fistfight between Durham's Keith Hagman and star Peninsula second baseman Juan Samuel, precipitated when Hagman slid hard into second base to break up a double play. Both players were ejected.

On June 6, Durham ended Peninsula's winning streak and moved back into first with a hard-fought 11–8 win. Pilots' manager Bill Dancy was ejected in Durham's three-run ninth for throwing dirt on the plate. The two teams moved back into a tie the next day when the Pilots beat the Bulls.

A few days later, the two contenders met in Durham for a crucial series, with the Bulls half a game ahead. They extended that lead with a 2–1 win in the first game behind the pitching of David Clay and Gary Reiter. The Bulls were aided by a crucial Peninsula mistake. In the fourth inning, Pilots catcher Darren Daulton rolled the ball back to the mound after what he thought was the third strike of the third out. However, home-plate umpire Frank Nieves ruled that Daulton had dropped the third strike. Batter Rick Siriano scampered to first, and the next hitter, Miguel Sosa, doubled in Durham's two runs. The Bulls won the next two contests by identical 6–3 scores to extend their lead to 3½. Peninsula salvaged the last game of the series, but the damage had been done. Durham held off Peninsula by two games to win the Southern Division.

Both clubs praised the pivotal, closely contested series as a classic. Durham skipper Bobby Dews called it the best series of Class A games he had ever seen. His Peninsula counterpart, Bill Dancy, was equally positive. Durham sportswriter Ron Morris called the games "a diet of well-played and contested games spiced with controversy and calculated strategy."

Alexandria was never challenged in the Northern Division during the first half, winning by eight games over Hagerstown. The hard-hitting Dukes had the league's leading hitter, second baseman Rick Renteria (.331, 14, 100), along with outfielder Joe Orsulak (.289, 28 stolen bases), designated hitter Ken Ford (.300, 24, 96), and outfielder Larry Sheets (.296). Fernando Gonzales (13–8, including a no-hitter) and Chris Green (9–1) were the primary beneficiaries of this offensive output. However, Alexandria's attendance continued to be mediocre.

Early contender Salem fell apart, losing 12 straight and 26 of 30 from May 19 to June 17. San Diego had another high Class A team in 1982, and its Salem affiliate got the short end of the player-development stick. Salem's best players were the double-play combination of shortstop Luis Quinones and second baseman Steve Garcia, although Quinones was promoted to the Texas League in midseason.

Winston-Salem was another disaster area. After 35 games, the Red Sox had a .204 batting average, an earned-run average of 4.53, and 77 errors. Winston-Salem had the same problem as Salem. Its parent team had a Class A team in Winter Haven, Florida, and split its talent between the two clubs. Catcher David Malpeso (.317, 29, 91) was the top Red Sox player. Although neither Salem nor Winston-Salem was as bad as the 1980 Rocky Mount club, both were about as ineffective as minor league teams can be with a full player development agreement.

Both Durham and Alexandria lost key pitchers to promotion at midseason, an all-too-common phenomenon. Atlanta promoted Rick Coatney and David Clay to AA but left first baseman Keith Hagman (.303), shortstop Miguel Sosa (.288, 25, 69), Andre Treadway (11–8) and Rick Hatcher (10–5) in Durham. The Dukes said good-bye to three pitchers with a combined 19–3 record, who shuffled off to Buffalo of the Eastern League.

Brian Fisher returned to action on July 4 in an 8–2 loss to Lynchburg. He never regained his preinjury velocity that season. He finished with a 6–6 record, a 2.77 earned-run average, and 129 strikeouts in 104 innings.

Durham found a way to win 10 of its first 13 in the second half but could not maintain that pace. Peninsula took over first place in early July. On July 17, the red-hot Pilots were 21–5 and led the Bulls by 3½ games. Peninsula was led by speedy outfielder Jeff Stone, who had set an organized baseball record of 123 stolen bases the previous season while playing at Spartanburg. Stone's unsuccessful chase after Albert Hall's Carolina League stolen-base record provided much of the drama in the Southern Division, especially after the Bulls lost 11 of 13 in late July. Stone ended the season with a .297 average and 94 stolen bases.

Peninsula closed July with a 29–9 mark, trailed by 23–14 Kinston and 21–16 Durham. The race never tightened in August, and Peninsula won by 6½ games over Kinston. In addition to Stone, Peninsula featured league Player of the Year Juan Samuel (.320, 28, 94, 111 runs, 64 stolen bases), catcher–first baseman Darren Daulton (.241, 11, 44), third baseman–catcher Mike Lavalliere (.275), Pitcher of the Year Charlie Hudson (15–5, 1.85), and 12-game winners Tony Ghelfi and Ed Wojna. Samuel and Daulton went on to become major league All-Stars, while several other members of the Peninsula club also enjoyed big-league careers.

Kinston moved past Durham into second place. Relief pitcher David Shipanoff saved 30 games for a starting staff that included John Cerutti (10–5 before being promoted to the Southern League), Tom Blackmon (11–6), and Tim Rogers (11–8). Less successful was former UCLA quarterback Jay Schroeder (.218, 15, 55), who eventually traded the burdens of hitting the professional curve ball for the dangers of dodging blitzing linebackers as an NFL quarterback with the Washington Redskins and the Los Angeles Raiders.

Although still not a contender, Winston-Salem improved in the second half after the addition of NCAA career home-run leader Jeff Ledbetter of Florida State University. Winston-Salem fans got a charge out of cheering the intriguingly nicknamed Tony "Buffalo" Beal, whose talent, unfortunately, failed to match the quality of his moniker.

Jay Schroeder
Courtesy of
the Kinston Indians

The Northern Division had three .500 teams and a still-awful Salem club. Hagerstown's Johnny Tutt provided some excitement. On July 29, he became the second player in league history to hit three triples in a game; in an August 24 contest, he stole five bases.

Salem continued to be a problem area. Most of San Diego's best young players were in Reno, while two of Salem's better prospects, Tim Gillaspie and Pat

Casey, were promoted to AA Amarillo at midseason, leaving the cupboard bare. On August 13, Salem was the victim of a seven-inning perfect game thrown by Durham's Rick Hatcher, a relief pitcher who was thrown into the starting rotation only because of injuries to the regular Durham starters. Hatcher threw only 76 pitches, 63 of which were strikes. Hatcher was hammered in several subsequent starts.

None of the other three Northern Division teams was able to take charge of a weak division, prompting Alexandria utility man Mike Quade to quip that the pennant would be "a question of who's gonna back in first." Hagerstown was the first to fall. Despite the presence of Pat Dumouchelle (.298) and Al Pardo (.289, 17, 86), the Suns lacked the firepower for a pennant. Alexandria crept into first place but dropped out with an August 26 doubleheader loss to Durham. Alexandria and Lynchburg took turns in first during the last week of August. On August 30, Alexandria dropped out of first for good with 1–0 loss to Kinston on a Tim Rodgers four-hitter, while Lynchburg nipped Winston-Salem 7–6 in 10 innings. Lynchburg lost its last game 9–8 to the Red Sox. With a chance to win the second-half title, Alexandria was thrashed by Kinston 9–2 behind a Chris Phillips two-hitter. Lynchburg had fulfilled Quade's prediction by backing into the title by half a game.

The Mets likely would have won with greater ease had they enjoyed the services of young third baseman Kevin Mitchell (.318, 1, 16). The future major league home-run champ was on the disabled list from July 24 until the conclusion of the season. First baseman Randy Milligan, catcher–third baseman Lloyd McClendon, outfielders LaSchelle Tarver (.308) and Herm Winningham (.295, 50 stolen bases), and Jody Johnston (12–3) took up the slack. The late-season acquisition of Roger McDowell, who won a pair of decisions, aided the Mets' pennant run.

The first round of the playoffs again consisted of a single game. In the Northern Division, Alexandria jumped to an 11–0 lead over Lynchburg after four innings and survived a spirited comeback to win 11–8. A three-run double in the fourth by Jim Felt was the big hit. In the Southern Division, the Bulls easily handled Peninsula 8–1, as Jeff Dedmon and Tom Waddell outdueled Pilots ace Charlie Hudson. The Bulls hit four home runs, including a grand slam by Keith Hagman.

Alexandria blasted Durham in three straight for the championship. In the opener, Rick Renteria drove in a pair of runs in a 5–2 Dukes victory. Fernando Gonzalez was the winning pitcher. Alexandria won game two 4–1, as former pro hockey player Rich Leggatt, a native of Canada, threw a four-hitter. Alexandria won the third game 8–5; catcher Buck Goldtorn's seventh-inning grand slam off Waddell broke a 4–4 tie and propelled Alexandria to its only Carolina League crown.

1982 Northern Division First-Half Final Standings

*Alexandria	45–20	playoff winner
Hagerstown	38–29	
Lynchburg	29–37	
Salem	22–48	

Southern Division First-Half Final Standings

Durham	43–25
Peninsula	41–27
Kinston	34–33
Winston-Salem	18–51

Northern Division Second-Half Final Standings

Lynchburg	36–34
Alexandria	35–34
Hagerstown	33–36
Salem	17–53

Southern Division Second-Half Final Standings

Peninsula	49–20
Kinston	42–26
Durham	37–31
Winston-Salem	27–42

——◆——

The 1983 season was dominated by the Lynchburg Mets, one of the handful of super teams in Carolina League history. The Mets not only won both Northern Division half-season championships—leaving a very good Hagerstown team in the lurch—they did so with a team that featured two future major league All-Stars and a half-dozen other future major league regulars.

The season certainly got off to an interesting start. On opening day in Durham, highly regarded prospect Duane Ward gave up seven runs in the top of the first to Peninsula. Ward retired only a single batter, walked four, committed a balk, and hit a pair of Pilots back to back. After the second beaning, both benches emptied, and the circumspect Ward fled to the safety of the Durham dugout. Another fight ensued in the seventh inning when a Durham fan poured beer into the Peninsula bullpen. A Bulls rally fell short, and Peninsula won 9–7.

Peninsula could have used some of that heat six days later when its home opener was snowed out.

Opening day was a harbinger for Durham. The Bulls lost six straight in early May to drop out of a short-lived stint at the top. On May 7, Durham's Tim Coles came in to pitch the seventh, pulled a hamstring, and never faced a batter. Later that week, the Bulls lost 20–4 to Hagerstown and 23–8 to Winston-Salem. The latter took over the lead from the slumping Bulls.

While the Bulls' pitching was collapsing in the Southern Division, Lynchburg was dominating the Northern Division. The Mets took over first place from Alexandria on May 7 in the middle of a 12-game winning streak which broke the pennant race open. On May 19, the New York Mets flew Lynchburg and Salem to New York to play a regular league game as a preliminary to a Mets–San Diego contest. Salem won 4–1, scoring all of its runs in the ninth. Highly regarded Mets pitcher Dwight Gooden lost the game, a rare occurrence that season.

The other Lynchburg pitchers didn't lose often, either. On May 14, the Mets were 23–9 and led Hagerstown by three games. They finished May with a mark of 34–14 after a 24–6 month. They completed the first half with a 49–20 record, 6½ games ahead of Hagerstown. Lynchburg had a devastating blend of power, speed, and pitching. Their best everyday player was speedy center fielder Lenny Dykstra, who stole 48 bases in his first 45 games. Drawing most of the raves, however, was the powerful Gooden, selected fifth in the first round of the 1982 draft and playing his first full year of professional baseball. Before the season was over, both would hold significant league records.

Dwight Gooden
Courtesy of BaseballAmerica

Winston-Salem maintained its lead in the Southern Division despite several injuries to key players. In mid-May, bonus baby Sam Horn hurt his wrist diving into second base and spent seven weeks on the disabled list. Shortly afterward, Mike Greenwell slipped making a turn at Lynchburg, tore knee cartilage, had surgery in Boston, and missed much of the middle of the season; Greenwell was batting .348 at the time of his injury. Another gruesome injury took place when Winston-

Lenny Dykstra
Courtesy of BaseballAmerica

Salem's Manny Jose collided with Alexandria catcher Alex Rodriguez at the plate. The unfortunate Rodriguez needed 47 stitches but returned after two weeks.

Veteran Winston-Salem skipper Bill Slack held the Red Sox together despite the injuries to Horn and Greenwell. They completed May with a two-game lead over Kinston. Winston-Salem never got far above .500, but none of the weak Southern Division teams could mount a strong challenge. Durham did win six straight to close to within 1½ games, but Winston-Salem beat Salem 2–1 in 10 innings in a key game to hold onto the first-half pennant.

Winston-Salem won seven of its first nine to break on top in the second half. The Bulls suffered a crucial loss when first baseman Bob Tumpane broke his right arm when a runner collided with him on a low throw. Former Bull Keith Hagman was sent back to Durham to take his place. The struggling Bulls lost 12 of their first 15 contests.

Hagerstown duplicated Winston-Salem's start with an early 7–2 record. The Suns had an outstanding pitching staff and the league's best slugger, Ken Gerhart. Lynchburg and Peninsula won six of their first nine games to stay close to Hagerstown.

League fans received an extra treat in the second half in the form of visits from a pair of well-known major league pitchers. The first was Doyle Alexander, signed by the Toronto organization after being released by the New York Yankees. Toronto checked out its new acquisition by sending him to Kinston, where he started against Salem on June 28. Alexander pitched six shutout innings and left with a big lead. He received no decision, however, as Salem rallied against the Kinston bullpen for a 7–6 win. Alexander was soon on his way back to the majors. The second major league visitor was Baltimore Oriole Jim Palmer, who gave Hagerstown several quality starts in a late-season attempt to rehabilitate a sore arm.

Palmer's appearances came in the midst of a hot race between Hagerstown and Lynchburg. At the end of July, Hagerstown was 25–12 and Lynchburg 22–

Jim Palmer's League Visit

Major league teams occasionally send big-league players to the minors to recover from injuries. Some of the more notable "rehab" players in the Carolina League over the years have been Dwight Gooden, Gene Conley, Marty Bystrom, Joey Jay, Brady Anderson, and Mike Devereux.

Perhaps the most celebrated such example was in August 1983, when Baltimore Orioles star Jim Palmer pitched for Hagerstown. By 1983, Palmer had established himself as one of the game's great pitchers, winning the Cy Young Award for the Orioles in 1973, 1975, and 1976. Palmer went on the major league disabled list on July 3, 1983, with tendinitis in his right arm; Baltimore sent him to nearby Hagerstown to rehabilitate the arm. In three appearances for the Suns, Palmer attracted huge crowds— over 6,000 in one appearance—and national media attention, including an article in *Sports Illustrated.* When Palmer beat Durham 8–6, Bulls manager Brian Snitker admitted that "our guys are excited. This might be the only big-leaguer they face in their careers." Since the Bulls were 12–32 at the time, this was a safe bet.

Palmer ended his brief Carolina League sojourn with a 2–0 record and a 3.46 ERA. Unfortunately, his arm troubles never completely cleared up. He retired in 1984 with a record of 268–152. He was elected to the Hall of Fame in 1989. By then, he had become almost as famous for his underwear advertisements as for his stellar major league career.

15. Hagerstown's pennant hopes were bolstered when it won a rare triple-header against Durham on August 6. The previous night's doubleheader had been suspended in the fifth inning of the first game when lightning knocked out the lights. That game was completed the next day, along with the second game of the August 5 doubleheader and the regularly scheduled August 6 game. Hagerstown won all three games; Gerhart hit three homers for the day. Palmer beat Durham the following day. Hagerstown led Lynchburg by three games on August 6. A week later, it still led by two.

Dwight Gooden kept Lynchburg in the race. After starting 3–3, Gooden was virtually unhittable. When he beat the Bulls 6–2 on August 17, he ran his record to 17–3. Around the same time, Dykstra had a 15-game hitting streak. On August 20, Lynchburg pulled within a game of Hagerstown. On the 21st, Lynchburg beat Winston-Salem 7–4 while Hagerstown lost to Peninsula 4–1, leaving both teams at 36-21. On the 23rd, Gooden struck out 10 in a rain-shortened five-inning win over Durham. This gave him 277 strikeouts for the season, two more than Ken Deal's 1947 league record. Gooden ran his record to 18–3 with the win and pushed Lynchburg percentage points ahead of the Suns in the standings. The following day, Dykstra hit a pair of homers to lead the Mets over Durham, while Hagerstown lost to Kinston 8–2. On August 25, Dykstra stole his 100th base as the Mets beat Durham again, this time by a 9–5 score. Around this time, Jim Mills denied a Salem protest and upheld a Lynchburg win from earlier in the season amid criticism that he had been pressured by the New York Mets. Lynchburg finished August with a three-game lead over Hagerstown. When they split a twin bill on September 1, the Mets clinched the title.

The Southern Division race was much more one-sided. Winston-Salem won 12 straight before losing 7–2 to Durham on July 13. This loss dropped them to 16–3. The Winston-Salem streak was sparked not by a young phenom, but rather by a 69-year-old interim manager. Early in the second half, Bill Slack had to return to his native Canada for his mother's funeral. He was replaced by Eddie Popowski, a diminutive coach-at-large who had been in the Boston system since 1937, including managerial stops at Roanoke, Greensboro, and Winston-Salem.

After its early surge, Winston-Salem played under .500, but no team in its division was able to challenge. At the end of July, Winston-Salem was the only team above .500 in the Southern Division.

While the pennant races were winding down, the league found itself embroiled in controversy, much of it falling on the shoulders of beleaguered league president Mills. Late in the season, Mills dismissed umpires Frank Nieves and Pete DeFlesco for stealing baseballs. Lynchburg and Winston-Salem then became involved in a controversy over playoff sites. Lynchburg had first choice by virtue of having the best overall record. The Mets initially decided to host the first two games in the best-of-five series because of a scheduling conflict with a high-school football game at their stadium. When the football game was moved, Lynchburg decided it preferred to host the final three games. Winston-Salem owner Erwin Oakley protested and was supported by Mills. However, the league directors overruled Mills in a meeting attended only by directors from the Northern Division. The playoff would begin in Winston-Salem.

A meager crowd of 392 saw a great first game at Ernie Shore Stadium. Led by Mark Carreon, who went four for six with four runs batted in, the Mets took a 9–3 lead into bottom of the ninth. The Red Sox mounted a furious comeback, scoring five times in the bottom of the ninth before Wes Gardner got Sam Nattile to ground out with a man on first to preserve a hard-fought 9–8 victory. Lynchburg won the second game easily, pounding Red Sox ace Mitch Johnson for a 14–6 win. Lynchburg closed out the championship series with a 4–3 win in game three. In that contest, Greenwell, fully recovered from his knee injury, hit a two-run double in the sixth inning to give Winston-Salem a 3–1 lead. The Red Sox held a 3–2 lead until Randy Milligan hit a two-run homer in the bottom of the eighth to give Lynchburg a 4–3 win.

The league's final statistics confirm Lynchburg's dominance. Dykstra ended up with a league-leading .358 batting average and a league-record 105 stolen bases, along with eight home runs, 81 runs batted in, and 14 triples. Gooden finished at 19–4, with a 2.50 earned-run average and 300 strikeouts. After the conclusion of the Carolina League season, he was promoted to the Mets' AAA team in Tidewater, where he pitched in that league's postseason. In 1984, he became the National League Rookie of the Year. Dykstra went on to become one of baseball's dominant players in the 1990s after being traded to Philadelphia. Mark Carreon (.334, 36 stolen bases), Dave Cochrane (.263, 25, 102), Randy Milligan (.292), Greg Olson (22 homers), Wes Gardner (6–3, 1.87, 15 saves), Jay Tibbs (14–8), and Jeff Bettendorf (13–4) complemented the two superstars.

The statistics for Winston-Salem's Greenwell (.278, 3, 21) and Horn (.240, 9, 29) reflect their long periods on the disabled list. First baseman Sam Nattile (.285, 21, 80) and catcher Denny Sheaffer took up the slack, while Mike Rochford and Mitch Johnson combined to win 31 games.

Hagerstown matched Lynchburg on offense but not in pitching strength. The Suns blasted a league-record 158 home runs, many of them by outfielders Ken Gerhart (.273, 31, 86, 131 runs) and Ron Salcedo (.290, 21, 93) and first baseman Jim Traber (14, 79). Bob Konopa (12–2) and Jeff Summers (9–2) were the top Hagerstown hurlers.

Alexandria's roster included a lightly regarded, undrafted outfielder named Bobby Bonilla (.256, 11, 59, 28 stolen bases), who eventually developed into one of the game's best players. His teammates included third baseman Jim Opie (.294, 20, 71), shortstop Sammy Khalifa, first baseman Lorenzo Bundy (.291, 25, 88), outfielder Nelson Delarosa (.290), Scott Bailes, and Jim Buckmier.

Fred McGriff (.243, 21, 57) was Kinston's best player. The slugging first baseman and future National League home-run king started the season in the South Atlantic League before being promoted to the Carolina League. Jay Schroeder (.206, 9, 43, 103 strikeouts) gave baseball one last try before going on to greater success in pro football. Speedsters Ken Kinnard and Alex Marte combined for 97 stolen bases. Second baseman Mike Sharperson and pitcher David Wells eventually joined McGriff in the majors.

Peninsula's top players included Rick Schu, Alan LaBouef, Jim Olander, and Gib Siebert (.305).

Durham was led by Inoncencio Guerrero (.332, 11, 44). Mediocre Bulls pitchers Zane Smith (9–15, 4.90) and Duane Ward (11–13, 4.29) eventually improved enough to make the majors.

Last-place Salem was led by outfielder Kevin Wiggins (.301, 10, 59) and Steve Murray (22 home runs). Keith Jones stole 67 bases.

The 1983 season was one of the most interesting in league history. Much of the stress of that season fell on the shoulders of Jim Mills, who was forced to make several controversial decisions, all of which seemed to alienate someone. At the October 29 league meeting, a motion to reelect Mills was defeated by a

6–2 margin. Nearly a decade later, Mills philosophically remarked that "when you run a league you don't make everybody happy."

1983 Northern Division First-Half Final Standings

* Lynchburg	49–20	playoff winner
Hagerstown	41–25	
Alexandria	35–32	
Salem	20–49	

Southern Division First-Half Final Standings

Winston-Salem	36–34
Durham	33–34
Kinston	32–36
Peninsula	26–42

Northern Division Second-Half Final Standings

Lynchburg	47–23
Hagerstown	43–27
Alexandria	34–36
Salem	30–40

Southern Division Second-Half Final Standings

Winston-Salem	38–32
Peninsula	32–38
Kinston	30–40
Durham	26–44

♦　♦　♦

Bernie Williams, 1988

Courtesy of Prince William Cannons

CHAPTER SEVEN
1984 — 88

♦   ♦   ♦

Sixteen candidates applied for Jim Mills's old job. The league hired John Hopkins, the general manager of the South Atlantic League's Greensboro Hornets. Hopkins took over a much different league in 1984 than had Jim Mills in 1977. The minor leagues were in the midst of a full-fledged revival in the 1980s. Attendance began an upswing in the early 1980s that has continued to the present.

A new president was not the only change for 1984. Alexandria moved to Prince William County, Virginia, taking over Alexandria's Pittsburgh PDC and playing in new, $2 million County Stadium. Peninsula talked about moving to Burlington, but the move never materialized. Salem switched its PDC from San Diego to Texas.

Given the nature of Class A minor league baseball in the modern era, anything resembling a dynasty is rare. A club's better players rarely come back for a second season, and many of the best don't even last an entire season before being promoted. A minor league roster is no stronger than the drafting and signing abilities of its major league supplier. Thus, it was a surprise that the Lynchburg Mets put together a 1984 roster every bit the equal of their 1983 powerhouse.

It didn't appear that way at the beginning of the season. The Mets started 7–12 and finished April six games behind Prince William. They hit their stride in May, however, when they went 23–8 and took over the lead. Lynchburg had the league's best hitters, including first baseman Dave Magadan (.350), catcher Barry Lyons (.316, 12, 87), outfielders Stanley Jefferson (.288, 45 stolen bases, 113 runs) and Jason Felice (.307, 20, 86), and designated hitter Paul Hollins (.277, 22, 100). In addition to leading the league with 758 runs scored, the Mets led the league with a 2.80 earned-run average, an unbeatable combination. Randy Myers (13–5, 2.06), Mitch Cook (16–4, 2.97), Jim Adamczak (11 saves), and Rick Aguilera (8–3, 2.34) were all among the league's best pitchers.

Still, there was competition. The Mets hit a bad patch in early June, losing seven straight. When Prince William won a pair of one-run decisions from the Mets on June 8, they led the defending champs by 2½ games. Responding to the challenge, Lynchburg righted itself and won its final eight games of the first half. On June 15, it beat Salem twice, while Prince William lost to Hagerstown. This left the clubs tied at 40–27. Prince William lost the first-half race by a game on the last day when it dropped the first game of a doubleheader to Hagerstown by a score of 3–1. Hagerstown's John Habyan hurled a three-hitter, while Billy Ripken's two-run double gave the Suns all the runs they needed.

The first-half race in the Southern Division belonged to the Durham Bulls. First baseman Bob Tumpane hit a dozen of his 27 home runs during May to spark his club to a 4½-game lead over Peninsula at the end of the month. He was supported by shortstop Andres Thomas, outfielder Mike Yastrzemski (Carl Yastrzemski's son), and Brian Aviles. The Bulls coasted to a six-game win over Kinston and Winston-Salem; Peninsula dropped to fourth in the final days.

Kinston had the league's most spectacular player. Burly first baseman Cecil Fielder hit 13 home runs in his first 26 games, a start that threatened every record on the books. Fielder couldn't maintain that pace, of course, but he did hit 19 home runs and drive in 49 runs in half a season before being promoted to AA Knoxville. In the early 1990s, Fielder became one of the most feared home-run hitters in the major leagues while playing for the Detroit Tigers.

Fielder wasn't the only significant

Cecil Fielder
Courtesy of Kinston Indians

midseason loss. Lynchburg lost standout pitchers Myers and Aguilera. They missed neither, however. After winning their last eight first-half contests, the Mets surged to a 14–2 start in the second half. By the end of July, they were 29–9 and on their way to an easy second-half pennant. At one point, Lynchburg was 38–11 before coasting to a 10-game margin over Salem. League batting leader Magadan broke his wrist on August 9 and missed the remainder of the season.

The Southern Division race was much more intriguing. What was perhaps the most interesting game of the year took place on July 11 in Durham. Otis Green, Kevin Sliwinski, Kash Beauchamp, and Rico Sutton hit consecutive solo homers for visiting Kinston in the top of the first inning against Bulls pitcher Aviles. Incredibly, Aviles settled down and allowed no more runs. The Bulls came back to win 5–4, although the gutty Aviles was not involved in the decision.

Kinston held onto first place for much of the second half despite the loss of Fielder. Beauchamp, the son of former major leaguer Jim Beauchamp, took up some of the slack, while Guillermo Valenzuela (11–4) and Luis Aquino (20 saves) anchored a solid pitching staff.

Peninsula, led by first baseman Randy Day (.265, 29, 103), third baseman Keith Miller (.323), Daryl Menard (11–5), and Wayne Stewart (9–3), won 14 of its final 18 games, 26 of its final 36. When the dust settled, it had left Kinston five games in the rear.

Lynchburg, the winner of both half-seasons in the Northern Division, sat and waited while Durham and Peninsula fought it out for the Southern Division title in the first round of the playoffs. Durham won game one 6–2 at Hampton's War Memorial Stadium behind pitcher Aviles and Mike Knox's four hits. Durham won the second game 8–6 as Peninsula self-destructed; the Pilots led 4–2 after six innings, but two costly errors helped the Bulls to a six-run seventh inning and the series sweep. The Bulls advanced to the championship round against Lynchburg.

The Mets won the opener 4–1 behind a Mitch Cook four-hitter. The Bulls evened the series in a dramatic second game. The contest was tied at five after nine innings. Each team scored single runs in the 14th and 16th. An RBI single by Tony Neuendorff with two outs in the bottom of the 17th finally gave Durham an 8–7 victory. Lynchburg turned the tables in game three. The contest was tied 4–4 after eight innings. The Bulls scored a pair of runs in the top of the ninth on a pinch-hit double by Dave Griffin to take a 6–4 lead. The Mets came back with three runs in the bottom of the ninth for a 7–6 win; a two-out single by Joe Redfield scored the last two runs. As exciting as the second and third games were, they paled alongside the fourth. Durham pitcher Todd Lamb, a former standout at nearby Duke University, took a no-hitter into the ninth inning of a scoreless game. A one-out double by star catcher Barry Lyons ruined the no-hitter, then a check-swing single by Jason Felice scored the game's only run and

The Revival of the Minors

The Carolina League underwent a dramatic revival during the 1980s. It was hardly alone. During that decade, the minor leagues reversed a 30-year decline to begin a period of resurgence that continues to this day.

The reasons for the revival are not entirely clear. Certainly, it was part of a general resurgence in interest in baseball. Aging baby boomers rediscovered the subtle joys of baseball during the 1980s, with the major leagues setting attendance records throughout the decade.

Yet paradoxically, the minor leagues also benefited from a reaction against major league ball. Many fans became increasingly disgruntled with high player salaries, greedy owners, pampered players, drug use, labor disputes, artificial turf, sterile stadiums, and high ticket prices. By contrast, the minors seemed to recall a simpler era. They offered well-scrubbed young players, compact, friendly ballparks, affordable ticket prices, and a touch of local color. The players didn't charge for autographs, and many actually spoke to their fans. All of a sudden, America fell back in love with minor league baseball. Sportswriter Steve Wulf observed in a 1990 *Sports Illustrated* article that the minors offered "good, clean, relatively inexpensive food and fun for the whole family. They are giving towns a sense of civic pride and providing them with their own piece of Americana." Articles praising the minor leagues appeared not just in the sporting press, but in such mainstream periodicals as *National Geographic* and *Time*, the latter hailing the "Bonanza in the Bushes."

Minor league baseball used sophisticated means to market nostalgia for a simpler age. To be sure, the minor leagues had always been more promotion-minded than the major leagues. The early days of the Carolina League featured touring baseball clown Al Schaact, cow-milking contests, and automobile giveaways. The league even sponsored a beauty contest in its early days. Yet the 1980s owners were more entrepreneurial than their earlier counterparts, many of whom viewed ownership as more of a civic duty than an avenue for profit. Clubs increasingly devoted more attention to marketing, promoting, and advertising. Long gone were the days when teams could put up a sign reading "Game Today" and expect people to show up.

The popularity of the 1988 movie *Bull Durham* created a run on Bulls merchandise and helped establish a market for other minor league clubs. By the end of the 1980s, Carolina League clubs were selling T-shirts, caps, jackets, souvenir drinking cups, and other merchandise, all of which displayed team logos and provided mobile advertising.

The growth of cable television gave the minors new broadcast opportunities. After years of resistance, the league finally decided it was better to join the television age than fight it. By the end of the decade, five of the eight league teams were broadcasting games, led by Lynchburg's 21 contests. Lynchburg publicity directory Shawn Holliday claimed that television was "like a two-hour commercial for us." This attitude was in marked contrast to that of earlier Carolina League executives, who decried television as a drain on the gate, and something to be avoided at all costs.

The success of these new promotional endeavors is evident. In 1979, the Carolina League drew 282,000 paying customers. A decade later, it drew in excess of a million.

clinched the title for Lynchburg. The Mets became the first Carolina League team since the 1950–51 Winston-Salem Cards to win back-to-back titles.

A couple of bizarre episodes made news away from the field.

In a special meeting on August 4, the league fined the Winston-Salem ownership $1,000 for "unprofessional" conduct in attempting to break Winston-Salem's longtime PDC with the Boston Red Sox. There was even some talk of formally revoking Winston-Salem's franchise, but nothing came of it.

Just as peculiar was an attempted midseason managerial change by Baltimore. The Orioles tried to switch Hagerstown manager John Hart with Charlotte manager Grady Little. The latter reported for only a few days, however, and Hagerstown replaced him with Len Johnston. Perhaps Little didn't want to deal with pitcher Rich Rice, who let everyone know that he always ate frog legs before pitching because "it makes my fastball jump."

Winston-Salem benefited from the return of injured 1983 prospects Mike Greenwell (.306, 16, 84) and Sam Horn (.313, 21, 89). A poor pitching staff doomed Winston-Salem's last Boston affiliate, although Steve Ellsworth (13–8) and Dana Kiecker did advance to the majors.

Hagerstown would have been more successful had it enjoyed the services of Ken Gerhart (.321 in 47 games), Jim Traber (.358 in 48 games), and John Habyan (9–4 in 13 games) for more than half a season. Cal Ripken's younger brother, Billy, batted only .230 but impressed with his fielding skills at second base.

Prince William had the league's best second baseman in Leon "Bip" Roberts (.301, 50 stolen bases), a future big-league All-Star. Dave Johnson (7–5, 1.32) started the season at Prince William but was promoted to the Eastern League at midseason. Former Cleveland Indians sensation Joe Charbonneau (.289, 8, 52) attempted a comeback for the Pirates but fell prey to a career-ending ankle injury.

Salem's best players were speedy outfielder George Crum (.268, 61 stolen bases) and Tim Henry (9–2, 3.47).

League attendance for 1984 was an impressive 681,000. Prince William hosted 8,879 on June 21 for a game against Lynchburg. On June 2, the Bulls had a crowd estimated in excess of 7,000. However, the tradition-minded Miles Wolff intentionally reported it as 6,225 so as to not threaten the existing Bulls record of 6,237, set on September 2, 1946.

The only problem area was Peninsula, which drew only 27,000 for the season. In December, Joe Buzas sold the franchise to Gil Granger, and the Hampton–Newport News Stadium Authority promised to improve aging War Memorial Stadium.

Both Fayetteville and Frederick, Maryland, made overtures about joining the league.

1984 Northern Division First-Half Final Standings

Lynchburg   43–27 playoff winner
Prince William   42–28
Hagerstown   32–38
Salem   28–42

Southern Division First-Half Final Standings

Durham   39–31
Kinston   33–37
Winston-Salem 33–37
Peninsula   30–40

Northern Division Second-Half Final Standings

Lynchburg   46–22
Salem   36–32
Prince William   33–37
Hagerstown   28–42

Southern Division Second-Half Final Standings

Peninsula   43–27
Kinston   38–32
Durham   29–41
Winston-Salem 25–45

—◆—

All eyes were focused on the Lynchburg Mets as the 1985 season began. If the Mets could win again, they would become the first team in league history to capture three straight titles. Keying the Mets' efforts was outfielder Shawn Abner, the first pick in the 1984 free-agent draft. Abner was considered a "can't miss" prospect. He ended the season with a .332 average, 16 homers, 89 RBIs, 30 doubles, 11 triples, and he led the league in total chances—in other words, he lived up to his billing.

Abner spent the entire season in Lynchburg. The Mets weren't be so lucky with several other prospects. Shortstop Kevin Elster (.295) and pitcher Kyle Hartshorn (17–4, 1.69) were almost as highly regarded as Abner; both were promoted before the end of the season. The Mets also lost reliever Tom Burns (2–0, 1.04, 10 saves) and Keith Miller (.302, 7, 54) at midseason. Nonetheless, Jeff Innis (2.34, 14 saves), Mike Weston (2.15, 10 saves), Jose Bautista

On the Way Down

For some players, the Carolina League is a steppingstone on the way to stardom. On rare occasions, however, it's a step on the way down. In 1980, Joe Charbonneau was voted Rookie of the Year in the American League. But the Cleveland outfielder was more than just a talented young prospect. He was a genuine personality. Charbonneau gained a measure of fame for drinking beer through his nose with a straw, after opening the bottle with an eye socket. He also dyed his hair red, white, and blue for the Fourth of July. He also scraped off a tattoo with a razor blade.

For win-starved Indians fans, Charbonneau was the reincarnation of late-1950s slugging star Rocky Colavito. For other fans, he was a breath of fresh air in an increasingly bland big-league environment.

Charbonneau's stay at the top was a short one. He hurt his back in spring training in 1981 and never recovered. He was demoted to the minors, underwent back surgery, and had a rash of bat-throwing temper tantrums. Fans turned on Charbonneau with a vengeance, and the frustrated Indians released him following the 1983 season. The Pittsburgh Pirates then signed Charbonneau and sent him to the Carolina League for a last chance. Charbonneau spent 1984 in Prince William County. He batted .289 and was on his best behavior. For much of the season, it seemed that Charbonneau was on his way back to the top. Yet a late-season ankle injury torpedoed his comeback and ended his big-league hopes.

Several years after the end of his once-promising career, a disappointed Charbonneau told *Sports Illustrated* that "baseball is full of peaks and valleys. When you're hurt, it's even valleyer."

(15–8, 2.34), Reggie Dobie (12–5, 2.63), and Dave Wyatt (8–1, 1.42) helped them compile an extraordinary team ERA of 2.42, along with a total of 18 shutouts.

It became obvious early in the season that there was a significant talent disparity between the league's Northern and Southern divisions. For much of the first half, every team in the Northern Division had a winning record and every team in the Southern Division had a losing mark.

Despite the strength of its competition, Lynchburg was more than up to the challenge. It finished April with a 13–6 record. Prince William and Hagerstown gave chase. Prince William faded, but Hagerstown and Salem continued to play well enough to win a pennant against ordinary competition.

Hagerstown was led by first

Shawn Abner
Courtesy of
Lynchburg Baseball Corp.

baseman Chris Padgett, shortstop D. L. Smith, and pitchers Eric Bell (11–6), Bill Lavelle, and Ricky Steirer.

Salem's standout players included second baseman Jerry Browne, third baseman Al Farmer (.300), Rick Knapp (13–7), and relief ace Paul Kilgus (3–1, 2.03, 10 saves). Future major league relief ace Mitch Williams (6–9, 5.45) showed how he achieved the nickname "Wild Thing"—he walked 117 batters in 99 innings while striking out 138. On May 25, Salem beat Durham 17–1 as Eli Ben hit two home runs in a nine-run eighth inning.

Despite their considerable talent, neither Hagerstown nor Salem could stay close to the powerhouse Mets. By the end of May, Lynchburg spurted to a 35–16 mark and led Hagerstown by six games and Salem by eight. Abner was especially impressive, hitting for average and power, running well, and fielding superbly. Lynchburg ended the first half with a 6½-game margin over Hagerstown. The highlight of Lynchburg's first half was a doubleheader at Prince William on May 26. In the first game, Jose Bautista threw a 6–0 no-hitter for the Mets. A bench-clearing brawl in the seventh inning of the second game resulted in four ejections. Prince William failed to score in either game.

The four Southern Division teams all struggled in the first half. On April 30, Peninsula was in first place despite a 10–10 record. Two weeks later, Peninsula (15–16) and Winston-Salem (14–15) led the division.

Gradually, Winston-Salem opened up a lead. The Spirits were in the first year of a PDC with the Chicago Cubs, after the previous year's break with Boston. Winston-Salem had an outstanding outfield prospect in Dave Martinez (.342, 38 stolen bases), a promising catcher in Damon Berryhill, and a solid pitching staff. Twenty-year-old southpaw Carl Hamilton (11–10, 2.72) pitched three shutouts in May and finished the month with a 6–0 record and an 0.41 earned-run average. Drew Hall (10–7) and Jamie Moyer (8–2, 2.30) also pitched well. Designated hitter J. D. Dickerson—a powerful five-foot-nine 175-pounder whose compact physique evoked comparisons with former major league player Jim Wynn—had 20 home runs by the end of June. He ended the season with 28 homers and 82 runs batted in.

Still, Winston-Salem was far from a powerhouse. In early June, it lost a doubleheader to Prince William to drop to 26–27, which nonetheless left it in first place in the weak Southern Division. Winston-Salem recovered to win five of its next six. It finished the first half with a mediocre 35–35 record but a three-game margin over second-place Durham; the Bulls again had Carl Yastrzemski's son Mike (.270, 11, 63).

There were several key roster moves around the league at midseason. Prince William lost relief ace Barry Jones (3–2, 1.21, 10 saves). Winston-Salem's Jamie Moyer was promoted around the same time, while Lynchburg lost a host of players. There were several key additions, including Hagerstown's acquisition of pitcher Bob Milacki from the Florida State League. Winston-Salem added David Masters, a six-foot-nine pitcher from the University of California at Berkeley, possibly the tallest player in Carolina League history.

The most highly publicized midseason addition was Prince William outfielder Barry Bonds (.299, 13, 37), the sixth pick in the 1985 draft. The son of former major league All-Star Bobby Bonds, Barry had been an All-American at Arizona State University. Late in July, Bonds was joined by first baseman–third baseman Bobby Bonilla (.262, 3, 11), an undrafted free agent who had played for Alexandria in 1983 and was slowly working his way up the Pirates' farm chain; Bonilla had been on the disabled list until mid-July. They joined defensive whiz Jose Lind, a shortstop who, with Bonds and Bonilla, went on to become part of Pittsburgh's championship teams in the late 1980s and early 1990s. Bonds and Bonilla became two of the game's most-publicized and best-paid major leaguers.

Yet even they couldn't carry Prince William to a second-half pennant. Lynchburg jumped on top again, with seven wins in its first 10 starts. Bonds sparked an eight-game Prince William winning streak in late July, but the Pirates dropped back in early August. Lynchburg used an 8–1 spurt around the same time to open up a gap on the rest of the Northern Division. The Mets finished with a commanding 13½-game gap over Salem. Prince William slumped to third.

The Southern Division improved its caliber of ball in the second half. Kinston and Peninsula were the main contenders. Each took its turn in first place during July and early August. On August 3, Kinston captured a pair of one-run decisions from Prince William to go into first place. Peninsula surged back on top and led by 2½ games on August 13. Pitchers Todd Frohwirth (7–5, 2.20, 18 saves) and Shawn Barton (12–4, 2.30) keyed its move to the top.

In the end, Kinston's speed was the deciding factor. The Blue Jays ended the

Barry Bonds
Courtesy of Baseball America

season with a league-leading 221 stolen bases. Eric Yelding (.260, 62 stolen bases), Glenallen Hill (.210, 20, 56, 42 stolen bases), and Nelson Liriano (.288, 25 stolen bases)—all future major leaguers—led the stolen-base onslaught. First baseman Pat Borders and third baseman Omar Malave (.288) concentrated on driving in the speedsters, while Omar Bencomo (10–8) paced the pitching staff. Hill's production came despite his striking out a league-record 211 times.

Kinston won 11 of its final 16 games, while

Peninsula lost eight of its last 15. Kinston clinched the second-half title on August 28 with a 4–0 win over Hagerstown, its ninth straight victory and third straight shutout.

Winston-Salem was never a factor in the Southern Division second half. In fact, it finished in the cellar with a dismal record of 23–46. *Winston-Salem Journal* columnist Dan Collins observed that the Spirits had been "lost in the ozone these past two months." They did prepare for the playoffs with the late-season acquisition of several new players, including first baseman Mark McMorris, who had batted .380 for Wytheville in the rookie Appalachian League.

Nonetheless, Winston-Salem appeared to be overmatched against Kinston. Yet the Spirits were destined for big things that September. Superb pitching gave them a two-game sweep over Kinston. Carl Hamilton won the opener 5–1, while Drew Hall won the second game 4–2.

The finals between Lynchburg and Winston-Salem were an even more apparent mismatch. Lynchburg had a regular-season record of 95–45, while the Spirits' record was 58–81. If the league had not had a split season, and if the two teams had been in the same division, Lynchburg would have finished 36½ games ahead of Winston-Salem. Lynchburg had won six consecutive Northern Division half-season titles and had been featured in such national publications as the *New York Times* and *USA Today*.

Yet the Spirits pulled off the biggest upset in league playoff history. Winston-Salem won the first game 4–2 at Lynchburg. Relief ace Dave Lenderman (3–4, 2.44, 15 saves), who had saved both wins against Kinston, salvaged the game for his third consecutive save. The key at-bat took place in the eighth inning when Abner came to the plate with two men on and one out. The league Player of the Year fouled off three 3–2 pitches before grounding out. Lenderman got out of the jam and preserved the win.

Winston-Salem won on the road again in game two, this time by a 7–3 score. A four-run Winston-Salem sixth inning overcame a 3–1 Lynchburg advantage. Jim Phillips pitched four perfect innings in relief while Lenderman rested. A modest crowd of 625 sat in stunned disbelief in Lynchburg's City Stadium as the Mets fell behind two games to none.

The wounded Mets rebounded to win the third game in Winston-Salem, pounding out a dozen hits in a 9–2 win. First baseman Andy Lawrence drove in three runs, while Abner went two for five.

The reprieve was short-lived. Winston-Salem closed out an improbable title with a 7–4 victory in game four. Andy Lawrence staked Lynchburg to a 2–1 lead with a third-inning single before the Mets fell apart. A routine ground ball got under shortstop Frank Moscat's glove in the third, leading to two unearned runs. A pair of wild pitches by Tom Eden led to two Winston-Salem runs in the fourth. Carl Hamilton carried a 7–3 lead through $6^{2/3}$ innings, at which time the reliable Lenderman came in to protect the victory and the title.

Many observers cited Lynchburg's overconfidence as a major contributing factor in its defeat. Mets manager Mike Cubbage was complimentary toward his team's opponent: "They just outplayed us in every phase of the game. They got the big hits, made the plays, made the pitches they had to make, and Cal [Emery] outmanaged me." Dave Martinez went five for twelve in the series, while the Winston-Salem bullpen was virtually perfect.

1985 Northern Division First-Half Final Standings

Lynchburg	48–22
Hagerstown	41–28
Salem	40–30
Prince William	32–37

Southern Division First-Half Final Standings

*Winston-Salem	35–35	playoff winner
Durham	32–38	
Peninsula	28–42	
Kinston	23–47	

Northern Division Second-Half Final Standings

Lynchburg	47–23
Salem	32–35
Prince William	33–37
Hagerstown	24–44

Southern Division Second-Half Final Standings

Kinston	41–26
Peninsula	39–26
Durham	34–36
Winston-Salem	23–46

—◆—

The league had no franchise changes during the off-season, but not for any shortage of discussion. Salem asked for league approval to move to Charleston, West Virginia, but was turned down. In December 1985, the Salem franchise was sold to Kelvin Bowles, a Rocky Mount, Virginia, businessman and local cable operator. Kinston was given permission to relocate to Wilson, Burlington, or Colonial Heights, Virginia, if it would prove helpful in acquiring a PDC.

Kinston eventually stayed put but operated as a co-op in 1986.

In the summer 1986 meeting, the league voted to expand to 10 teams if PDCs could be secured. Wilson, Colonial Heights, Charleston, Fayetteville, and southern Maryland were all possibilities for expansion—further evidence of the increased popularity of minor league baseball. The question of expansion to 10 teams was to come up periodically over the next few years, but the absence of PDCs and/or useable ballparks always derailed the idea.

The Kinston Eagles had the most interesting games in the early part of the 1986 season. On April 28, they beat Prince William 10–9 in 17 innings. Three days later, they lost to Salem 13–12, almost overcoming a 9–2 deficit. That game featured a bench-clearing brawl in the top of the seventh when Salem's Jose Vargas took exception to a pair of inside pitches.

Hagerstown and Winston-Salem may have had less excitement than Kinston, but they more than compensated with solid teams that won their respective first-half titles comfortably. Hagerstown's win in the Northern Division ended Lynchburg's streak of six consecutive half-season titles. Lynchburg again had the league's top prospect, highly touted shortstop Gregg Jefferies, but lacked the balance of the Suns, whose lineup included second baseman Pete Stanicek (.317, 77 stolen bases, 115 runs), third baseman Craig Worthington (.300, 15, 102), outfielders Sherwin Cijntje (.303), Scott Khoury, Dan Norman (77 RBIs), and Norm Roberts (.305), Geraldo Sanchez (13–6), Chester Stanhope (14–3), Greg Talamantez (12–6), and highly touted former Stanford All-American Jeff Ballard.

Hagerstown jumped ahead of Lynchburg early. At the end of April, it was 13–6 and led the Mets by three games. By the second week in May, Hagerstown was 22–8 and the only team in the division with a winning record. Lynchburg made a late run to close the final first-half margin to a deceptively close three games.

The two clubs did produce some fireworks. On June 7, Lynchburg manager Bobby Floyd and Hagerstown manager Bob Molinaro came to blows when Lynchburg bunted with a 7–0 lead. Lynchburg took the position that Hagerstown had been doing such things regularly. Two days later, Hagerstown's Dave Falcone hit a pair of grand slams and drove in a league-record 11 runs in a 21–3 win over Salem.

The Peninsula White Sox looked like the Southern Division winner for much of the first half. Peninsula, in the first year of a PDC with the Chicago White Sox, jumped to a 14–7 start and led Winston-Salem through the third week in May before falling behind the Spirits. Winston-Salem won 24 of its final 34 first-half games to pull away from Peninsula and win by five games. Winston-Salem's run to the title was sparked by outfielder Doug Dascenzo, catcher Hector Villanueva, and pitchers Dave Pavlas and Les Lancaster. Future Chicago Cubs skipper Jim Essian managed the Spirits.

The league had its usual additions and departures at midseason. Prince William added University of Arkansas All-American Jeff King, the first selection of the free-agent draft. Atlanta promoted Dave Justice and Jeff Wetherby from Sumter to Durham late in the first half. Former University of North Carolina catcher Matt Merullo was signed by the Chicago White Sox and assigned to Peninsula. The most significant roster deletions were suffered by Hagerstown, which lost Ballard (9–5, 1.85) to AA Charlotte, and Winston-Salem, which lost Lancaster (8–3, 2.78) to AA Pittsfield.

Despite the loss of pitching aces Ballard and Lancaster, Hagerstown and Winston-Salem were able to repeat their pennant-winning performances.

Hagerstown led virtually the entire way again. A 10–2 Lynchburg streak enabled the Mets to briefly tie Hagerstown at 15–8 on July 12. However, the Mets lost first baseman Ron Gideon for three weeks with an ankle injury and fell off Hagerstown's hot pace. The Suns were slowed down only by a family of skunks, which established a home underneath the left-field bleachers at Municipal Stadium and almost caused cancellation of an August 12 game before being removed. Skunks notwithstanding, Hagerstown pulled away to an 8½-game win over Lynchburg.

Winston-Salem's road to a repeat title was much rockier. Peninsula again jumped to an early lead before losing 11 of 13 to drop out of the race for good. It was replaced at the top by the Durham Bulls. The Bulls had never been a factor in the first half but were revitalized by the addition of Justice and Wetherby and the resurgence of second baseman Ronnie Gant, who batted only .237 in the first half before exploding in the second. Gant and Justice went on to become two of the National League's most feared sluggers for Atlanta in the 1990s, Gant after a move to the outfield.

Durham finished July with a 1½-game lead over Winston-Salem. The Spirits overtook Durham in early August and opened up a 4½-game margin. The Bulls fought back. On August 25, they swept Salem, while Prince William beat Winston-Salem 1–0 to reduce the Spirits' lead to 1½. Two more losses to Prince William left Durham and Winston-Salem in a virtual tie entering a season-ending four-game series at Winston-Salem's Ernie Shore Field.

Because of two Winston-Salem rainouts, it was necessary for the Bulls to capture three of the four games to secure the title. The Bulls won the opener 10–3, scoring six runs in the eighth inning; Jeff Blauser, Justice, and Gant all homered for the victors. Wetherby and Gant combined for five hits to lead the Bulls to a game-two victory, Durham's 14th win in 16 games. The Bulls led by two and could clinch the second-half title with a win in either of the last two games.

The third game of the series went into extra innings. In the top of the 11th, Gant singled in a run to give the Bulls a 6–5 lead. He then went quickly from hero to goat in the bottom of the inning, committing back-to-back errors—

Ron Gant
Courtesy of BaseballAmerica

both on ground balls—to put runners on second and third. Villanueva singled in both runners off Durham relief ace Maximo Del Rosario to give the Spirits a 7–6 win.

The deciding fourth game was also a nail-biter. A bloop RBI double by Derrick Hardamon in the seventh broke a 4–4 tie and led to a 6–4 Winston-Salem victory. Spirits manager Essian described Hardamon's blast as a "well-placed finesse shot." Winston-Salem ended the second half with a .574 winning percentage, .003 ahead of Durham.

The finals matched Hagerstown, with a 91–48 regular-season record, and Winston-Salem, with an 82–56 record. The favored Suns won the first game 6–5 after trailing 3–1. A three-run homer in the sixth by Scott Khoury gave the Suns a 6–3 lead. Winston-Salem scored two runs in the bottom of the ninth, but Hagerstown relief ace Bill Lavelle put out the fire with baserunners on first and second. Only 183 fans paid to see the game on a cool, damp night.

The next two games were equally riveting.

Winston-Salem won the second game of the series 5–4 in 12 innings when Tom DiCeglio's line drive off the wall drove in the winning run. However, the big hit for the Spirits was J. D. Dickerson's two-run homer in the four-run seventh; hampered by arm trouble, Dickerson had suffered through a poor season. Laddy Renfroe pitched $2^{1/3}$ scoreless innings in relief.

Winston-Salem won game three 5–3 in 17 innings, scoring three times in the top of the inning. Dascenzo went six for eight and scored the go-ahead run in the top of the 17th when Khoury slipped chasing a Brian Williams single. Renfroe pitched seven scoreless innings in relief before giving up a solitary run in the bottom of the 17th.

Winston-Salem closed out the series with a 7–0 win in game four. Former University of North Carolina hurler Roger Williams pitched a one-hitter, allowing only a seventh-inning double by former big leaguer Ken Smith. Winston-Salem broke it open early with a five-run third inning. Dascenzo drove in two runs and ended the four-game series with 11 hits.

Dascenzo's playoff heroics mirrored a superb regular season. The switch-hitting outfielder batted .327, drove in 83 runs, stole 57 bases, and scored 107 runs. Villanueva (.318, 13, 100), second baseman Bryan House (65 stolen bases), and shortstop Julius McDougal supported Dascenzo. Dave Pavlas (14–6), Jeff Pico (12–8), Roger Williams (12–7), and Laddy Renfroe (21 saves) supplied the pitching.

Hagerstown's unexpected postseason loss took some of the luster off a campaign in which it compiled the best overall record in the league and batted a league-leading .290.

Lynchburg's Jefferies (.354, 11, 80, 43 stolen bases) gave the Mets their fourth consecutive Player of the Year despite the fact that he spent the first month of the season with Columbia of the South Atlantic League. Outfielder Marcus Lawton (56 stolen bases), first baseman Ron Gideon (77 RBIs), and third baseman Zoilio Sanchez (.296, 14, 85) helped give the Mets a potent offense. Mediocre pitching held them back.

Prince William's Jeff King (.235, 6, 20) struggled in his abbreviated rookie season in the pros. Shortstop Felix Fermin (40 stolen bases), first baseman Lance Velen (.293, 18, 88), outfielder Jeff Cook (.301), Jose Melendez (13–10), Chris Ritter (14–9), Rob Russell (13–5), and John Smiley (14 saves) had more success. Smiley eventually moved out of the bullpen to become a standout major league starter.

Salem had a dismal club that finished a distant last. Nonetheless, outfielder–first baseman Kevin Reimer (76 RBIs) and catcher Chad Kreuter later advanced to the majors.

Durham's pennant hopes were undermined by a 4.80 team earned-run average. Gant (.277, 26, 102, 35 stolen bases) showed the combination of speed and power that later made him a star in Atlanta. Shortstop Jeff Blauser (.286, 13, 52), Justice (.279, 12, 44), and Jeff Wetherby (.299) also exhibited the skills that would take them to the majors. Third baseman Mike Nipper batted .379 in 52 games.

Peninsula was led by catcher Matt Merullo (.303) and outfielders Ron Scheer and Darrell Pruitt (.299, 36 stolen bases).

The co-op Kinston Eagles benefited from the presence of Pat Borders (.328) for 49 games before he ended his season in Knoxville. Designated hitter Gino Gentile (.267, 25, 85) had previously played as high as AAA Pawtucket. Marty Reed (16–6) was the top Kinston hurler.

1986 Northern Division First-Half Final Standings

Hagerstown	46–24
Lynchburg	38–22
Prince William	32–38
Salem	20–49

Southern Division First-Half Final Standings

*Winston-Salem	43–27	playoff winner
Peninsula	38–32	
Durham	32–38	
Kinston	30–39	

Northern Division Second-Half Final Standings

Hagerstown	45–24
Lynchburg	37–33
Prince William	35–34
Salem	25–44

Southern Division Second-Half Final Standings

Winston-Salem	39–29
Durham	40–30
Kinston	30–37
Peninsula	22–42

—♦—

The Kinston franchise came close to moving to Waldorf, Maryland, during the 1986–87 off-season, but the plan fell through when the southern Maryland community's city council voted against placing a stadium referendum on the local ballot. Danville again expressed interest in rejoining the league, but in the absence of a useable stadium, the town attracted little interest from league officials.

The four 1987 pennant races were all one-sided. In the first half, Hagerstown and Winston-Salem repeated their 1986 triumphs, thus running their streaks to three consecutive half-season titles. Of course, both accomplished this feat with rosters largely revamped from the previous season.

Hagerstown was led by .300 hitters Leo Gomez (110 RBIs), Terry Crowley, and Tim Richardson and pitchers Blaine Beatty (11–1) and Bob Walton (8–2). It finished April tied for first with Salem at 13–8 and took over the lead for good in early May. Gomez, a hard-hitting Puerto Rican third baseman, was the mainstay of the balanced Suns attack, while the left-handed Beatty established himself as the league's top hurler.

The biggest shocker in the Northern Division was the inept performance of the Lynchburg Mets. Much of the team had played the previous season for

South Atlantic League champ Columbia, and Lynchburg officials expected a return to pennant contention at the very least. Yet the Mets lost 15 of their first 19 games. At the end of April, they had a team earned-run average of 6.03 and a batting average of .227 and were committing an average of two errors per game. Promising outfielder Angelo Cuevas broke his foot, and manager John Tamargo lost his temper in several locker-room explosions.

Tamargo's tactics may have worked, at least for a time. The Mets got Ron Gideon from AA Jackson to replace Cuevas and fought back to .500 before fading to last place.

Hagerstown ended the first half with a 6½-game margin over Salem. The Suns were the only Northern Division team with a winning record.

Although never in contention in the first half, Prince William, now affiliated with the New York Yankees, had two of the league's most publicized players. Third baseman Hensley Meulens was a native of Curaçao, Netherlands Antilles, and a slugger of such talent that he was nicknamed "Bam-Bam." One of his teammates was Mickey Tresh, whose father, Tom, and grandfather Mike had both been major league standouts. Mickey was attempting to make the Treshes major league baseball's first three-generation family. He eventually fell short of his goal.

Also attracting a brief flurry of attention was Dwight Gooden, who drew over 5,000 in a solitary appearance for Lynchburg during a short-lived rehabilitation. Major league vet Marty Bystrom made a brief rehab appearance for Prince William, as did Tippy Martinez for Hagerstown.

Like Hagerstown in the Northern Division, Winston-Salem led its division virtually the entire first half. The Spirits were led by catcher Joe Girardi, outfielder Cedric Landrum (79 stolen bases), relief pitcher Jeff Hirsch (3–1, 1.50, 16 saves), and starting pitchers Bill Kazmierczak (9–5) and Bill Danek (10–3). The latter won his first five starts before losing to the Bulls on May 9.

Winston-Salem's run to the pennant was aided by a series of injuries that devastated the Durham Bulls. The most serious ended the season for Kent Mercker, a first-round draft pick and the league's most highly regarded pitching prospect. Mercker suffered a partial tear of his left ulnar collateral ligament in his third start and underwent surgery on April 28. Elbow surgery also sidelined Rick Siebert, another well-thought-of pitching prospect, while Eddie Matthews (4–1, 1.94) was promoted to Greenville early in the season.

Winston-Salem completed the first half with a 41–29 record and a seven-game margin over Peninsula.

Hensley Meulens
Courtesy of Prince William Cannons

It was the only team in its division with a winning record, meaning that six of the league's eight clubs posted losing marks during the season's first half.

Any thoughts Hagerstown and Winston-Salem had about establishing a Lynchburg-style mini-dynasty were short-lived. Hagerstown lost Beatty to AA, while Winston-Salem lost both Danek and Hirsch. Kinston lost speedy second baseman Tommy Hinzo (49 stolen bases) to Williamsport. Later in the season, Hinzo was promoted to Cleveland, making him one of the few players, excluding injury rehabs, to go from the Carolina League to the majors in a single season. Lynchburg lost Cuevas, who had recovered from his injury well enough to bat .349, to AAA Tidewater.

The second-half pennant races belonged to a pair of clubs undergoing revitalization. The Salem Buccaneers were affiliated with the Pittsburgh Pirates for the first time since 1980, renewing a relationship that had sent such standouts as Dave Parker, John Candeleria, Ozzie Olivares, Kent Tekulve, and Miguel Dilone through Salem on their way to the majors. After a 6–6 second-half start, the Bucs exploded. On July 18, they were 17–10 and owned a four-game lead over Lynchburg. At the end of the month, they were 28–12 and the only team in the division with a winning record.

Salem had a number of highly regarded prospects. Jeff King's 1986 Carolina League debut at Prince William had been less than scintillating. The Pirates decided to keep him in the Carolina League, this time with their new farm team at Salem. King showed considerable improvement, hitting .277 and collecting 26 homers and 71 RBIs before being promoted to Harrisburg late in the season. Outfielders Tony Chance (.318, 23, 96, 26 stolen bases) and John Rigos (.287, 31 stolen bases) also provided home-run punch, while midseason acquisition Jeff Cook (.339, 39 stolen bases) and second baseman Steve Moser (.297, 31 stolen bases) set the table. Mike Walker (12–5) started the season at AA, but after losing his first two decisions, he was sent down to Salem, where he became the ace of the staff. The Bucs were managed by Steve Demeter, a longtime minor league presence and a former Carolina League player. Salem ended the second half with a 47–23 record, which placed it 14 games ahead of 33–37 Prince William.

Prince William's Meulens was promoted to Fort Lauderdale late in the season, but not before having a three-homer game against Winston-Salem in late July. He ended his Carolina League campaign with a .300 average, 28 home runs, and 103 RBIs.

Meulens's three-homer explosion wasn't the only indignity suffered by the Southern Division's first-half champ. Minus Danek and Hirsch, Winston-Salem finished in the cellar in the second half.

Meanwhile, the Kinston Indians dominated. Kinston was in the first season of a PDC with the Cleveland Indians. This proved a profitable relationship for

Kinston despite the fact that Cleveland had long been something of a major league joke. To Kinston's benefit, Cleveland's last-place finishes and habitually small crowds left it no way to acquire talent other than its minor league system. Third baseman–designated hitter Casey Webster (.318, 20, 111), first baseman Milt Harper (.312, 20, 97), outfielders Kerry Richardson (87 RBIs) and Scott Jordan, and pitcher Andy Ghelfi (12–6) led Kinston. Manager Mike Hargrove, a former major leaguer, was also considered a comer.

Webster, the league RBI leader, had his bat impounded on August 17 for drilling out the barrel end an eighth of an inch, which can increase bat speed. This incident proved to be the only roadblock in Kinston's path. The Indians jumped to a 7–2 start in the second half. Peninsula and Durham stayed close for a few weeks, but Kinston pulled away during August for an easy victory over the White Sox and Bulls. Durham added Atlanta's first-round draft pick, Derek Lilliquist, a left-handed pitcher from the University of Georgia, but it was too late to influence the race. As with the three other half-season races, only the first-place team posted a winning record. A sidelight to the end of the season was the termination of Lynchburg's PDC with the New York Mets. Early in the season, the parent Mets had announced that they were building a minor league complex in Port St. Lucie, Florida, and in the interest of efficiency would transfer their high-level Class A franchise to the Florida State League. This ended a working relationship that had produced some of the best teams in Carolina League history.

Salem and Kinston continued their hot play in the playoffs. Salem took a pair from Hagerstown to advance to the best-of-five final. Kinston swept Winston-Salem 11–6 and 10–7, the latter in 12 innings. The Spirits hurt their cause with 11 errors in their two loses, resulting in nine unearned Kinston runs. Three errors led to four Kinston runs in the top of the 12th inning of the second game.

Salem won the championship opener 6–2 behind Bill Sampen; Kinston pitcher Mike Walker struck out 10 in six innings and gave up only four hits, but all at the wrong time. Salem won the second contest 7–1 behind newly acquired pitcher Mike York, just up from the South Atlantic League. Salem finished an impressive three-game sweep with a 5–2 win.

The four clubs that failed to capture a half-season title all finished with losing records.

Durham was led by second baseman Mark Lemke (.292, 20, 68) and outfielder Alex Smith (.323).

Peninsula's top talent included Mark Davis (.294, 16, 72, 37 stolen bases), shortstop Craig Grebeck, third baseman Dan Rohrmeier (.329 in 68 games), outfielder Aubrey Waggoner (52 stolen bases), and Bryce Hulstrom (9–2, 2.88).

Mickey Tresh ended the season with a disappointing .247 average. His more successful Prince William teammates included first baseman Rob Sepanek (.306, 25, 106) and Aris Tirado (8–1, 3.09).

The Mets finished their final season in Lynchburg with the league's worst record. Ron Gideon (25 homers, 92 RBIs) and Kurt DeLuca (.340 in 58 games) were the best of their players.

1987 Northern Division First-Half Final Standings

Hagerstown	40–30
Salem	33–36
Prince William	33–37
Lynchburg	32–37

Southern Division First-Half Final Standings

Winston-Salem	41–29
Peninsula	34–36
Kinston	33–37
Durham	33–37

Northern Division Second-Half Final Standings

* Salem	47–23	playoff winner
Prince William	33–37	
Hagerstown	32–38	
Lynchburg	31–39	

Southern Division Second-Half Final Standings

Kinston	42–28
Durham	32–38
Peninsula	32–38
Winston-Salem	31–39

———◆———

With the Mets out of the Carolina League, Lynchburg signed a PDC for 1988 with the Boston Red Sox, placing that organization back in the league after an absence of three seasons. Peninsula lost its agreement with the White Sox and was forced to operate as a co-op. It renamed itself the Virginia Generals but had little more success than most co-op teams.

The Southern Division had an exciting first-half race between Kinston and

Durham. The Bulls' pitching staff was anchored by Kent Mercker, fully recovered from his arm trouble and anxious to pitch himself back into Atlanta's plans. First baseman Mike Bell (84 RBIs), outfielder Andy Tomberlin (.301), and third baseman Ken Pennington (.316) keyed Durham's batting attack, while Danny Weems (13–8), Doug Stockham (8–3, 2.52), and relief ace Jim Czajkowski (8–5, 17 saves) added strength to the pitching staff. The Bulls finished April with a 15–7 mark, leading Kinston by half a game.

Despite a mediocre start, Winston-Salem had the league's early sensation. Pitcher Bill Kazmierczak won his first three starts with a microscopic earned-run average of 0.36. One of those starts was a 1–0 seven-inning no-hitter against Salem on April 13. On May 20, he threw another no-hitter in an 11–0 win over Virginia. This made him the first—and so far the only—Carolina League hurler to throw two no-hitters in the same season.

The no-hitter against Virginia probably should have come with an asterisk. The undermanned Generals were simply awful. They were in the middle of a 15-game losing streak when Kazmierczak threw his second gem. In August, they had a 14-game losing streak. In early June, Virginia pitcher Clyde Reichard quit baseball, saying he wouldn't play for a team that didn't have a catcher who could catch the ball. The Generals responded by winning four straight.

Durham maintained its lead in the south. On May 7, it was 3½ games ahead of Winston-Salem and four ahead of Kinston. Two weeks later, it was 29–13 and led Kinston by three.

The Bulls and the Spirits developed some bad blood during the early part of the season, involving, of all people, Bulls coach and former major league catcher Joe Pignatano. In a late-May game, Pignatano exchanged words with Winston-Salem pitcher Shawn Boskie. Spirits designated hitter Butch Garcia added fuel to the fire when he told a local paper, "We don't like each other. That's the bottom line. They've got a lot of mouth on that team. Even their coaches talk too much. . . . When you're as old as he [Pignatano] is you should get out of the game. . . . He's too old." Not surprisingly, Garcia spent the rest of the series dodging fastballs.

About the same time, Kinston suspended outfielder Joey Belle, who went AWOL after announcing the game was no longer fun. Belle was leading the league in runs batted in at that juncture.

The game wasn't much fun for Salem pitcher Scott Hemon on May 31, when he took a Theron Todd line drive off his forehead. The ball hit Hemon with such force that it bounced into the dugout for a double. Hemon lay motionless on the ground for several minutes before being taken to a Durham hospital. He suffered a concussion but made a full recovery. The Bulls won the joyless game 7–5 to run their record to 33–18; Kinston and Winston-Salem continued to give chase.

Despite leading virtually the entire first half, Durham couldn't shake Kinston. In the absence of Belle (.301, 8, 39), outfielder Beau Allred and first baseman Mike Twardowski (.322, 6, 87) led the Indians' attack. Kinston's real strength was a balanced starting rotation and a sterling relief staff of Kevin Bearse (10–8, 1.31, 22 saves) and midseason acquisition Steve Olin (5–2, 8 saves).

Kinston caught Durham in mid-June. When the Bulls lost 4–3 to Hagerstown on June 15, they dropped a game behind the Indians. The two teams concluded the first half with a four-game series in Kinston. The series opened with a double-header. The Bulls won the first game 4–3 behind Mercker, but Kinston overcame a 4–1 deficit to win the nightcap 8–4 to remain a game ahead. The Bulls won the next day 7–0 behind Weems and Czajkowski to move into a tie going into last day of the first half. Again, Kinston came from behind to win. Durham led 5–1 after 4½. Kinston tied the game 5–5 on a three-run Allred homer in the sixth. Kinston scored the winning run on a double, a balk by Bulls pitcher Paul Morak, and a sacrifice fly by Ever Magallenes. Kevin Bearse threw 4²/₃ innings of scoreless relief to secure the first-half pennant.

The Northern Division race lacked the dramatics of the Southern Division race. Nonetheless, it was closely contested between Salem and Hagerstown. Prince William started off well, paced by outfielder Bernie Williams, who finished April with a .432 batting average, and slugging first baseman Kevin Maas. However, Maas, who hit 12 home runs in 29 games for Prince William, was promoted to AA early in May, and Prince William dropped back.

Considering the hardships faced by the Hagerstown pitching staff, it's surprising that the Suns didn't drop back also. Pitcher Chris Myers, Baltimore's first-round pick in the 1987 draft, was hampered by tendonitis; Anthony Telford was out with nerve damage; and Craig Lopez blew out his arm. Several other pitchers were promoted to AA, including standout reliever Greg Olson, who finished the season in Baltimore and eventually became one of the game's bullpen aces. Baltimore did send pitcher Brian Dubois (14–9) to Hagerstown to help fill out the depleted staff. On May 26 in his first start, he pitched a no-hitter against Prince William for 8²/₃ innings before giving up a single to Mitch Lyden. In his next start, Dubois gave up five runs in six innings against the usually weak-hitting Virginia Generals.

The injuries to Hagerstown gave Salem an opening. The Bucs had a balanced attack led by outfielders Wes Chamberlain and Tony Longmire, third baseman Orlando Merced (.292), infielder Kevin Burdick (.321), shortstop Tommy Shields (.314), and pitchers Mike York (9–2) and Stan Belinda (14 saves). They gradually pulled away from Hagerstown in June and ended the first half 3½ games ahead of the Suns.

Salem lost many of its better players to midseason promotions, including leading hitter Kevin Burdick. Winston-Salem lost Kazmierczak (9–2, 1.34) to

Pittsfield. Lynchburg added Boston's first-round draft pick, pitcher Tom Fischer, a nephew of Boston pitching coach and former major league pitcher Billy Fischer. Prince William added New York's fifth-round draft pick, third baseman Dan Sparks. Joey Belle ended up in Waterloo of the Midwest League, where he was suspended for disciplinary reasons. He eventually changed his first name to Albert and made the major leagues, where he has continued to confound observers with his blend of All-Star talent and erratic behavior.

The Northern Division had a great pennant race between Hagerstown and Lynchburg during the second half. Lynchburg had finished the first half with a dismal 25–45 mark. But the addition of Fischer, pitchers Dan Gabriele (10–6) and Mike Clarkin from Harrisburg, and John Abbott from Winter Haven fueled a remarkable turnaround. Those players joined holdovers David Walters (11–6), Jeff Plympton, outfielder Mickey Pina (.273, 21, 108), first baseman Jim Orsag (.324, 12, 69), third baseman Scott Cooper (.298), and outfielder Bob Zupcic (.297, 13, 97). Lynchburg won 10 of its first 13 in the second half. Later in the campaign, it had an 11–1 run. Cooper batted .362 with 23 runs batted in during the month of July. Gabriele won 10 games in a half-season.

Yet Hagerstown continued to match Lynchburg win for win. The Suns had strong hitters in first baseman Dave Bettendorf (.327), first baseman–designated hitter Craig Faulkner, and outfielder David Segui. They also had tremendous speed in second baseman Don Buford, Jr. (77 stolen bases), and outfielder Walt Harris (53 stolen bases). Buford's father and namesake was a former Baltimore Oriole, while Harris, a former Stanford football star, had played that sport professionally for the San Diego Chargers.

The race went down to the wire, with Lynchburg sweeping a three-game series from Salem to edge the Suns by one game. Hagerstown ended the season with the best combined regular-season record in the Northern Division but missed the playoffs.

Prince William's second half was an unmitigated disaster. In mid-July, Bernie Williams injured his thumb and wrist running into the wall at Hagerstown. The 19-year-old Puerto Rican star missed the rest of the season. He did, however, have enough at-bats to qualify for the league batting title, which he won at .335; Williams recovered well enough

Bernie Williams
Courtesy of Prince William Cannons

to eventually become the starting center fielder for the Yankees. Prince William also lost designated hitter Mitch Lyden, infielder Dan Roman (.311), catcher John Ramos (.304), and Art Calvert to Albany. Steve Adkins and Scott Kamieniecki tried to stay the course. On August 27, the depleted Yankees lost to Durham 21–0, giving up 14 hits and 15 bases on balls. Starter Doug Gogolewski gave up seven runs on two hits and six walks in only one inning.

Durham's chances of taking the second-half title in the Southern Division were undermined when Mercker (11–4, 2.68, 159 strikeouts in 128 innings) was promoted to AA early in the second half. So dominating had Mercker been that he continued to lead the league in strikeouts until the final two weeks of the season. An appearance by outstanding prospect Brian Hunter (.347 in 13 games) came too late to help the Bulls.

Winston-Salem was also unable to replace its midseason losses. Outfielder Derrick May (.305, 8, 65) and Shawn Boskie (12–7, 3.39) went on to make the majors in two seasons.

Kinston managed to duplicate its first-half Southern Division title despite losing some solid players to promotion. It also lost infielder Rob Swain for the season with a broken wrist. Yet it added some valuable assets, most notably relief pitcher Steve Olin, who was promoted from the Midwest League at midseason. Olin combined with Kevin Bearse to give Kinston an almost unhittable bullpen. The team won its last nine games to finish five ahead of Durham.

Kinston got a bye in the first round of the playoffs and awaited the winner of the Salem-Lynchburg series. Lynchburg won the first contest 4–3 in 10 innings, coming back from 3–0 deficit. Scott Cooper scored the winning run when he walked with two outs, went to third on a wild pitch, and scored on a second wild pitch. Salem won the next game, but Lynchburg captured the series with a 5–0 win in game three.

The Kinston-Lynchburg championship series was an outstanding matchup. Greg Michael and Bearse pitched Kinston to a 3–1 win in the opener.

Lynchburg evened the series with a riveting and controversial 4–3 win in game two. The game started as a pitching duel between the hard-throwing Gabriele and Kinston sinker-ball specialist Mark Giles. Gabriele took a no-hitter and a 1–0 lead into the bottom of the eighth. Two walks and a sacrifice bunt prompted Lynchburg manager Dick Berardino to pull Gabriele despite his no-hitter. Following an intentional walk, relief pitcher Bart Haley struck out Jim Richardson on a 3–2 count and retired Darren Epley on a hard grounder to third to end the inning. Kinston manager Glenn Adams then replaced Giles because of his high pitch count. The usually reliable Olin gave up three runs in the top of the ninth, making the score 4–0. Kinston rallied in the bottom of the inning. An out, a walk, and another out left Lynchburg only one out from a playoff no-hitter. But a bunt single by Kinston's Mark Pike quickly ruined that plan. Then

The Real Crash Davis

Crash Davis
Courtesy of Duke University Sports Information

In the mid-1980s, minor league baseball became cool. Nothing better exemplified that new image than the 1988 Orion movie *Bull Durham*, which starred Kevin Costner and Susan Sarandon. Much of the movie was filmed in the autumn of 1987 at Durham Athletic Park. It was a commercial and artistic success and was hailed by many observers as one of the best baseball movies ever made. It also made the Durham Bulls famous. They reaped a financial gold mine from the movie, selling Bulls T-shirts, caps, and jackets across the country by mail. Bulls general manager Rob Dlugozima observed that his team was "the hottest minor league team in the country in terms of fan recognition."

The movie also brought some belated attention to a Carolina League veteran of an earlier era. In 1987, Ron Shelton, a former minor league baseball player turned movie director, was glancing through a Carolina League media guide when he came across a name that attracted his attention. The name was Crash Davis, and Shelton knew he wanted to use it in the baseball movie he was planning. Shelton contacted Crash Davis and received permission to use his name. The following year, Shelton's *Bull Durham* became a smash success, and Kevin Costner made Crash Davis a household name.

Lawrence Davis was born in Georgia but grew up in Gastonia, North Carolina. When he was 16, he led his Gastonia American Legion team to a national championship. He acquired his nickname because he resembled a character named Crash in the comic strip "Freckles." Davis starred at Duke University under the coaching of Jack Coombs. From 1940 through 1942, he played second base and batted .230 for the Philadelphia Athletics, managed by the legendary Connie Mack.

As was the case with most pro players, World War II interrupted Davis's career. He spent much of the war years as a naval ROTC instructor and played a little minor league ball in Massachusetts under the name Chuck Leary. He returned to Philadelphia after the war but was released in spring training in 1947. He later recalled that "it was a real blow. I'll never know what role the war played in that, being removed from the scene and so forth."

After playing in New England in 1947, Crash Davis returned to his native North Carolina in 1948. His years in the big leagues had made Davis an unusually polished player for the Carolina League, and he used his smarts well. In 1948, the Durham Bull led the league with 50 doubles, fielded exceptionally well, and hit two home runs in the league's first All-Star Game.

Davis finished his pro career with the Raleigh Caps in 1952. He returned to Gastonia, where he coached Gastonia High School to the state baseball title in 1953, 1954, and 1955. He also coached the Gastonia American Legion team to a second-place finish in the 1954 Little World Series. Davis worked 30 years for Burlington Industries before retiring.

What did he think of *Bull Durham*? According to the real-life Crash Davis, Kevin Costner's characterization of him was "closely related, except for the steamy sexual scenes." At the movie's premiere in Durham, Davis wore a button which read "Crash Davis is not Kevin Costner."

Darryl Landrum hit an electrifying three-run homer to make the score 4–3. Jeff Plympton relieved for Lynchburg and struck out Ray Williamson on a full count to preserve the win.

Kinston recovered and won game three 7–2 thanks to some help from Mark Pike. After hitting a solo homer, Pike preserved a 4–2 lead with a big defensive play in the sixth. With speedy Tom Buheller on second and one out, Scott Cooper singled to center; Pike made a perfect throw to nip Buheller, and Cooper was doubled up trying to go to second.

Lynchburg won game four 3–2 in 10 innings to even the series again. Bart Haley threw five hitless innings in relief to get the win. The decisive run scored on a walk, a sacrifice bunt, a throwing error by Epley, and a single by Buheller.

Because of a conflict with a high-school football game, the deciding fifth game was scheduled at Lynchburg on a Friday afternoon. The game was rained out, however, and played the following night. Kinston disappointed the home crowd by defeating Lynchburg 3–1, with Olin pitching $3^{1}/_{3}$ perfect innings in relief. Landrum and Richardson had solo homers for the champs. This was Kinston's first title since 1962.

Tragically, Kinston relief ace Steve Olin was later killed in a 1993 spring-training boating accident.

1988 Northern Division First-Half Final Standings

Salem	40–29
Hagerstown	37–33
Prince William	31–38
Lynchburg	25–45

Southern Division First-Half Final Standings

*Kinston	45–25	playoff winner
Durham	44–26	
Winston-Salem	39–31	
Virginia	18–52	

Northern Division Second-Half Final Standings

Lynchburg	43–27
Hagerstown	42–28
Salem	33–37
Prince William	24–46

Southern Division Second-Half Final Standings

Kinston	43–27
Durham	38–32
Winston-Salem	34–36
Virginia	23–47

✦   ✦   ✦

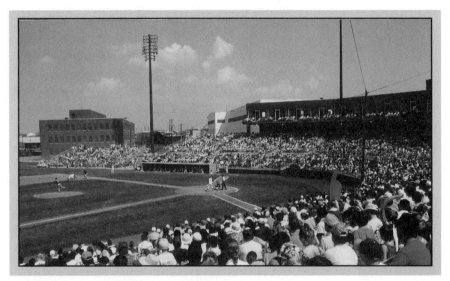

Judy Johnson Field, home of the Wilmington Delaware Blue Rocks

CHAPTER EIGHT
1989 — 93

♦ ♦ ♦

Following the 1988 season, Hagerstown left the Carolina League for greener pastures. It was replaced by another Maryland city, Frederick. The Keys, as they were dubbed, also took Hagerstown's working agreement with Baltimore. The Virginia Generals became the Peninsula Pilots. Again they were unable to procure a working agreement and were forced to operate as a co-op, with predictably dismal results.

The Durham Bulls dominated the 1989 early going. Indeed, they got off to the most spectacular start in league history. Their opener, against the new kids on the block from Frederick, was rained out twice. They were finally able to get under way with an April 9 doubleheader. In the opener, Durham's Dennis Burlingame threw a 4–0 perfect game, believed to be the only opening-day perfect game in professional baseball history. In the nightcap, his teammate Steve Avery took a no-hitter into the sixth inning before giving up two hits in a 1–0 win.

Burlingame and Avery were both considered outstanding prospects, but their paths diverged dramatically. Avery, a hard-throwing first-round draft pick, made the major leagues the following season and achieved stardom in the early 1990s. Burlingame, on the other hand, came down with arm trouble, which short-circuited his major league ambitions. When he first experienced elbow trouble in early May, he was 4–0 with an earned-run average of 0.43.

The Bulls rode their opening-day momentum through April. Later in the month, they swept a three-game series with Salem by scoring 34 runs. Third baseman Ken Pennington and outfielders Andy Tomberlin (.281, 35 stolen bases), Al Martin, and Theron Todd (79 RBIs) gave the balanced Bulls the league's best offense, while Pat Tilmon (11–4), Steve Ziem (9–0, 1.66, 7 saves), and Jim Czajkowski (0.99, 14 saves) supported Burlingame and Avery on the mound. The Bulls completed April with a commanding 17–4 record. Winston-Salem trailed by four, while Kinston was already 6½ games off the lead.

Kinston's slow start came despite a talent-filled roster which included short-stop Mark Lewis, the second pick in the 1988 draft; pitcher Charles Nagy, a former University of Connecticut star and a standout on the 1988 United States Olympic team; and pitcher Jeff Mutis (7–3, 2.62), a former third-round draft pick who had pitched briefly in Kinston the previous season. Mark Gilles (6–3, 2.53), Rick Surhoff (14 saves), and Tommy Kramer (9–5, 2.60) also had fine seasons on the mound.

In mid-May, Kinston began to close the gap when Durham lost five of eight. On May 16, the Bulls lost 6–2 to Salem, while Kinston split a pair with Lynchburg to cut Durham's lead to two. On May 20, Durham was 27–14, Kinston 25–15, and Winston-Salem 23–17.

Durham regained its momentum late in May and began to reopen the lead. A six-game winning streak enabled the Bulls to finish May with a 37–16 mark and a four-game lead over Kinston. Durham finished the first half 3½ games ahead of Kinston.

Winston-Salem faded badly down the stretch and finished a dozen games back. Like Kinston, Winston-Salem had a fine pitching staff, led by Pat Gomez (11–6), Julio Strauss (17 saves), and Frank Castillo, but little hitting.

The co-op Pilots finished in last place again. However, they did so with an intriguing roster. Three of their players were on loan from Hiroshima Toyo Carp of the Japanese Central League: pitcher Wataru Adachi, infielder Kohichi Ogata, and outfielder Tetsuya Katahira. Among their top players were outfielder Scott Jaster, on loan from the Mets; former Bull Dodd Johnson, released by the Atlanta organization; and pitcher Tim Kirk, a former University of North Carolina player released by the Pirates over the winter. Kirk pitched so well for the Pilots that he was signed in midseason by Atlanta and sent to Greenville. Mickey Tresh (.269) gave it another try. This ragtag assemblage was managed by 26-year-old Jim Thrift, a son of longtime big-league executive Syd Thrift.

The Northern Division lacked a standout team but was well balanced. The Frederick Keys appeared to be on their way to a pennant much of the first half. The Keys led Prince William by four games in late May before losing nine straight. The loss of catcher Dan Simonds and pitchers Mike Linsky and Bob Williams to Hagerstown hurt, as did an altercation between star second baseman Luis Mercedes (.309) and several of his teammates. First baseman David Segui (.317), outfielder Jack Voigt (77 RBIs), and infielder Rod Lofton (62 stolen bases) hit well for the Keys; Pete Rose, Jr. (.179), didn't, his famous name notwithstanding. Andres Constant (10–4), Dave Miller (13–4), and Mike Borgatti (7–0, 0.86, 9 saves) paced the pitching.

The Keys briefly righted themselves with a four-game winning streak and regained first place. On June 10, Lynchburg was 31–31 and Frederick 31–32 going into a crucial three-game series. Lynchburg won all three games to run its winning streak to seven and Frederick's losing streak to six. The Keys ended up losing 17 of 22 and ended the first half with a losing mark, 1½ games behind the Red Sox.

Lynchburg's pennant run was led by outfielder Phil Plantier, who hit .339 during May and ended the first half with the league lead in all three triple-crown categories. Outfielder Mike Kelly and pitchers David Owen (13–9), Derek Livernois, and Freddie Davis (2.37, 13 saves) also performed well.

Salem finished third, only two games behind Lynchburg. Its team included outfielder Moises Alou (.302, 14, 53), a player with one of baseball's most distinguished lineages. In the 1960s, Dominican Republic brothers Felipe, Matty, and Jesus Alou were three of the game's finest outfielders. In 1992, Moises Alou's father, Felipe, was to become his son's manager in Montreal. Third baseman John Wehner (.301), second baseman Terry Crowley, and pitchers Randy Tomlin (12–6), Joe Pacholec (12–7), and Jose Ausanio (20 saves) were other key Bucs.

Last-place Prince William made an unusual managerial switch early in the season, replacing the intense Mark Weidemaier with the more laid-back Stump Merrill. The most exciting Prince William player in the first half may well have been pitcher Frank Seminara. On May 3, he beaned three consecutive Salem batters in an 8–2 loss. The third, Robert Harris, suffered a broken jaw.

Lynchburg's chance of a second-half repeat was dealt a severe jolt when standout shortstop Tim Naehering (.301) was pro-

Phil Plantier
Courtesy of Baseball America

Moises Alou
Courtesy of Salem Buccaneers

moted to Pawtucket at midseason. He was replaced by John Valentine, who was promoted from Winter Haven. Kinston lost ace pitcher Nagy (8–4, 1.51) to AA Canton-Akron, along with outfielder Jim Bruske. Durham lost Avery (6–4, 1.45) to promotion.

Kinston started 10–1 in the second half, which gave it a substantial early lead over the Bulls. Surprising Peninsula, led by Scott Jaster, held onto second place for several weeks before dropping back. The Bulls returned to contention in mid-July, closing the gap to one game. Durham outfielder Andy Tomberlin went 16 for 35 during the week of July 9–15, with 8 homers and 17 runs batted in. On July 9, he hit three homers and drove in six runs in an 11–3 pounding of Frederick. Burlingame attempted to come back, but his arm failed to respond, and he returned to the disabled list.

Durham moved into a virtual tie for first on July 29 when it beat Peninsula 4–1 while Kinston was losing 1–0 to Prince William. At the end of July, all four Southern Division teams were bunched closely, led by Durham at 21–18. However, a four-team race never materialized. Peninsula, then Winston-Salem, and finally Kinston dropped back, leaving the Bulls alone at the top. Durham ended the second half with a mediocre 37–31 record but a 3½-game margin over Kinston.

The Northern Division second half belonged to Prince William, whose early-season managerial switch paid dividends. Second baseman Pat Kelly, third baseman Don Sparks, outfielder Gerald Williams, shortstop Bob DeJardin (38 stolen bases), and pitchers Mike Draper (14–8) and Alan Mills (6–1, 0.91, 7 saves) helped Prince William overcome its last-place first-half finish. Frederick and Lynchburg provided stiff competition, but Prince William's 42–27 mark was good enough for a 2½-game margin over Frederick. Like Hagerstown the previous season, Frederick ended with the best overall record in the Northern Division but missed the playoffs.

There were a number of highlights in the latter part of the second half.

Lynchburg's Phil Plantier hit two home runs in one inning against Salem on August 20. A week later, his teammate John Valentine hit three home runs against

Alan Mills   Courtesy of Prince William Cannons

Peninsula. Peninsula's Kohichi Ogata stole a record-equaling five bases on August 18.

Salem finished last in the Northern Division but did provide one highlight. On July 3, Domingo Merego, Moises Alou, John Wehner, and Al Molina homered in a single inning in a 7–6 win over Lynchburg.

Plantier came up just short in his triple-crown bid. He led the league with 27 home runs and 105 RBIs but finished third with a .300 batting average. In 1993, after being traded from Boston to San Diego, he emerged as one of baseball's top sluggers.

Winston-Salem second baseman Rusty Crockett set a dubious league mark by being hit by 24 pitches, breaking Fred Valentine's 1958 mark by four.

The league also hosted brief visits from two interesting personalities. After 10 weeks of negotiations, Ben McDonald, the first pick in the 1989 draft, signed with Baltimore for an estimated $1 million. McDonald, a six-foot-eight All-American pitcher from Louisiana State University, was assigned to Frederick. He pitched only two games for the Keys, amid extensive publicity, and was not involved in a decision. About the same time, Atlanta sent pitcher Turk Wendell from Burlington, Iowa, to Durham. Wendell eventually became something of a cult figure for his eccentricities, which included talking to the ball and brushing his teeth between innings.

Having won both half-season titles, Durham sat out the first round of the playoffs.

Prince William won the first game of its series 4–1, with Andy Cook the winning pitcher; Alan Mills picked up the save. Lynchburg rallied from a 4–1 deficit to win the second game 5–4. Prince William won the third game 4–2 to take the series, as Mills acquired another save.

Mills, who had joined Prince William in midseason, continued his sterling work in the finals. He got the win in Prince William's 4–1 opening-game victory by hurling 2²/₃ innings of shutout relief; the Bulls pounded out 11 hits but left the bases loaded twice. Durham evened the series with a 3–2 win in game two, as Matt Turner saved the win for Pat Tilmon when he got Mitch Lyden to ground out with two on in the bottom of the ninth. Prince William then went to Durham and captured a pair of games for the title. Mills was the undisputed hero. He saved the third game 3–2 for Mike Draper and saved the fourth for Wade Taylor 4–2. In the eighth inning of game four, Mills fought off Ken Pennington for 11 pitches before striking him out. He pitched 5²/₃ hitless innings in the championship series, winning one game and saving two. Mills either won or saved every Prince William victory in the playoffs.

The Carolina League passed a significant milestone in 1989. Announced attendance exceeded the million mark for only the second time; the first was in 1947. Durham again paced the league with 272,000, a new record. The league total was even more impressive in light of the sparse 20,000 who ventured to Peninsula's aging War Memorial Stadium.

1989 Northern Division First-Half Final Standings

Lynchburg	*35–34*
Frederick	*34–36*
Salem	*33–36*
Prince William	*30–39*

Southern Division First-Half Final Standings

Durham	*47–23*
Kinston	*42–25*
Winston-Salem	*35–35*
Peninsula	*20–48*

Northern Division Second-Half Final Standings

*Prince William	*42–27*	*playoff winner*
Frederick	*39–29*	
Lynchburg	*35–32*	
Salem	*30–39*	

Southern Division Second-Half Final Standings

Durham	*37–31*
Kinston	*34–35*
Winston-Salem	*29–36*
Peninsula	*24–41*

—◆—

The 1990 season belonged to the Frederick Keys. The second-year Carolina League team opened the new $5-million Harry Grove Stadium. In a league dominated by classic old stadiums, such as Salem's Municipal Field, Durham Athletic Park, and Peninsula's War Memorial Stadium, the high-tech Grove Stadium attracted a good deal of attention. It wasn't without controversy. Construction on 17 skyboxes continued through the 1990 season while local officials and the team squabbled over how to pay for cost overruns. However, Frederick fans obviously loved the stadium, flocking to the park to the tune of 277,000.

The Keys, an Orioles farm club, also thrived on the field. Although they lacked both speed and home-run power, they managed to capture both half-season titles in the Northern Division. During the first half, Frederick jumped to a 19–7 start and led by eight games after only a month. The Keys couldn't put the field away so easily, however. Late in the first half, they lost star first baseman–designated hitter Ken Shamburg (.321) to AA.

A Lynchburg run late in May, coupled with a Frederick slump, enabled the Red Sox to catch up. When Lynchburg beat Frederick on June 2, the two clubs were tied at 27–23. Having fought its way to the top, Lynchburg promptly collapsed, losing nine of 12 and leaving Frederick alone at the top. The slumping Red Sox lost 14 of their final 20 contests.

Kinston's road to a first-half title in the tougher Southern Division paralleled Frederick's run. The Indians blasted out of the gate with a 16–5 start. Pitcher Jerry Dipoto started off 4–0 with an 0.79 earned-run average. Kinston had a powerhouse lineup, led by outfielder Ken Ramos (.345), catcher Jesse Levis (.296), first baseman Jim Orsag (.296), shortstop Lindsay Foster, and pitchers Ty Kovach (12–3), Todd Gonzales (11–4), Scott Neil (8–3), Greg Ferlenda (23 saves), and Dipoto (11–4).

After a slow start, Winston-Salem made a charge for the top. The fine play of third baseman Gary Scott (.295), designated hitter Doug Welch (.320), and John Salles (14–5) propelled Winston-Salem into a tie for first on June 6 after consecutive victories over Kinston. Kinston regained the lead the following day with a 3–1 win over the Spirits.

The two clubs fought it out down the stretch. On June 18, Kinston's Kovach beat Frederick 3–0 for his 10th win, while Salem dropped Winston-Salem 7–2.

This extended Kinston's lead to two games. Kinston beat Frederick 6–3 the next day to clinch the title, ending up one game ahead of Winston-Salem.

Frederick and Kinston repeated their titles in the second half, although not without difficulty.

The Frederick offense struggled with the loss of Ken Shamburg. Indeed, it finished the season with a minuscule 50 home runs, five fewer than Muscle Shoals hit by himself in 1949. The lack of competition in the Northern Division helped the Keys stay close to the top. As late as July 21, a full month into the second half, all four teams in the division had losing records.

Prince William broke on top late in the month but was unable to pull away. On August 11, the Cannons were in first place despite a mark of 22–23. One week later, Frederick beat Kinston 13–10 to move into first place with a 25–26 record, half a game ahead of Prince William. From that point, the two clubs went in opposite directions. Frederick won 11 of its final 16, while Prince William lost 12 of its final 18 to finish well behind the Keys. The late-season acquisition of first baseman Mel Wearing (.329 in 22 games) and designated hitter T. R. Lewis (.325 in 22 games) was an important reason for Frederick's impressive late-season performance.

Kinston won despite a dizzying number of roster changes. Ramos was promoted to AA, although not before going to bat enough times to qualify for the batting title. Orsag and Dipoto were also promoted, while Kovach missed much of the second half with a leg injury. Pitcher Chris Cole broke his wrist when he slipped while jogging before a game in Salem.

Yet the replacements sent to Kinston by Cleveland were more than adequate. Among them was Cleveland's 1990 first-round draft pick, first baseman Tim Costo, who batted .316 and drove in 42 runs in half a season. Pitcher Oscar Munoz was promoted from the New York–Penn League in midseason and went 7–0 with a 2.39 ERA. Third baseman Jim Thome was promoted from Burlington of the rookie Appalachian League and batted .308 in 33 games, while late-season acquisition Tracy Sanders batted .438 in 10 contests.

Possibly because of the roster turnover, Kinston got off to a slow start in the second half. Peninsula jumped to an unaccustomed good start and actually led the division for two weeks. Winston-Salem and Durham took turns in first place during the second half of July. A nine-game Kinston winning streak late in the month got the Indians back in the race. On August 4, they moved into first when they beat Frederick. The Spirits regained the top spot for a brief time but were unable to hold on. Kinston pulled away in the last two weeks to beat Winston-Salem handily. Winston-Salem's runner-up finish was especially frustrating, as the Spirits' superb mark of 86–54 was the league's second best but did not qualify them for the postseason.

On paper, Kinston owned a substantial edge over Frederick going into the playoffs. Kinston's regular-season mark was 14½ games better than Frederick's, and the Indians had won 12 of the 17 games between the two clubs. Yet once again, the Carolina League postseason defied expectations.

Kinston's opening-game loss would have devastated a less resilient team. Oscar Munoz took a 4-0 lead into the ninth inning. When a two-run homer by Tyrone Kingwood cut the margin in half, Kinston skipper Brian Graham went to his bullpen. Six Frederick singles later, the Keys were on their way to a 6–4 win.

The Indians fought back with an 8–4 win in game two to even the series; Jesse Levis and Rick Falkner each had three runs batted in.

Frederick jumped back in front with a dramatic win in game three. Kinston starter Todd Gonzalez and Frederick starter Pat Leinen traded scoreless frames into extra innings. Both were gone by the time the game entered the 11th. In the bottom of that inning, a walk and a balk put Frederick shortstop Ricky Gutierrez on second base. Tyrone Kingwood lifted a looping fly ball to Kinston right fielder Fabio Gomez, who dropped the ball for an error and a 1–0 loss.

Again, Kinston came back. Its 8–5 win in game four was another nail-biter. Trailing by three, Frederick loaded the bases with two outs in the bottom of the ninth. Kingwood hit a sinking liner to left field, which a sprinting Sanders caught just above his shoestrings to preserve the victory. Had Sanders missed the ball, the game likely would have been tied. Frederick manager Wally Moon pronounced Sanders's gamble a "foolish play." Kinston skipper Graham called it a "tremendous catch."

Kinston carried the momentum of game four to an early 5–0 lead in the deciding contest and appeared poised to take the title before its bullpen fell apart. A three-run homer by Tim Holland in the sixth gave Frederick a 6–5 lead. It held on for a 7–5 win and the title.

Sportswriter Dean Gyorgy wrote in *Baseball America*, "Years from now, when fans of the Frederick Keys look back, they'll want to say they were there in 1990. It was a magical year for all associated with the team." Frederick was led by the smooth-fielding Gutierrez and the batting of Holland (.302) and Kingwood (.335). The real strength of the team was a pitching staff which included Zachary Kerr (14–7), Mike Oquist (9–8, 170 strikeouts), and Todd Stephan (8–2, 1.32, 17 saves). Baltimore Orioles Brady Anderson and Mike Devereux made brief appearances while recovering from injuries. Third baseman Pete Rose, Jr., batted a mediocre .232.

Kinston ended the season with the league's best record, a league-best 697 runs scored, a league-best 3.04 team earned-run average, and the bitter memories of a close playoff loss.

Durham became the first team in league history to go over 300,000 in attendance. Those fans saw two of the minors' most highly regarded prospects, six-foot-three, 225-pound first baseman Ryan Klesko (.274, 7, 47 after a midseason promotion from Sumter) and outfielder Keith Mitchell (.294).

Peninsula suffered through a shaky first year with its Seattle PDC. Second baseman Brett Boone and catcher Jim Campanis were each attempting—as had Mickey Tresh a few years earlier—to establish the first three-generation family in major league history. Boone, the son of Bob Boone and the grandson of Ray Boone, won the race when Seattle promoted him to the major leagues late in the 1992 season.

Lynchburg finished well below .500. Former first-round draft pick Greg Blosser (.282, 18, 62) led the league in homers with an unusually low total.

Prince William's best players were pitchers Frank Seminara (16–8, 1.90) and shortstop Dave Silvestri (37 stolen bases). Smooth-fielding first baseman J. T. Snow, son of former NFL star Jack Snow, batted a disappointing .256 but still maintained his stature as a top prospect.

Salem had the worst record in the league, a distinction largely attributable to an awful pitching staff. Shortstop Mike Huyler (.296 in 67 games), outfielder Darwin Pennye (.284), and catcher Armando Romero (.291, 17, 90) gave the Bucs some runs, but only Paul Miller (8–6, 2.45) retired opposing batters with any consistency.

1990 Northern Division First-Half Final Standings

*Frederick	39–31	playoff winner
Prince William	33–37	
Lynchburg	33–37	
Salem	25–45	

Southern Division First-Half Final Standings

Kinston	46–24
Winston-Salem	45–25
Durham	37–33
Peninsula	22–48

Northern Division Second-Half Final Standings

Frederick	35–31
Prince William	31–38
Salem	30–39
Lynchburg	25–43

Southern Division Second-Half Final Standings

Kinston	42–23
Winston-Salem	41–29
Peninsula	35–35
Durham	34–35

—♦—

The major leagues and the minor leagues engaged in sometimes bitter negotiations during the 1990–91 off-season. The Professional Baseball Agreement expired in January 1991, and the major leagues played hardball in an attempt to force the minor leagues to pay a larger share of the cost of player development. The majors even threatened to completely withdraw their support of the minors. The result was a new agreement that did indeed shift more money from the newly lucrative minor leagues to the majors. Few minor league operators liked the new agreement, but the reality was that they had to accept it. Many predicted ticket-price increases and deferred stadium maintenance as a result. The new agreement also explicitly recognized the right of the commissioner of major league baseball to reverse decisions of the National Association in "the best interests of baseball."

The Carolina League was officially designated a "high-A" or "advanced-A" league, as opposed to "low-A." The Florida State League and the California League also achieved the "high-A" designation, formalizing a pecking order long recognized by baseball officials.

Another change took place during the off-season when Miles Wolff sold the Durham Bulls to Raleigh television executive Jim Goodmon. Although the price was not announced, estimates ranged around $4 million. There was little doubt that Wolff had made a sizable profit from his 1979 investment of $2,417 for Carolina League franchise rights.

After finishing 1990 with the best regular-season record in the league but losing the playoffs, the Kinston Indians dominated the 1991 season. Kinston jumped off to a 16–8 start and held off a late run by Winston-Salem to win the Southern Division first-half title.

The Indians and the Spirits were two of the more talented teams of recent years.

Kinston was led by second baseman Miguel Flores, outfielder Brian Giles (.310), and pitchers Chad Allen, Scott Morgan (7–2, 2.54), and Curt Leskanic (15–8). The real stars of the team, however, were two unlikely professional players, outfielder Tracy Sanders (.266, 18, 63) and relief pitcher Mike Soper (3–2, 2.47).

The President Visits the Carolina League

Until the Washington Senators moved to Texas following the 1971 season, United States presidents were frequent visitors to major league baseball games, particularly for the ceremonial opening-day first pitch. Minor league teams have hosted presidential visits less often. Twice in recent years, however, President George Bush attended Carolina League games in Frederick, Maryland.

President Bush's first appearance was on June 8, 1991, when he and his grandson, also named George Bush, attended a Durham-Frederick contest. The visit took place after a day-long Washington parade honoring the veterans of Operation Desert Storm and came at the peak of Bush's popularity. The president attracted considerable attention from players and fans alike and left after five innings. Durham won the contest 8–1.

President Bush made another visit the following season on August 14, 1992. He and his wife, Barbara, were part of a crowd of 6,205 which saw Durham beat the home team by a 4–0 count. Bush's reception this time was polite but more subdued than that of the previous year.

George Bush is believed to be the only United States president to have attended a Carolina League game while in office. However, on April 30, 1993, Vice President Al Gore attended a game at Prince William County Stadium, where the home team defeated Winston-Salem 4–2. Gore was accompanied by his son Albert and a group from St. Albans School.

President Bill Clinton has not attended a Carolina League game but has been photographed playing golf wearing a Durham Bulls cap.

With Carolina League teams based near the nation's capital and major league baseball still absent from Washington, presidential visits to league ballparks may become a common occurrence.

Sanders, who had played briefly for Kinston the previous season, was a 58th-round 1990 draft pick out of tiny Limestone College in Gaffney, South Carolina, where his coach had been Hall of Fame pitcher Gaylord Perry. Soper was a 1989 37th-round pick out of the University of Alabama. Once in the pros, Soper developed a baffling submarine-style delivery that produced a regular supply of ground balls and made him virtually untouchable in save situations.

The stars of the Winston-Salem team were 19-year-old right-handed pitcher Ryan Hawblitzel (15–2, 2.42), a 1990 second-round draft pick; Troy Bradford (9–5); slugging third baseman Pete Castellano (.303, 10, 87), a native of Venezuela; and designated hitter Chris Ebright (.280). The Spirits trailed Kinston by 8½ games with three weeks left in the first half but won 17 of their final 20 to finish a deceptively close two games out of first.

Durham had a sporadic offense but a standout pitching staff, led by David Nied (8–3, 1.56) and Scott Taylor (10–3, 2.18). The Colorado Rockies later made Nied the first pick in the 1992 major league expansion draft. When the Bulls went their first 11 games without a home run, manager Grady Little instituted a clubhouse pool for the first homer. Outfielder Tony Tarasco eventually won the $56 prize. Dennis Burlingame (11–7), who had spent the previous season in Sumter, pitched the entire season with Durham in his comeback from elbow surgery. Catcher Javy Lopez, outfielder Melvin Nieves, and second baseman Ramon Carabello (53 stolen bases) were also highly regarded prospects.

Prince William won the Northern Division almost by default. After three weeks, it was 15–6 and the only team in the division with a winning record. The Cannons were keyed by pitcher Sam Militello (12–2, 1.22), a former standout at the University of Tampa. He won his first four starts and pitched 29 consecutive scoreless innings to help stake Prince William to a lead they never relinquished. Militello's curveball was so formidable that some scouts compared him to long-time major league standout Bert Blyleven. Reliever Mark Ohlms (26 saves), Kirt Ojala, and Jeff Hoffman (12–5, 2.87) augmented a first-rate pitching staff. The Cannons were another team with mediocre hitting. Catcher Brad Ausmus impressed with his defensive skills before being promoted to Albany.

The other three Northern Division clubs were well below .500. Second-place Lynchburg completed the first half at 30–39, 7½ games behind Prince William.

There were some fine individual performances in the first half in the Northern Division.

Salem outfielder Ben Shelton had a streak in which he drove in 23 runs in 11 games. His teammate Scott Bullett (.333 in 39 games) was called up to Pittsburgh late in the season and used mainly as a pinch runner; Bullett is the younger brother of basketball star Vicky Bullett, a member of the 1988 and 1992 United States women's Olympic basketball teams. Salem hurler Tim Smith (12–9, 2.16) led the league in earned-run average, while Paul List (.318) was second in batting.

Sam Militello
Courtesy of Prince William Cannons

Lynchburg outfielder Boo Moore homered in five consecutive games. Speedy Jeff McNeely (.322, 38 stolen bases) and first baseman Willie Tatum (.287) also helped power the Red Sox. However, in one especially bleak period, Lynchburg scored only three runs in 50 innings.

Frederick featured shortstop Manny Alexander (47 stolen bases) and pitchers Kip Vaughan (11–8) and John O'Donoghue, Jr., the latter of whom had a 14-strikeout game. O'Donoghue's pitching coach was his father, John O'Donoghue, Sr., a former big-league hurler.

Kinston repeated its first-place finish in the second half, prevailing in a tight three-team race over Durham and Winston-

Salem. Again, the Indians jumped off to a quick start, winning 16 of their first 22. Hawblitzel and Castellano kept Winston-Salem in the thick of the race, however. On August 11, Kinston led the Spirits by only half a game. Kinston then surged to a 17–6 finish, while Winston-Salem came in 13–9 down the stretch. Durham finished strong to overtake Winston-Salem for second place, three games behind Kinston.

Mike Soper was the key for Kinston. He ended the season with 41 saves, which not only shattered the Carolina League record but also equaled the minor league record set by Mike Perez in 1987 in the Midwest League. Their co-record was broken the following season.

Durham's late run featured a memorable acquisition. Atlanta made Arizona State All-American outfielder and 1990 *Baseball America* College Player of the Year Mike Kelly (.250, 6, 17) the number-two pick in the 1991 draft. After protracted negotiations, he signed with the Braves and was assigned to Durham. Kelly showed signs of rustiness early but displayed his considerable talents as his short season progressed.

The season progressed into disaster for Peninsula. Late in the campaign, the Pilots lost 22 consecutive games, breaking the old league record of 19 set by Fayetteville in 1950. The Pilots ended the streak with a win on the last day of the season. A number of Peninsula losses could have made a horror highlight film. The Pilots committed six errors in one inning of a 12–5 loss to Frederick. On another occasion, Salem committed eight errors against the Pilots but still won 12–7. Winston-Salem's Steve Trachsel no-hit Peninsula on July 12. On August 24, Durham scored 11 runs in the bottom of the sixth inning to defeat the Pilots 15–6. The following night, the Bulls scored 15 runs in the first inning against Peninsula on the way to a 21–6 win.

Peninsula did have one big-name prospect, outfielder Mark Merchant, the number-two pick in the 1987 draft. Ken Griffey, Jr., the only player selected ahead of Merchant that year, achieved big-league stardom in short order, but Merchant disappointed in the Pittsburgh organization and was traded to Seattle. A mediocre .252 season with Peninsula left him no closer to the majors. Pitcher Jim Converse, outfielder Ron Pezzoni (.289), and first baseman Damon Saetre were the most effective Pilots.

All four Northern Division teams spent the second half bunched around the .500 mark. There were several key injuries. Militello missed three weeks with an inflamed knuckle, while league batting champ Jeff McNeely missed much of the second half with an assortment of injuries. A major addition to the Northern Division was Frederick outfielder Mark Smith, a former University of Southern California Trojan picked ninth in the first round of the 1991 draft by Baltimore. Like Mike Kelly, Smith demonstrated a mixture of rustiness and raw talent in his brief Carolina League tenure.

The most dramatic ride on the baseball roller coaster was taken by Frederick pitcher Erik Schullstrom. On July 3, he threw a no-hitter against Kinston, winning 2–0. In his next start, Salem's Roman Rodriguez, Paul List, Alberto de los Santos, and Ken Trusky pounded him for consecutive first-inning home runs; Salem won the game 8–3.

Salem led the Northern Division much of the second half before an 11–3 Lynchburg run propelled the Red Sox into the lead. Lynchburg held on for a 3½-game victory over Prince William.

Lynchburg swept Prince William in the first round of the playoffs by scores of 4–3 and 6–4; the Cannons hurt their cause with six errors in the opener.

Lynchburg's luck ran out against the hot Indians in the final. Kinston won the first two games on the road by one-sided scores. The third game was much more competitive. Lynchburg starter Ed Riley took a 1–0 lead and a one-hitter into the ninth, but a two-out single by Paulino Tena sent the game into extra innings. Kinston won the game and the title in the 12th when reliever Tony Mosely hit Brian Giles with the bases loaded.

Frederick won a title of a different nature. The Keys drew an astonishing 318,000 fans, by far the best single-season mark in league history. Durham also surpassed the 300,000 mark, while Prince William surpassed 200,000. The league totaled an impressive 1.3 million in attendance.

1991 Northern Division First-Half Final Standings

Prince William	*38–32*
Lynchburg	*30–39*
Salem	*30–40*
Frederick	*26–44*

Southern Division First-Half Final Standings

* Kinston	*45–23*	*playoff winner*
Winston-Salem	*43–27*	
Durham	*38–29*	
Peninsula	*27–43*	

Northern Division Second-Half Final Standings

Lynchburg	*37–33*
Prince William	*33–36*
Salem	*33–37*
Frederick	*32–38*

Southern Division Second-Half Final Standings

Kinston	44–26
Durham	41–29
Winston-Salem	40–30
Peninsula	19–50

—◆—

The Peninsula Pilots were the story of the 1992 season.

The hapless Pilots had finished the 1991 season playing genuinely bad baseball in an old stadium before sparse crowds. Plans were made in the off-season to move the club to Wilmington, Delaware. These plans were canceled hastily when a deal to build a new facility in that city fell apart. Two potential Virginia investors announced a plan to buy the club and build a privately funded stadium, but that deal also fell apart.

There was some good news, however. The Peninsula Stadium Authority spent $200,000 on renovations to Municipal Stadium, built in 1948. More important, the parent Seattle Mariners made a commitment to send players to the Tidewater community. As one team official put it, Seattle had made a conscious decision in 1991 to make its high-A San Bernadino club in the California League "as competitive as we could." As for the team's other high-A club in Peninsula, the Mariners vowed only to "see what we could do." What they did was produce one of the worst clubs in Carolina League history.

Things were dramatically different in 1992, as was evident on opening day, when Greg Bicknell and Chuck Wiley combined for a no-hitter against Salem. The revived Peninsula team won its first three contests and seven of its first 11, the latter mark matched by the Durham Bulls. Only a few days into the season, the Pilots were the victim of a 9–0 no-hitter thrown by four Bulls pitchers. The first of these was Mike Hostetler, a former Georgia Tech standout.

Durham and Peninsula battled on relatively even terms for the Southern Division title throughout the first half. Despite the presence of the league's best pitching staff, which included Bicknell (10–7), John Cummings (16–6, 2.57), Wiley, LaGrande Russell, and Todd Youngblood (7–3), Peninsula's star attraction was burly first baseman–designated hitter Bubba Smith. The 230-pound former University of Illinois star hit more tape-measure home runs than any Carolina League player in recent memory. A three-homer game against Winston-Salem in May served notice to the league's pitchers and gave Smith ammunition against critics who argued that he was too slow to be a top prospect. He ended the season with 32 home runs and 93 runs batted in. In the best slugger's tradition, he also fanned 138 times. Outfielder Darren Bragg (44 stolen bases),

Bubba Smith
Courtesy of Winston-Salem Spirits

second baseman Ruben Santana, and catcher Miah Bradbury also had good seasons for the Pilots.

If Smith attracted the most attention, Durham countered with the league's best prospect, shortstop Chipper Jones (.277), the top selection in the 1990 amateur draft. Jones, third baseman Tim Gillis (21, 84), outfielders Lee Heath (52 stolen bases) and Brian Kowitz (.301), and Hostetler (9–3, 2.15) kept Durham slightly ahead of Peninsula most of the first half before a late slump dropped the Bulls into the league's first half-season tie since 1970. The loss of talented outfielder Melvin Nieves (.302), who was promoted to AA after a month, hurt the Bulls.

Under league rules, the next regular-season meeting between Peninsula and Durham would count as both a regular game and a one-game playoff. The Atlanta Braves made the unusual move of delaying the promotion of Jones and pitcher Brad Woodall (4 saves) to AA until after the playoff. This widely hailed move was no help to Durham when Peninsula's Bicknell shut down the Durham bats 2–0 for the first-half title.

In the Northern Division, Frederick jumped to an early lead, sparked by designated hitter T. R. Lewis (.307) and outfielders Stanton Cameron (.247, 29, 92) and Jim Wawruck (.309), the latter a former University of Vermont baseball and soccer star. In early June, Frederick right-hander Stacy Jones struck out 13 Bulls in six innings, including eight straight. Shortly afterward, he was promoted to AA.

The Keys were overtaken in late May by the Lynchburg Red Sox, who held on for the first-half title. Lynchburg's championship run was keyed by two top prospects, right-handed pitchers Frank Rodriguez (12–7) and Aaron Sele (13–5). Rodriguez was one of the league's more intriguing stories. A multitalented athlete, he was considered a major league prospect as either a pitcher or a position player. In 1991, he hurled Howard (Texas) Junior College to the 1991 Junior World Series championship with a 17-strikeout performance in the final game. Sele, a self-proclaimed "finesse power pitcher," had been a college star at Washington State. In 1990 as a member of Team USA, Sele threw a memorable 1–0 victory over the Cuban team. He then endured a mediocre 1991 season with an awful Winter Haven club in the Florida State League and began 1992 anxious to regain his stature as a top prospect.

Both Rodriguez and Sele pitched superbly for Lynchburg, as did less publicized Tim Vanegmond (12–4, 3.42). Rodriguez and reliever Joe Caruso no-hit Winston-Salem on April 30, the third Carolina League no-hitter that month. At midseason, Sele appeared to be a good bet to become the league's first 20-game winner since Robbie Snow in 1966. Shortly afterward, however, he was promoted to AA New Britain of the Eastern League. Infielder John Malzone (.306), third baseman–designated hitter Luis Ortiz, and outfielder Boo Moore (19 home runs) provided a solid attack.

Peninsula and Lynchburg repeated their titles during the second half, both facing down challenges from first-half also-rans.

Peninsula led the Southern Division race virtually from the beginning. A nine-game Durham winning streak kept the Bulls in the race early, while a 10-game losing streak dropped Kinston back. Both streaks ended on July 15 when Kinston's Herbert Perry, a former University of Florida quarterback, hit three home runs to propel the Indians to an 8–3 win over the Bulls.

The Winston-Salem Spirits made a late run at the Pilots. When they captured a doubleheader from Durham on August 30, the Spirits pulled within a single game of Peninsula with two games left. However, Winston-Salem lost to Durham the next day by a 7–4 margin, and Peninsula finished the second half with a half-game lead.

On August 28, the Bulls lost their home finale to Prince William 15–3 before 6,492 fans, a new record for venerable Durham Athletic Park. During the off-season, plans were finalized to replace the stadium with a new facility in Durham, putting to rest the possibility that the franchise might move closer to Raleigh.

Much of league president John Hopkins's attention was focused on an unusually large number of brawls. The bench-clearing episodes began early. A brawl on April 17 between Winston-Salem and Peninsula resulted in eight ejections, four from each team. Hopkins, who was in attendance, noted that the two clubs got in "some pretty good licks. It was definitely not a dance."

The most serious altercations, however, involved Durham and Salem. On July 7, Durham finished a three-game sweep of the Buccaneers with a 20–3 mauling that created bad blood. The two clubs met later in the month in Salem, shortly after the All-Star break. An exchange of beanballs on July 24 led to a brawl and the ejection of nine players. The teams went at it again the following night, when nine more players, along with Salem manager John Wockenfuss and Durham skipper Leon Roberts, were ejected. By the time the dust settled, Hopkins had levied fines on both managers and 14 of their players.

Since Lynchburg and Peninsula had won both half-season titles in their respective divisions, there were no first-round playoff. The first all-Virginia finals

Durham Athletic Park

Courtesy of Miles Wolff

Farewell to DAP

The 1988 movie *Bull Durham* helped make Durham Athletic Park the country's most famous minor league ballpark. Much of the movie was filmed in the 1939 structure, built following a fire which destroyed its predecessor. By the late 1970s, however, it had deteriorated to such an extent that one minor league official suggested that the structure would best be served by a small atomic bomb. A decade later, the refurbished ballpark was transformed from relic to icon and lauded for its ambiance, its architecture, and its downtown charm.

Its popularity, however, ultimately helped spell its demise. Capacity crowds accentuated its lack of modern facilities, including parking, concession areas, and adequate locker rooms. Durham voters turned down several proposals to build a new stadium, and plans were well under way for a new ballpark midway between Durham and Raleigh. At the last minute, this was averted, and plans were made for a new ballpark in Durham in time for the 1994 season.

Durham officials made plans to send DAP out in style. The 1993 season became a year-long farewell, with player reunions, commemorative souvenirs, and extensive national media attention. Even *Sports Illustrated* lamented the closing of DAP.

Imagine the embarrassment when the time came to finalize the construction contracts for the new ballpark. In late September, general construction, electrical, mechanical, and plumbing contracts came in a whopping $4.7 million over budget. Work ground to a halt, and city and team officials reluctantly agreed that the new park could not be completed in time for opening day.

As of this writing, it appears that the Bulls will spend at least the entire 1994 season at DAP, giving minor league fans one last chance to see the historic ballpark.

since 1978 turned out to be closely contested and extremely controversial. Lynchburg was the favorite. Not only did it have the best regular-season record in the league, it also had the home-field advantage, as the last three games of the five-game series were scheduled for Lynchburg. Further bolstering Lynchburg's chances were a superb bullpen and a propensity for winning close contests, as evidenced by its superb 36–11 mark in one-run games.

Lynchburg captured the opener 5–4 after jumping to a 5–0 lead on the strength of a three-run homer by designated hitter Luis Ortiz. It held off a Peninsula rally when outfielder Jim Morrison threw out the tying run at the plate in the bottom of the seventh. Reliever Joe Caruso (6–4, 1.98, 15 saves) held the Pilots in check in the eighth and ninth to save the game for ace Frank Rodriguez.

Lynchburg dissipated its advantage with a horrible second-game performance. Peninsula scored five unearned runs to break a 4–4 tie in the bottom of the eighth on four singles, a walk, two errors, and a pair of wild pitches by Cory Bailey (league-leading 23 saves). The final score was 9-4.

The clubs moved to Lynchburg, where, after a pair of rainouts, Lynchburg captured game three 6–4. The Red Sox hit Peninsula ace Greg Bicknell hard and benefited from a superb bullpen effort by Caruso.

Lynchburg sent Rodriguez to the mound to wrap up the series in game four, but instead, the Pilots' bats exploded for an 8–3 rout. Second baseman Ruben Santana, a native of Puerto Rico, keyed the assault with two singles, a double, and a triple.

This set the stage for a dramatic fifth game. The Red Sox knocked out league Pitcher of the Year John Cummings with a run in the first and three in the second. Peninsula fought back to a 4–4 tie with two runs in the third and single runs in the fifth and sixth; the tying run scored in part because of a balk called on Caruso. The game was still tied when Bailey came on for Lynchburg in the top of the eighth with one out and runners on first and third. Before he threw his first pitch, second-base umpire Bruce Dreckman called him for a balk, which scored the go-ahead run. Peninsula's Jeff Darwin preserved the 5–4 win when he struck out the side on nine pitches in the eighth inning and fanned two in the ninth.

Lynchburg manager Buddy Bailey and his players were incredulous that a balk had been called in such a crucial situation. After the game, the furious Lynchburg skipper charged that "one bad call cost us the game—that's our season."

Lynchburg and Peninsula were the only teams in the league to win more than they lost. Durham finished at .500, while Frederick and Prince William were two games below that mark.

Prince William overcame a poor first half to finish only 2½ behind Lynchburg in the Northern Division second half. The Cannons had a strong pitching staff led by Bruce Prybylinski, Richard Hines (11–7), and Rich Polak (22 saves). Second baseman Kevin Jordan (.311) paced a modest batting attack. A hand injury sidelined talented Prince William outfielder Lyle Mouton for much of the season.

Salem finished with the league's worst overall mark, largely because of a 4.05 team ERA. Outfielders Keith Thomas and Midre Cummings (.305, 14, 75), first baseman Rich Aude, and shortstop Ramon Martinez paced the Pirates, while Marty Neff hit 15 home runs in 59 games following his promotion.

Winston-Salem's late run for the second-half Southern Division title was keyed by first baseman Andy Hartung (.278, 23, 94), third baseman Jose Viera, designated hitter Corey Kapano (.318), Chuck Kirk (10–6), and Aaron Taylor (10–7, 20 saves). Top prospect Earle Cummings was demoted after striking out 54 times in fewer than 100 at-bats.

Usually potent Kinston was torpedoed by erratic pitching. Herbert Perry ended the season with 19 home runs. Outfielder Omar Ramirez (.299), Alan Embree (10–5), and Chad Ogea (13–3) also merited watching.

In the end, Peninsula's title was not enough to save that franchise. In the off-season, new Peninsula ownership—which included former New York Mets player and manager Bud Harrelson—announced plans to move the franchise to Wilmington, Delaware, for the 1993 season.

1992 Northern Division First-Half Final Standings

Lynchburg	39–30
Frederick	35–34
Salem	33–36
Prince William	31–38

Southern Division First-Half Final Standings

* Peninsula	37–32	playoff winner
Durham	37–32	
Kinston	35–34	
Winston-Salem	29–40	

Northern Division Second-Half Final Standings

Lynchburg	38–28
Prince William	38–33
Frederick	34–37
Salem	31–40

Southern Division Second-Half Final Standings

Peninsula	37–32
Winston-Salem	37–33
Durham	33–38
Kinston	30–37

—◆—

The Carolina League's move into Delaware was a success both on and off the field. Enthusiastic fans poured into newly constructed Judy Johnson Field at Legends Stadium to watch a competitive Wilmington Blue Rocks team.

Salem moved to the Southern Division with the relocation of the Peninsula franchise, with Wilmington taking a spot in the Northern Division. The move also created the longest road trips in league history.

Wilmington was virtually unbeatable at home during the early going. The Kansas City farm team was led by second baseman Michael Tucker (.305), a star of the 1992 United States Olympic team. Third baseman Gary Caraballo (.303), outfielder Hugh Walker (21 home runs), shortstop Shane Halter (.299), and pitchers Brian Bevil (7–1) and Brian Harrison (13–6) helped the Blue Rocks steamroll their Northern Division competition during the first half.

The Southern Division first-half race was much closer. Kinston, Durham, and Salem spent much of the campaign around .500, with Winston-Salem lagging behind. Kinston pulled away down the stretch, while Salem faded badly to last place. The Indians were led by outfielder Marc Marini (.300), second baseman Pat Maxwell (.293), and first baseman Clyde "Pork Chop" Pough, a fan favorite. The pitching staff included Ian Doyle (5–1, 23 saves) and the league's top hurler, Julian Tavarez (11–5, 2.42).

Wilmington was unable to continue its scintillating pace in the second half. Halter and Tucker were promoted, while Caraballo was sidelined by a bad back.

Frederick swept Wilmington in a three-game series early in the second half to establish its dominance. The first game was perhaps the most unusual contest of the season. Frederick hurler Vaughn Eshelman threw a no-hitter through seven innings but still trailed 1–0. The Keys took the lead in the bottom of the seventh on a two-run homer by Brad Seitzer. Eshelman tired in the top of the eighth and was removed by skipper Pete Mackanin. The no-hitter held until the ninth, when Wilmington's Andy Stewart doubled off reliever Joe Borowski with one out in the ninth. Frederick catcher Troy Kallman threw the ball into center field in an unsuccessful attempt to pick off pinch runner Brady Stewart, who scampered home to apparently tie the game. However, umpire Joel Fincher ruled that third-base coach Ron Johnson had helped push Stewart home and called the runner out. Frederick held on for a controversial 2–1 victory.

The Keys cruised to a comfortable second-half win. Frederick outfielder Curtis Goodwin (.281, 61 stolen bases) was considered the league's top prospect. His

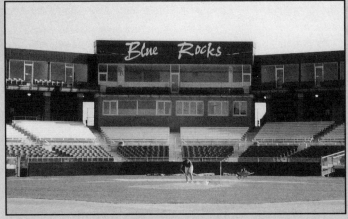

Judy Johnson Field at Legends Stadium

The Carolina League Goes to Delaware

The Carolina League was established as a North Carolina–Virginia circuit and maintained that status for over a third of a century. In 1981, it made a successful move into Maryland. Those geographical limits remained until 1993, when the troubled Peninsula franchise was moved to Wilmington, Delaware.

Delaware certainly seemed ripe for minor league baseball. Wilmington had last hosted a minor league team in the 1952 Interstate League. Yet Delaware baseball fans were within a short drive of major league baseball in Baltimore and Philadelphia. Having not been in the minor league habit for more than 40 years, how would they respond?

The answers were all positive. Taxpayers funded a new ballpark, Judy Johnson Field at Legends Stadium, which opened to favorable reviews. Johnson, a former star in the Negro Leagues, is the only Delaware native in the Hall of Fame. Even more important was the enthusiastic response of area fans. Five hundred turned out for a "Meet the Blue Rocks" banquet shortly before opening day. The home opener was sold out a month in advance; more than 5,000 jammed the stadium that day.

It also helped that the parent Kansas City Royals gave the Blue Rocks a solid club, featuring top prospects such as former United States Olympian Michael Tucker. Wilmington captured the Northern Division first-half championship and made it to the finals of the playoffs before losing to Winston-Salem.

Even though the Blue Rocks lost five games to rainouts, they still drew 332,000 fans, an average of more than 5,000 per game. That placed them third nationally among all A and AA clubs.

The only drawback to Wilmington's presence in the league appears to be the longer road trips—but after all, long bus rides are part of the charm of minor league baseball.

outfield running mates, Alex Ochoa (90 RBIs, 34 stolen bases) and Basilio Ortiz, were not far behind. Rick Forney, Jimmy Haynes, and Scott Klingenbeck combined for 39 wins. Bullpen ace Dave Paveloff (15 saves) was promoted early in the second half but was ably replaced by Joe Borowski (11 saves).

Kinston looked like a repeat winner in the Southern Division for much of the second half. However, the slugging Winston-Salem Spirits stayed close. The Spirits, in the first year of a PDC with Cincinnati, had a spectacular group of sluggers who collected a league-record 160 home runs. However, they finished as also-rans in the first half because of poor pitching. Cincinnati responded by sending better pitchers to start the second half.

Leading the Winston-Salem batting attack was a familiar figure, Bubba Smith, the league Player of the Year the previous season at Peninsula. Smith started the 1993 season at AA in the Seattle organization, but following a trade to Cincinnati, he was sent back to the Carolina League. Smith (.301, 27, 81) responded to the challenge by leading the league in home runs despite playing only 92 games. He repeated as league Player of the Year, the first man to accomplish that feat. Outfielders Chad Mottola (.280, 21, 91), who was the fifth pick in the 1992 draft out of the University of Central Florida, Eugene "Motorboat" Jones (.300), and Cleveland Laddell and first baseman Tim Belk (.306) added to the potent Spirits' lineup. Reliever John Hrusovsky saved 25 games.

Winston-Salem trailed Kinston by a single game when it hosted the Indians for a crucial three-game series late in August. The Spirits pounded the Indians 12–6, 14–3, and 9–2 and pulled away in the final week. The disheartened Indians faded to third.

Winston-Salem continued its hot play by edging Kinston in a closely contested first-round playoff series. Motorboat Jones hit a two-out, three-run homer in the bottom of the eighth to give the Spirits a 4–3 win in the opener. Kinston came back with a 3–2 win in game two, but Winston-Salem captured game three and the series 3–2 on a ninth-inning solo home run by Bobby Perna.

In the Northern Division playoff, Wilmington upended Frederick with surprising ease, 11–0 and 3–0.

The Blue Rocks were unable to cap their dream season with a title, however, losing the championship to Winston-Salem. The Blue Rocks captured a marathon 14-inning opener 6–5 but lost the next three games. Winston-Salem sent the final game into extra innings with a run in the bottom of the ninth and finished it off in the 11th on an RBI single by shortstop Ricky Gonzalez, a 23-year-old Venezuelan who had been acquired from the South Atlantic League on August 21. Gonzalez was named the Most Valuable Player of the championship series.

Although they missed the playoffs, the Durham Bulls had solid seasons from second baseman Tony Graffanino, outfielders Vince Moore and Mike Warner (.319), first baseman Doug Wollenburg (.299), and Canadian Dominic Therrien (.300). Hard-throwing left-handed phenom Terrell Wade (2–1) stopped in the Bull City long enough to fan 47 batters in 31 innings en route from low-A Macon to AA Greenville.

Salem's first venture into the Southern Division resulted in two last-place finishes, despite the efforts of sluggers Michael Brown, Jon Farrell, and Ken Bonifay, who combined for 59 home runs. Shortstop Tony Womack (.299, 28 stolen bases) excelled before being promoted to AA after half a season.

Prince William featured slugging first baseman Tate Seefried (21 home runs, 89 RBIs) and ace left-hander Andy Pettitte (11–9, 3.04).

Lynchburg's top players were Doug Hecker (21 home runs) and Scott Bakkum (12 wins).

The Carolina League finished the 1993 season with record attendance of 1.74 million. Frederick drew over 350,000, while Wilmington and Durham also surpassed the 300,000 mark. The league drew almost three times as many fans as it had only a decade earlier. Further demonstrating the ongoing popularity of minor league baseball were National Association figures showing that minor league attendance had increased for the 11th consecutive season.

As the Carolina League prepares to enter its second half-century, its popularity and reputation have never been higher.

1993 Northern Division First-Half Final Standings

Wilmington	45–24
Frederick	35–35
Lynchburg	32–37
Prince William	30–40

Southern Division First-Half Final Standings

Kinston	37–32
Durham	35–34
Winston-Salem	33–37
Salem	31–39

Northern Division Second-Half Final Standings

Frederick	43–27
Prince William	37–33
Lynchburg	33–37
Wilmington	30–40

Southern Division Second-Half Final Standings

* Winston-Salem	39–31	playoff winner
Durham	34–35	
Kinston	33–36	
Salem	30–40	

✦   ✦   ✦

Appendix 1 Carolina League Leaders

Batting Average

1945 Glenn Brundis, Danville .366
1946 Tom Wright, Durham .380
1947 Harry Sullivan, Raleigh .391
1948 Eddie Morgan, Martinsville .373
1949 William Brown, Danville .361
1950 Bill Evans, Burlington .338
1951 Ray Jablonski, Winston-Salem .363
1952 Emil Karlik, Durham .347
1953 Bill Radulovich, Durham .349
1954 Guy Morton, Greensboro .348
1955 Danny Morejon, High Point-Thomasville .324
1956 Curt Flood, High Point-Thomasville .340
1957 Eddie Logan, High Point-Thomasville .327
1958 Fred Valentine, Wilson .319
1959 Carl Yastrzemski, Raleigh .377
1960 Phil Linz, Greensboro .321
1961 Gates Brown, Durham .324
1962 Cesar Tovar, Rocky Mount .329
1963 Donald Bosch, Kinston .332
1964 Michael Page, Winston-Salem .344
1965 Ed Stroud, Portsmouth .341
1966 Jose Calero, Winston-Salem .330
1967 Van Kelly, Kinston .323
1968 Carlos May, Lynchburg .330
1969 Ken Huebner, High Point-Thomasville .324
1970 Rennie Stennett, Salem .326
1971 Art Howe, Salem .348
1972 Dave Parker, Salem .310
1973 Terry Whitfield, Kinston .335
1974 Frank Grundler, Lynchburg .335
1975 Ted Cox, Winston-Salem .305
1976 Rogers Lee Brown, Peninsula .349
1977 Ozzie Olivares, Salem .370
1978 Ronald MacDonald, Lynchburg .325
1979 Pat Kelly, Kinston .309
1980 Will Culmer, Peninsula .369

1981 Brad Komminsk, Durham .322
1982 Rick Renteria, Alexandria .331
1983 Lenny Dykstra, Lynchburg .358
1984 Dave Magadan, Lynchburg .350
1985 Dave Martinez, Winston-Salem .342
1986 Gregg Jefferies, Lynchburg .354
1987 Leo Gomez, Hagerstown .326
1988 Bernie Williams, Prince William .335
1989 Luis Mercedes, Frederick .309
1990 Ken Ramos, Kinston .345
1991 Jeff McNeely, Lynchburg .322
1992 Corey Kapano, Winston-Salem .318
1993 Tim Belk, Winston-Salem .306

Home Runs

1945 August Granzig, Leaksville; Tommy Kirk, Martinsville;
      Jerome Gutt, Martinsville; Maurice Abrams, Martinsville 12
1946 Gus Zernial, Burlington 41
1947 Eugene Petty, Danville 31
1948 Russell Sullivan, Danville 35
1949 Leo Shoals, Reidsville 55
1950 Fred Vaughan, Greensboro 27
1951 Ray Jablonski, Winston-Salem; Carl Miller, Reidsville 28
1952 Dale Powell, Danville 25
1953 Jack Hussey, Raleigh 29
1954 Jim Pokel, Fayetteville 38
1955 Harold Holland, Danville 31
1956 Leon Wagner, Danville 51
1957 Gene Oliver, Winston-Salem; Bob Perry, Danville 30
1958 Bert Barth, Wilson; Jackie Davis, High Point-Thomasville 25
1959 Don Lock, Greensboro 30
1960 Ed Olivares, Winston-Salem 35
1961 Chuck Weatherspoon, Wilson 31
1962 Bert Barth, Rocky Mount 33
1963 Walt Matthews, Durham 30
1964 Ed Chasteen, Raleigh 28
1965 Mike Derrick, Kinston 28
1966 Barry Morgan, Kinston 28
1967 Hal King, Asheville 30
1968 Tony Solaita, High Point-Thomasville 49

1969 Greg Luzinski, Raleigh-Durham 31
1970 Cliff Johnson, Raleigh-Durham 27
1971 Charlie Spikes, Kinston 22
1972 Robert Gorinski, Lynchburg 23
1973 Jim O'Bradovich, Lynchburg; Terry Whitfield, Kinston 18
1974 Randy Bass, Lynchburg 30
1975 Jim Morrison, Rocky Mount 20
1976 Marshall Brant, Lynchburg 23
1977 John Hughes, Peninsula 22
1978 Ozzie Virgil, Peninsula 29
1979 Gary Pellant, Alexandria 18
1980 Craig Brooks, Winston-Salem 24
1981 Gerald Davis, Salem 34
1982 David Malpeso, Winston-Salem 29
1983 Ken Gerhart, Hagerstown 31
1984 Randy Day, Peninsula 29
1985 J. D. Dickerson, Winston-Salem 28
1986 Ronnie Gant, Durham 26
1987 Hensley Meulens, Prince William 28
1988 Mickey Pina, Lynchburg 21
1989 Phil Plantier, Lynchburg 27
1990 Greg Blosser, Lynchburg 18
1991 Tracy Sanders, Kinston 18
1992 Bubba Smith, Peninsula 32
1993 Bubba Smith, Winston-Salem 27

Runs Batted In

1945 John Carenbauer, Danville 121
1946 Woody Fair, Durham 161
1947 Bill Nagel, Leaksville 128
1948 Russell Sullivan, Danville 129
1949 Leo Shoals, Reidsville 137
1950 Woody Fair, Danville 103
1951 Ray Jablonski, Winston-Salem 127
1952 Dale Powell, Danville; Paul Owens, Winston-Salem 105
1953 Don Buddin, Greensboro 123
1954 Guy Morton, Greensboro 120
1955 Harold Holland, Danville 121
1956 Leon Wagner, Danville 166
1957 Inocencio Rodriguez, Danville 114

1958 Allen Milley, Danville 97
1959 Don Lock, Greensboro 122
1960 Ed Olivares, Winston-Salem 125
1961 Chuck Weatherspoon, Wilson 123
1962 Bert Barth, Rocky Mount 136
1963 Jim Price, Kinston 109
1964 Steve Whitaker, Greensboro 100
1965 Mike Derrick, Kinston 103
1966 Barry Morgan, Kinston 104
1967 Ron Allen, Portsmouth 100
1968 Tony Solaita, High Point-Thomasville 122
1969 Greg Luzinski, Raleigh-Durham 92
1970 Cliff Johnson, Raleigh-Durham 91
1971 Craig Kusick, Lynchburg 91
1972 Dave Parker, Salem 101
1973 Chuck Erickson, Winston-Salem 101
1974 Randy Bass, Lynchburg 112
1975 Luther Wrenn, Salem 97
1976 Marshall Brant, Lynchburg 93
1977 Eugenio Cotes, Salem 102
1978 Ozzie Virgil, Peninsula 98
1979 Mike Fitzgerald, Lynchburg 75
1980 Julio Franco, Peninsula 99
1981 Brad Komminsk, Durham 104
1982 Rick Renteria, Alexandria 100
1983 Dave Cochrane, Lynchburg 102
1984 Randy Day, Peninsula 103
1985 Shawn Abner, Lynchburg 89
1986 Craig Worthington, Hagerstown 105
1987 Casey Webster, Kinston 111
1988 Mickey Pina, Lynchburg 108
1989 Phil Plantier, Lynchburg 105
1990 Armando Romero, Salem 90
1991 Pete Castellano, Winston-Salem 87
1992 Andy Hartung, Winston-Salem 94
1993 Chad Mottola, Winston-Salem 91

Wins

1945 Art Fowler, Danville 23
1946 Roy Pinyoun, Raleigh; Frank Paulin, Leaksville 19

1947   Ken Deal, Burlington   23
1948   Lewis Hester, Reidsville   25
1949   Eddie Neville, Durham   25
1950   Lee Peterson, Winston-Salem; Pete Angell, Danville   21
1951   Mike Forline, Reidsville   21
1952   Leonard Matarazzo, Fayetteville   22
1953   Ramon Monzant, Danville   23
1954   Bob Cruze, Durham; Curt Barclay, Danville   19
1955   Woody Rich, High Point-Thomasville   19
1956   Jack Taylor, High Point-Thomasville   22
1957   George Moton, Winston-Salem   18
1958   Jack Taylor, High Point-Thomasville   19
1959   Bill Spanswick, Raleigh; Don Dobrino, Wilson   15
1960   Lee Stange, Wilson   20
1961   Bill MacLeod, Winston-Salem; Willie Jones, Wilson; Ed Merritt, Greensboro; Al Eisele, Burlington   15
1962   Frank Bork, Kinston   19
1963   Chuck Kovach, Burlington; Gerry Merz, Rocky Mount   17
1964   Donald Hagen, Raleigh   16
1965   Jim Morio, Peninsula; Wayne McAlpin, Wilson   16
1966   Robbie Snow, Winston-Salem   20
1967   Harold Clem, Raleigh; Gary Jones, Greensboro; Mike Daniel, Asheville; Jon Warden, Rocky Mount   15
1968   Jerry Cram, Wilson; Charlie Hudson, Raleigh-Durham; Ed Smith, Lynchburg   16
1969   John Penn, Raleigh-Durham   15
1970   Lynn McGlothen, Winston-Salem   15
1971   Richard Fusari, Peninsula   19
1972   James Minshall, Salem   16
1973   Bill Stiegemeier, Lynchburg; Roy Thomas, Rocky Mount   15
1974   Don Aase, Winston-Salem   17
1975   Oliver Bell, Rocky Mount; Warren Brusstar, Rocky Mount; Allen Ripley, Winston-Salem   14
1976   Don Fowler, Peninsula; Ed Whitson, Salem   15
1977   Jeff Schneider, Peninsula   15
1978   Marty Bystrom, Peninsula; Henry Mack, Peninsula   15
1979   Bryan Clark, Alexandria; Thomas Hart, Peninsula   14
1980   LeRoy Smith, Peninsula   17
1981   Mike Brown, Winston-Salem   14
1982   Charles Hudson, Peninsula; Jonathan McKnight, Kinston   15
1983   Dwight Gooden, Lynchburg   19

1984 Mitch Cook, Lynchburg 16
1985 Kyle Hartshorn, Lynchburg 17
1986 Marty Reed, Kinston 16
1987 David Miller, Durham 15
1988 Mike Sander, Hagerstown; Brian Dubois, Hagerstown; Phil Harrison, Winston-Salem 14
1989 Mike Draper, Prince William 14
1990 Frank Seminara, Prince William 16
1991 Ryan Hawblitzel, Winston-Salem; Curt Leskanic, Kinston 15
1992 John Cummings, Peninsula 16
1993 Rick Forney, Frederick 14

Earned-Run Average

1945 Charlie Timm, Raleigh 2.36
1946 Harold Brown, Greensboro 2.42
1947 Harvey Haddix, Winston-Salem 1.90
1948 Al Henencheck, Raleigh 2.24
1949 Adam Twarkins, Danville 2.07
1950 Woody Rich, Greensboro 2.41
1951 Jim Lewey, Winston-Salem 2.65
1952 Eddie Neville, Durham 1.72
1953 Duane Wilson, Greensboro 2.21
1954 John Patula, Greensboro 1.58
1955 Jack Taylor, High Point-Thomasville 1.78
1956 Cleo Lewright, Kinston 2.38
1957 David Reed, Durham 2.04
1958 Don Aehl, Durham 1.86
1959 Bill Spanswick, Raleigh 2.49
1960 Jim Bouton, Greensboro 2.73
1961 Bill MacLeod, Winston-Salem 2.31
1962 Steve Blass, Kinston 1.97
1963 Sherman Jones, Raleigh 2.10
1964 Tom Moser, Burlington 2.47
1965 Dock Ellis, Kinston 1.98
1966 Robbie Snow, Winston-Salem 1.75
1967 Harold Clem, Raleigh 1.64
1968 Bill Champion, Tidewater 2.03
1969 Gordy Knutson, Raleigh-Durham 1.90
1970 Dan Bootcheck, Rocky Mount 1.92
1971 Richard Fusari, Peninsula 2.19

1972 Dave Pagan, Kinston 2.53

1973 Roy Thomas, Rocky Mount 2.24

1974 Don Aase, Winston-Salem 2.43

1975 T. Frederick Jones, Winston-Salem 2.11

1976 Peter Manos, Peninsula 1.16

1977 Jeff Schneider, Peninsula 2.50

1978 Jose Martinez, Peninsula 2.07

1979 Thomas Hart, Peninsula 2.22

1980 James Wright, Peninsula 1.85

1981 Mike Brown, Winston-Salem 1.49

1982 Charles Hudson, Peninsula 1.85

1983 Dwight Gooden, Lynchburg 2.50

1984 Randy Myers, Lynchburg 2.06

1985 Kyle Hartshorn, Lynchburg 1.69

1986 Jeff Ballard, Hagerstown 1.85

1987 Charles Scott, Kinston 2.69

1988 Kent Mercker, Durham 2.75

1989 Ray Mullino, Winston-Salem 2.32

1990 Frank Seminara, Prince William 1.90

1991 Tim Smith, Lynchburg 2.16

1992 Joe Caruso, Lynchburg 1.98

1993 Jason Fronio, Kinston 2.41

Player of the Year

1948 Lewis Hester, Reidsville

1949 Leo Shoals, Reidsville

1950 Bill Evans, Burlington

1951 Ray Jablonski, Winston-Salem

1952 Leonard Matarazzo, Fayetteville

1953 Ramon Monzant, Danville

1954 Guy Morton, Greensboro

1955 Danny Morejon, High Point-Thomasville

1956 Curt Flood, High Point-Thomasville

1957 Fred Van Dusen, High Point-Thomasville

1958 Fred Valentine, Wilson

1959 Carl Yastrzemski, Raleigh

1960 Ed Olivares, Winston-Salem

1961 Chuck Weatherspoon, Wilson

1962 Rusty Staub, Durham

1963 Jim Price, Kinston

1964 Ed Stroud, Tidewater
1965 Bobby Murcer, Greensboro
1966 Robbie Snow, Winston-Salem
1967 Don Money, Raleigh
1968 Tony Solaita, High Point-Thomasville
1969 Luther Quinn, Salem
1970 Cliff Johnson, Raleigh-Durham
1971 Richard Giallella, Peninsula
1972 Dave Parker, Salem
1973 Terry Whitfield, Kinston
1974 Miguel Dilone, Salem
1975 Luke Wrenn, Salem
1976 Marshall Brant, Lynchburg
1977 Ozzie Olivares, Salem
1978 Ozzie Virgil, Peninsula
1979 Bob Dernier, Peninsula
1980 Julio Franco, Peninsula
1981 Brad Komminsk, Durham
1982 Juan Samuel, Peninsula
1983 Lenny Dykstra, Lynchburg
1984 Barry Lyons, Lynchburg
1985 Shawn Abner, Lynchburg
1986 Gregg Jefferies, Lynchburg
1987 Casey Webster, Kinston
1988 Mickey Pina, Lynchburg
1989 Phil Plantier, Lynchburg
1990 Gary Scott, Winston-Salem
1991 Pete Castellano, Winston-Salem
1992 Bubba Smith, Peninsula
1993 Bubba Smith, Winston-Salem

Pitcher of the Year

1979 Thomas Hart, Kinston
1980 LeRoy Smith, Peninsula
1981 Mike Brown, Winston-Salem
1982 Charles Hudson, Peninsula
1983 Dwight Gooden, Lynchburg
1984 Randy Myers, Lynchburg
1985 Kyle Hartshorn, Lynchburg
1986 Dave Pavlas, Winston-Salem

1987 Blaine Beatty, Hagerstown
1988 Kent Mercker, Durham; Kevin Bearse, Kinston
1989 Charles Nagy, Cleveland
1990 Frank Seminara, Prince William
1991 Sam Militello, Prince William
1992 John Cummings, Peninsula
1993 Julian Tavarez, Kinston

Manager of the Year

1987 Mike Hargrove, Kinston
1988 Dick Berardino, Lynchburg
1989 Grady Little, Durham
1990 Wally Moon, Frederick
1991 Brian Graham, Kinston
1992 Marc Hill, Peninsula
1993 Dave Keller, Kinston; Pete Mackanin, Frederick

Appendix 2 Carolina League All-Star Games

In 1933, Arch Ward, sports editor for the *Chicago Tribune*, came up with one of the most enduring ideas in American sports. In the depths of the Great Depression, he persuaded wary major league baseball owners to agree to a game between stars from the American League and the National League. The two "All-Star" teams met in Chicago as part of that city's Century of Progress Exposition. The game, which featured a two-run homer by an aging Babe Ruth, was so successful that the major leagues made it an annual event, with the provision that the site be moved every year.

Major league baseball's All-Star Game has spawned numerous imitators. Not surprisingly, the minor leagues have been among them. The Carolina League did not have an All-Star Game for its first three seasons but soon came around. In the summer of 1947, Raleigh sportswriter Neale Patrick argued that "the will of the fans definitely is being disregarded—unless the folks who pay the freight in our loop are just a mite different from the fans elsewhere around the land. The All-Star game is essentially a fan-pleaser and the majority of the followers go heavily for the fielding of mythical teams."

The league directors evidently agreed. They voted to have an All-Star Game for the 1948 season.

Without a natural division, the league had several options. One was to divide the league into an east-west or north-south split for the All-Star Game only. A second option was to have the defending champion or midseason leader play a squad of players from the other seven teams. A third option was to pit Carolina League stars against stars from another league or against a team from a higher league. Over the years, the Carolina League has tried all of these approaches.

Until 1985, the league sponsored the game and pocketed the profits, if any. Since that time, the host city has paid a fee to the league and kept the profits.

Following are brief synopses of the league's All-Star clashes.

1948 The East routed the West 19–2 in the inaugural Carolina League All-Star Game. Durham second baseman Crash Davis's first-inning grand slam keyed the winning team's efforts. The 19 runs remain a league All-Star Game record, as does the 17-run margin.

East	730	001	314—19
West	020	000	000—2

Attendance in Greensboro: 3,961

1949 Two errors led to the only runs in this pitching duel. Three Danville pitchers combined on a 2–0 three-hitter.

All-Stars	000	000	000—0
Danville	200	000	00x—2

Attendance in Danville: 5,337

1950 No game was held.

1951 The All-Stars scored eight runs in the eighth to break open a close contest en route to a 12–4 win. Winston-Salem first baseman and future big-league standout Joe Cunningham hit two home runs in the inning, the only Carolina League player to accomplish that in an All-Star game. Greensboro's Jack Mitchell and Reidsville's Bob Falk each had four hits. The game was hastily moved to Greensboro when Reidsville general manager Herb Brett was unable to convince Reidsville officials to lift a town ordinance against Sunday baseball.

All-Star	000	013	080—12
Reidsville	001	030	000—4

Attendance in Greensboro: 4,378

1952 Raleigh ace Ben Rossman pitched a complete-game five-hitter in defeat. Burlington sensation "Rocket" Ron Necciai was the winning pitcher in the 1–0 contest.

All-Stars	000	010	000—1
Raleigh	000	000	000—0

Attendance in Raleigh: 5,350

1953 The All-Stars jumped to a big lead and held off a late Burlington rally for a 7–5 win.

All-Stars	122	100	001—7
Burlington	100	031	000—5

Attendance in Graham: 3,125

1954 Greensboro second baseman Jake Charvatt's four hits led the All-Stars to a 9–6 come-from-behind win over Burlington. Reidsville's Bill Evans added three hits for the winners, who banged out 16 hits. Hi-Toms outfielder Danny Morejon became the first black to play in the All-Star Game.

All-Stars	030	011	031—9
Burlington	204	000	000—6

Attendance in Graham: 3,433

1955 For the first time, the Carolina League held two All-Star Games. The All-Stars won the traditional game 5–1, led by Greensboro's Dick McCarthy and Winston-Salem's Tom McDonald, each of whom had three hits. Future big-league skipper Jack McKeon managed Fayetteville.

All-Stars	121	000	010—5
Fayetteville	001	000	000—1

Game held in Fayetteville: (figures not available)

In the other All-Star Game that year, and for the only time, the Carolina League matched rookies against veterans. Winston-Salem pitcher Stan Johnson's two-run single in the seventh broke a 1–1 tie and led the veterans to a 3–2 win. The gradual disappearance of veterans from the Carolina League quickly rendered this All-Star option obsolete.

Rookies	000	000	110—2
Veterans	000	100	20x—3

Game held in Thomasville: (figures not available)

1956 Again, the league had a pair of games.

The traditional game was played July 18. The All-Stars again jumped to an early lead and held on 4–2. Hi-Toms ace Jack Taylor pitched three scoreless innings for the All-Stars.

All-Stars	300	100	000—4
Wilson	000	010	010—2

Game held in Wilson: 3,583

The second contest that year was an East-West matchup, the first since 1948. It was played about a month after the first game. The West scored five runs in the fourth inning on a flurry of walks, errors, hit batters, bunt singles, sacrifices, and wild pitches en route to an 8–1 win. Danville first baseman Willie McCovey went three for four for the West, including a home run.

East	100	000	000—1
West	100	500	20x—8

(figures not available)

1957   High Point-Thomasville's Fred Van Dusen hit an eighth-inning homer to break a 5–5 tie with Durham. Van Dusen drove in three runs for the winning All-Stars, while Tom Futch had four hits and two RBIs for losing Durham in the 7–6 contest.

All-Stars	022	001	011—7
Durham	013	100	001—6

Attendance in Durham: 1,964

1958   All-Star pitching held the Hi-Toms to five hits in a 4–1 victory. Durham's Dick Day got the win in relief, while Danville's Bobby Hoffman had three hits. Day struck out the first four batters he faced.

All-Stars	000	002	002—4
Hi-Toms	000	000	010—1

Attendance in Thomasville: 1,878

1959   No game was held.

1960   Greensboro ended an eight-game All-Star winning streak with a come-from-behind 9–7 victory. Jim Bouton, the only Carolina League All-Star to become famous as an author, was the winning pitcher. The All-Stars botched Bouton's sacrifice bunt in Greensboro's six-run sixth inning.

All-Stars	310	000	021—7
Greensboro	030	006	00x—9

Attendance in Greensboro: 2,502

1961 In one of the most dramatic Carolina League All-Star Games ever, the Wilson Tobs scored twice in the bottom of the ninth for a 3–2 victory. Joe McCabe's double drove in the tying run, while Juan Visteur's drag-bunt single scored the winner.

All-Stars	000	010	100—2
Wilson	000	000	102—3

Attendance in Wilson: 2,240

1962 The All-Stars scored twice in the top of the ninth for a 5–3 victory over Kinston. Durham star Rusty Staub scored the last run when he stole home on a delayed steal. His teammate Wally Wolf turned in a superb relief stint for the win.

All-Stars	000	300	002—5
Kinston	101	000	010—3

Attendance in Kinston: 2,799

1963 With the league now divided into two divisions, it tried another East-West matchup. Durham's Bob Rikard hit a 400-foot three-run homer in the seventh to lead the West to a 4–1 victory. The winners garnered only three hits, the losers five.

West	000	010	300—4
East	000	100	000—1

Attendance in Kinston: 1,322

1964 Despite the natural East-West rivalry, the league went back to a matchup between an All-Star squad and the league leaders. The result was the first extra-inning contest in the game's history. Burlington's Ron Durham drove in Raleigh's Coco Laboy with the winner in the top of the 10th. Laboy had three hits for the All-Stars in their 4–3 win.

All-Stars	100	000	020	1—4
Kinston	001	030	000	0—3

Attendance in Kinston: 2,020

1965 Greensboro's Jim Palma hit a two-run homer in the top of the first, and the All-Star pitching staff, including winner Dock Ellis of Kinston, made it stand up for an easy 4–0 win over Durham. The All-Stars outhit the Bulls 13–2.

All-Stars	300	000	001—4
Durham	000	000	000—0

Attendance in Durham: 2,046

1966 Bernie Carbo of Peninsula, Al Oliver of Raleigh, and Dick Billings of Burlington homered to stake the All-Stars to a big lead. When Winston-Salem scored three times in the bottom of the ninth to make the game a one-run affair, Durham's Wally Wolf came in to put out the fire and preserve the 6–5 victory.

All-Stars	010	001	121—6
Winston-Salem	001	000	103—5

Attendance in Winston-Salem: 4,891

1967 Again, the league tried a pair of All-Star games, this time matching each division leader against a team of stars from that division. Both games were played on the same day.

The East game was a close All-Star victory. Portsmouth's Larry Hisle went three for three with a pair of runs batted in for the winners, while Don Money had a two-run double for the Raleigh Caps in a 7–6 loss.

East	201	040	000—7
Raleigh	001	030	000—6

Attendance in Raleigh: 1,307

The West game was more one-sided. Asheville's Danny Walton had two home runs and five runs batted in to lead the All-Stars to a 10–3 rout of Greensboro.

West	024	001	201—10
Greensboro	000	001	020—3

Attendance in Greensboro: 2,346

1968 The league went back to a one-game format. Salem hosted the first All-Star Game played outside North Carolina since 1949. The Buccaneers posted a 6–1 win, one of the most impressive victories over an All-Star team in the game's history. John Jeter hit a two-run homer for the Bucs.

All-Stars	000	000	010—1
Salem	330	000	00x—6

Attendance in Salem: 2,528

1969 Five All-Star pitchers combined for a six-hit 2–0 shutout over Rocky Mount. Raleigh-Durham third baseman Bob Boone hit a fourth-inning sacrifice fly that gave the All-Stars the only run they would need.

All-Stars	000	100	010—2
Rocky Mount	000	000	000—0

Attendance in Rocky Mount: 1,685

1970 Raleigh-Durham's Cliff Johnson, the league's best slugger, hit a three-run homer in the first inning off Winston-Salem's Lynn McGlothen, the league's best pitcher, to spark the All-Stars to an easy 8–1 victory.

All-Stars	410	001	002—8
Winston-Salem	000	001	000—1

Attendance in Winston-Salem: 2,054

1971 Lynchburg's Mark Carlson scored the game-winning run in the top of the 11th on a throwing error. Peninsula shortstop Sterling Coward had three singles for the All-Stars in a 2–1 win.

All-Stars	000	010	000	01—2
Kinston	001	000	000	00—1

Attendance in Kinston: 1,061

1972 Pat Cluney singled in an unearned run in the bottom of the 14th to win the longest Carolina League All-Star Game ever for Burlington, 3–2. The sloppy game was marred by nine errors. Salem's Dave Parker went three for seven for the All-Stars. Major league commissioner Bowie Kuhn was among the spectators.

All-Stars	200	000	000	000	00—2
Burlington	000	001	100	000	01—3

Attendance in Burlington: 915

1973 Four Lynchburg batters had four hits apiece as the Twins blasted the All-Stars 9–3. The winners totaled 15 hits.

All-Stars	002	010	000—3
Lynchburg	120	110	130—9

Attendance in Lynchburg: 1,496

1974 A late-game surge enabled the All-Stars to win a 14–9 slugfest over Salem. Rocky Mount left fielder Dan Fitzgerald went three for four, including a grand slam, and drove in six runs for the visitors. Salem hit four home runs in a losing effort. Salem starter John Candeleria struck out nine in six innings and left with a 6–2 lead, but his bullpen collapsed.

All-Stars	001	001	651—14
Salem	100	023	021—9

Attendance in Salem: 1,273

1975 The four-team Carolina League played against its Class A rival and partner, the Western Carolina League. Lonnie Smith went three for four for the Western Carolina League, while four of his teammates held the Carolina League to four hits in a 7–0 shutout.

Western Carolina League	200	050	000—7
Carolina League	000	000	000—0

1976 For the first of four years, a team of Carolina League All-Stars hosted a team from the AAA International League. The All-Stars pounded Charleston (W.V.) 11–5. Lynchburg's Marshall Brant and Winston-Salem's Ron Evans each drove in three runs, while Salem's Ed Whitson picked up the win.

Charleston	000	022	010—5
All-Stars	024	111	02x—11

Attendance in Salem: 711

1977 The Carolina League All-Stars won another slugfest, this time 9–7 over Pawtucket. Peninsula's John Hughes hit a fourth-inning grand slam, while Salem's Ozzie Olivares hit safely three times.

Pawtucket	110	210	200—7
All-Stars	320	400	00x—9

Attendance in Winston-Salem: 1,276

1978 A two-out single by Lynchburg's Chuck Valley gave the Carolina League All-Stars a hard-fought 5–4 win over Tidewater. The All-Stars outhit the AAA club 12–6.

Tidewater	003	001	000—4
All-Stars	021	001	10x—5

Attendance in Lynchburg: 1,258

1979 The Tides got their revenge and gave the International League its only victory in the series, pounding out a dozen hits to take an easy 9–2 victory.

Tidewater	104	220	000—9
All-Stars	000	001	100—2

Attendance in Hampton: 1,081

1980 With the league back to eight teams and two divisions, it returned to an intraleague All-Star Game. A 10th-inning home run by Rocky Mount's Jim Gabella gave the North Carolina Division an extra-inning win. Durham's Rick Behenna was the winning pitcher.

Virginia Division	100	001	000	0—2
North Carolina Division	000	020	000	1—3

Attendance in Kinston: 1,299

1981 This game belonged to Hagerstown's John Stefero. His two home runs produced four runs and led the North to a 9–3 win over the South. Future big leaguer David Rivera also had a big game for the winners. Because of the baseball strike, the game was televised by a Durham station.

North	014	100	012—9
South	020	000	100—3

Attendance in Durham: 4,011

1982 A bases-loaded double by Hagerstown's Al Pardo scored three runs in the bottom of the first and helped stake the North to a 5–0 lead. Peninsula's Jeff Stone closed the gap to 5–3 with a three-run homer in the seventh, but the South could come no closer.

South	000	000	300—3
North	400	100	00x—5

Attendance in Alexandria: 1,817

1983 In the first All-Star Game played in Maryland, Winston-Salem's Sam Nattile drove in four runs with two hits for the South in a 5–2 victory.

South	004	000	100—5
North	000	000	011—2

Attendance in Hagerstown: 1,043

1984 Kinston's Kash Beauchamp had one of the best individual All-Star Games in league history. The Kinston outfielder hit a home run, a triple, and two singles, scored four times, and drove in four runs. Luis Quinones added three hits, including a triple, for the South in an 11–6 victory. Lynchburg's Dave Magadan had three hits for the North.

South	214	010	003—11
North	010	002	030—6

Attendance in Salem: 731

1985 Winston-Salem's J. D. Dickerson hit a two-run single in the first inning to give the South a lead it never relinquished. Durham outfielder Chris Baird had a double, a single, and two runs batted in and threw a runner out at the plate for the South in a 5–2 win.

North	002	000	000—2
South	212	000	000—5

Attendance in Winston-Salem: 7,358

1986 The North ended a four-game losing streak as five pitchers held the South to four hits in a 3–1 contest. Lynchburg outfielder Marcus Lawton stole two bases and threw out a runner at the plate to preserve the victory.

South	000	001	000—1
North	020	000	01x—3

Attendance in Lynchburg: 855

1987 Kinston third baseman Casey Webster broke a 1–1 tie with a solo homer in the seventh inning. Two errors by the North then led to two more runs and a 4–1 South win.

North	000	100	000—1
South	100	000	300—4

Attendance in Hampton: 2,631

1988　Pitching dominated this game. A two-run homer by Hagerstown's Craig Faulkner was one of only three hits by the victorious North. The South had five hits in a 2–1 loss. Lynchburg's Enrique Rios was the winning pitcher.

North	000	200	000—2
South	000	000	010—1

Attendance in Kinston: 2,614

1989　This was another pitching duel. Kinston shortstop Mark Lewis homered for the South in a 2–1 win. Salem's John Wehner had three of the North's five hits.

North	000	000	100—1
South	000	011	00x—2

Attendance in Durham: 5,120

1990　The star of this game was Winston-Salem third baseman Gary Scott, who had two doubles and an inside-the-park homer in the South's 5–4 victory. The winning pitcher was Peninsula's Len Pilkington, an infielder by trade, who was used in desperation by South manager Brian Graham.

South	100	001	200	1—5
North	300	000	001	0—4

Attendance in Woodbridge: 5,947

1991　The South used a four-run sixth to break a 2–2 tie en route to a 6–5 win. Durham's Scott Taylor pitched a perfect eighth and ninth inning for the win.

South	020	004	000—6
North	002	000	300—5

Attendance in Frederick: 5,612

1992 The North scored all the runs it needed in the second inning of this 5–2 contest. Lynchburg outfielder Midre Cummings was named the game's MVP on the basis of a double, a single, and an RBI. Eight North pitchers held the South to only six hits.

South	000	011	000—2
North	030	000	20x—5

Attendance in Salem: 4,219

1993 Game MVP Curtis Goodwin and Tate Seefried hit late home runs to help the North to a come-from-behind 6–3 win.

North	100	010	301—6
South	011	100	000—3

Attendance in Winston-Salem: 3,581

Bibliography

Primary Sources
Minutes of the Carolina League Board of Directors Meetings, 1961–92

Interviews and Correspondence
Duke, Willie
Falwell, Calvin
Hopkins, John
Horner, Jack
Jessup, Bill
Mills, Jim
Wolff, Miles

Newspapers
Baseball America
CL Beat
Durham Morning Herald
Durham Sun
Fayetteville Observer
Greensboro Daily News
Kinston Daily Free Press
Lynchburg Daily Advance
Lynchburg News
Norfolk Pilot
Raleigh News and Observer
Raleigh Times
Reidsville Review
Sporting News
Washington Post
Winston-Salem Journal

Books
Aaron, Henry, with Lonnie Wheeler. *I Had a Hammer: The Hank Aaron Story*. New York: Harper Collins, 1991.
Alexander, Charles C. *Our Game: An American Baseball History*. New York: Henry Holt and Company, 1991.
Anderson, Jean Bradley. *Durham County*. Durham: Duke University Press, 1990.
Beam, John Mark III. *They Played Here: Sports History of the High Point Area*. High Point: High Point Historical Society, 1990.
Bench, Johnny, and William Brashler. *Catch You Later: The Autobiography of Johnny Bench*. New York: Harper and Row, 1979.
Benson, Michael. *Ballparks of North America: A Comprehensive Historical Reference to*

Baseball Grounds, Yards and Stadiums, 1845 to Present. Jefferson, N.C., and London: McFarland and Company, 1989.

Blake, Mike. *The Minor Leagues: A Celebration of the Little Show.* New York: Wynwood Press, 1991.

Bosco, Joseph. *The Boys Who Would Be Cubs: A Year in the Heart of Baseball's Minor Leagues.* New York: William Morrow and Company, 1990.

Cairns, Bob. *Pen Men: Baseball's Greatest Bullpen Stories Told by the Men who Brought the Game Relief.* New York: St. Martin's Press, 1990.

Carew, Rod, with Ira Berkow. *Carew.* New York: Simon and Schuster, 1979.

Chrisman, David F. *The History of the Piedmont League (1920–1955).* Bend, Oreg.: Maverick Press, 1987.

———. *The History of the Virginia League (1900–1928; 1939–1951).* Bend, Oreg.: Maverick Press, 1988.

Cohen, Joel H. *Joe Morgan: Great Little Big Man.* New York: G. P. Putnam's Sons, 1978.

Daniels, Jonathan. *Tar Heels: A Portrait of North Carolina.* New York: Dodd, Mead, and Company, 1941.

Davis, Paxton. *Being a Boy.* Winston-Salem: John F. Blair, Publisher, 1988.

Dolson, Frank. *Beating the Bushes.* South Bend, Ind.: Icarus Press, 1982.

D'Orso, Mike. "Beyond Bull Durham." In *Best Sports Stories of 1989*, edited by Tom Barnidge. St. Louis: The Sporting News, 1989.

Finch, Robert L., L. H. Addington, and Ben M. Morgan. *The Story of Minor League Baseball: A History of the Game of Professional Baseball in the United States, with Particular Reference to Its Growth and Development in the Smaller Cities and Towns of the Nation.* Columbus, Ohio: National Association of Professional Baseball Leagues, 1953.

Flood, Curt, with Richard Carter. *The Way It Is.* New York: Trident Press, 1970.

Goldblatt, Abe, and Robert W. Wentz, Jr. *The Great and the Near Great: A Century of Sports in Virginia.* Norfolk and Virginia Beach: The Donning Company, 1976.

Goldstein, Richard. *Spartan Seasons: How Baseball Survived the Second World War.* New York: Macmillan Publishing Company, 1980.

Gooden, Dwight, with Richard Woodley. *Rookie: The Story of My First Year in the Major Leagues.* Garden City, N.Y.: Doubleday and Company, 1985.

Greenberg, Hank. *The Story of My Life.* Edited by Ira Berkow. New York: Times Books, 1989.

Guidry, Ron, with Peter Golenbock. *Guidry.* Englewood Cliffs, N.J.: Prentice-Hall, 1980.

Hall, Donald, with Dock Ellis. *Dock Ellis in the Country of Baseball.* New York: Coward, McCann and Geoghegan, 1976.

Harville, Charlie. *Sports in North Carolina: A Photographic History.* Norfolk: The Donning Company, 1977.

Hieman, Lee, Dave Weiner, and Bill Gutman. *When the Cheering Stops.* New York and London: Macmillan Publishing Company, 1990.

Hoie, Bob. "The Minor Leagues." In *Total Baseball*, edited by John Thorn and Pete Palmer. New York: Baseball, Inc., 1989.

Holway, John. *Voices from the Great Black Baseball Leagues.* New York: Dodd, Mead, and Company, 1975.

Johnson, Arthur T. *Minor League Baseball and Local Economic Development.* Champaign: University of Illinois Press, 1993.

Johnson, Lloyd, and Miles Wolff, eds. *The Encyclopedia of Minor League Baseball.* Durham: Baseball America, Inc., 1993.

Jones, Cleon, with Ed Hershey. *Cleon.* New York: Coward-McCann, 1970.

Kahn, Roger. *Good Enough to Dream.* Garden City, N.Y.: Doubleday and Company, 1985.

Kirkland, Bill. *Eddie Neville of the Durham Bulls.* Jefferson, N.C.: McFarland and Company, 1993.

Klein, Dave. *On the Way Up: What It's Like in the Minor Leagues.* New York: Julian Messner, 1977.

Kuhn, Bowie. *Hardball: The Education of a Baseball Commissioner.* New York: Times Books, 1987.

Kuralt, Charles. *Southerners: A Portrait of the People.* Birmingham, Ala.: Oxmoor, 1986.

Lamb, David. *Stolen Season: A Journey Through America and Baseball's Minor Leagues.* New York: Random House, 1991.

Leyburn, James G. *The Way We Lived: Durham, 1900–1920.* Elliston, Va.: Northcross House, 1989.

Lyle, Sparky, and Peter Golenbock. *The Bronx Zoo.* New York: Crown Publishers, 1979.

Lyttle, Richard B. *A Year in the Minors: Baseball's Untold Story.* Garden City, N.Y.: Doubleday and Company, 1975.

Miller, James Edward. *The Baseball Business: Pursuing Pennants and Profits in Baltimore.* Chapel Hill and London: University of North Carolina Press, 1990.

Minor League Baseball Stars. Cooperstown, N.Y.: Society for American Baseball Research, 1978.

Minor League Baseball Stars II. Manhattan, Kans.: Society for American Baseball Research, 1985.

Minor League Baseball Stars III. Cleveland: Society for American Baseball Research, 1992.

Morgan, Joe, and David Falkner. *Joe Morgan: A Life in Baseball.* New York: Norton, 1993.

Obojski, Robert. *Bush League: A History of Minor League Baseball.* New York: Macmillan Publishing Company, 1975.

Pallone, Dave, with Alan Steinberg. *Behind the Mask: My Double Life in Baseball.* New York: Viking, 1990.

Palmer, Howard. *The Real Baseball Story.* New York: Pageant Press, 1953.

Parramore, Thomas C. *Express Lanes and Country Roads: The Way We Lived in North Carolina, 1920–1970.* Chapel Hill: University of North Carolina Press for the North Carolina Department of Cultural Resources, 1983.

Peary, Danny, ed. *Cult Baseball Players: The Greats, the Flakes, the Weird, and the Wonderful.* New York: Simon and Schuster, 1990.

Pinella, Lou, and Maury Allen. *Sweet Lou.* New York: G. P. Putnam, 1986.

Rader, Benjamin G. *American Sports: From the Age of Folk Games to the Age of Televised Sports.* Englewood Cliffs, N.J.: Prentice-Hall, 1990.

———. *Baseball: A History of America's Game.* Urbana and Chicago: University of Illinois Press, 1992.

Reidenbaugh, Lowell. *Cooperstown: Where Baseball's Legends Live Forever.* St. Louis: The Sporting News, 1983.

Ryan, Bob. *Wait Till I Make the Show: Baseball in the Minor Leagues.* Boston: Little, Brown, 1972.

Seymour, Harold. *Baseball: The Early Years.* New York: Oxford University Press, 1960.

———. *Baseball: The Golden Age.* New York: Oxford University Press, 1971.

Slaughter, Enos, with Kevin Reid. *Country Hardball: The Autobiography of Enos "Country" Slaughter.* Greensboro: Tudor Publishers, 1991.

Starr, Bill. *Clearing the Bases: Baseball Then & Now.* New York: Michael Kesend Publishing, 1989.

Strawberry, Darryl, with Art Rust, Jr. *Darryl.* New York: Bantam Books, 1992.

Sullivan, Neil J. *The Minors: The Struggle and Triumph of Baseball's Poor Relation from 1876 to the Present.* New York: St. Martin's Press, 1990.

Sumner, Jim L. *A History of Sports in North Carolina.* Raleigh: North Carolina Department of Cultural Resources, 1990.

Tiant, Luis, and Joe Fitzgerald. *El Tiante: The Luis Tiant Story.* Garden City, N.Y.: Doubleday and Company, 1976.

U.S. Congress. *Organized Baseball.* Report of the Subcommittee on Study of Monopoly Power of the Committee on the Judiciary Pursuant to House Resolution 95. Washington: U.S. Government Printing Office, 1952.

———. *Organized Professional Team Sports.* Hearings Before the Antitrust Subcommittee of the Committee on the Judiciary, House of Representatives. Washington: U.S. Government Printing Office, 1957.

Voigt, David Quentin. *American Baseball: From Gentleman's Sport to the Commissioner System.* Norman: University of Oklahoma Press, 1966.

———. *American Baseball: From Postwar Expansion to the Electronic Age.* University Park, Pa., and London: Pennsylvania State University Press, 1983.

———. *American Baseball: From the Commissioners to Continental Expansion.* Norman: University of Oklahoma Press, 1970.

———. *Baseball: An Illustrated History.* University Park, Pa., and London: Pennsylvania State University Press, 1987.

Wilber, Cynthia J. *For the Love of the Game: Baseball Memories from the Men Who Were There.* New York: William Morrow and Company, 1992.

Yastrzemski, Carl, with Al Hirshberg. *Yaz.* New York: Viking Press, 1968.

Yastrzemski, Carl, with Gerald Eskenazi. *Yaz: Baseball, the Wall, and Me.* New York: Doubleday and Company, 1990.

Journal and Magazine Articles
Carry, Peter. "Bonanza in Red Springs: Minor League Owner Matt Boykin." *Sports Illustrated* 31 (July 28, 1969): 42–43.

Delsohn, Steve. "Beers with Jack McKeon." *Sport* 80 (July 1989): 19–24.

Hersch, Hank. "His Life is a Movie." *Sports Illustrated* 69 (August 8, 1988): 67.

———."Time for Big Ben." *Sports Illustrated* 70 (May 29, 1989): 54–55.

Hufford, Thomas D. "Leo 'Muscle' Shoals." *Baseball Research Journal* 3 (1974): 102–6.

Jordan, Pat. "Kid K." *Sports Illustrated* 66 (June 1, 1987): 82–86.

Lamb, David. "A Season in the Minors." *National Geographic* 179 (April 1991): 40–73.

Lidz, Franz. "Flashes in the Pan." *Sports Illustrated* 76 (May 4, 1992): 56–61.

LoBello, Steven G. "Physically Handicapped Players in Major League Baseball." *Nine: A Journal of Baseball History and Social Policy Perspectives* 1 (Spring 1993): 207–13.

O'Conner, Adrian. "Baseball Coverage in Charlotte." *Baseball Research Journal* 10 (1980): 173–79.

Rudolph, Barbara. "Bonanza in the Bushes." *Time* 132 (August 1, 1988): 38–39.

Simpson, William S., Jr. "1908: The Year Richmond Went 'Baseball Wild.'" *Virginia Cavalcade* 26 (Spring 1977): 184–92.

Smith, Claire. "National League President Bill White: Baseball's Angry Man." *New York Times Magazine* (October 13, 1991): 28–31, 53, 56.

Smith, Leverett T. "Minor League Baseball in Rocky Mount." *Baseball Research Journal* 7 (1978): 12–17.

Smith, Scott. "Take Me Out to the Ballgame." *The State* 59 (July 1991): 18–19.

Sumner, Jim L. "Baseball at Salisbury Prison Camp." *Baseball History Annual* 1 (1988): 19–27.

———. "The North Carolina State Professional Baseball League of 1902." *North Carolina Historical Review* 64 (July 1987): 247–73.

———. "Virginia–North Carolina League: A Fascinating Failure." *Baseball Research Journal* 18 (1989): 38–40.

———."William G. Bramham: The Czar of Minor League Baseball." *Carolina Comments* 37 (July 1989): 116–22.

Swift, E. M. "It's Been Some Rocky Year." *Sports Illustrated* 53 (September 1, 1980): 58–59.

Ward, Harry M. "Richmond Sports at Flood Tide: Mayo Island, 1921–1941." *Virginia Cavalcade* 34 (Spring 1985): 182–91.

Wulf, Steve. "Biggest Bird in the Bushes." *Sports Illustrated* 59 (August 15, 1983): 44–45.

———. "Down on the Farm." *Sports Illustrated* 73 (July 23, 1990): 32–43.

Guides

Baseball America's Almanac. Durham: Baseball America, 1986–92.

Baseball Guide and Record Book. Saint Louis: Charles C. Spink and Son, 1945–92.

Carolina League Media Guide and Record Book. Various publishers, 1948–92.

Index